# The
# Country
# Diaries

ALAN TAYLOR is a journalist for the *Sunday Herald* and is Editor
of the *Scottish Review of Books*. Formerly, he worked for *Scotland
on Sunday* and the *Scotsman*, where he was Managing Editor. He is
co-editor of two other anthologies, *The Assassin's Cloak: An Anthology
of the World's Greatest Diarists* and *Those Who Marched Away:
An Anthology of the World's Greatest War Diaries*, both published by
Canongate. For the past decade he has been half of the Scottish
team on Radio 4's *Round Britain Quiz*.

# THE COUNTRY DIARIES

## A YEAR IN THE BRITISH COUNTRYSIDE

EDITED BY ALAN TAYLOR

CANONGATE

*Edinburgh · London · New York · Melbourne*

This paperback edition published in 2010 by Canongate Books

1

Copyright © Alan Taylor, 2009

Illustration copyright © John Hinchcliffe, 2009

The moral right of the author has been asserted

First published in Great Britain in 2009 by Canongate Books Ltd, 14 High Street,
Edinburgh EH1 1TE

www.meetatthegate.com

For Permissions Acknowledgements, please see page 345

*British Library Cataloguing-in-Publication Data*
A catalogue record for this book is available on
request from the British Library

ISBN 978 1 84767 326 8

Typeset in Bembo by Palimpsest Book Production Ltd,
Grangemouth, Stirlingshire

Printed and bound in Great Britain by Clays Ltd, St Ives plc

# Contents

# Introduction

Where I grew up, in Musselburgh, which is six or so miles from Edinburgh, the countryside was so near you could sense its presence even if you couldn't quite touch it. I lived on a small housing estate which had a farm as its neighbour. My great-uncle was employed as a farm labourer and I would watch him trudge home for lunch, his haversack slung over his back, his dungarees clagged with the clay-like mud that was more fertile than a biblical patriarch.

For obscure bureaucratic purposes, Musselburgh is now officially in East Lothian but in those days it was part of Midlothian. East Lothian, as anyone journeying north by train on the east coast line will attest, is a prosperous county. At harvest time the fields produce enough cereal and vegetables to feed Scotland's population. In spring, the Lammermuir Hills are alive with new lambs baa-ing weakly like a string section tuning up. Hirsute Highland heifers graze in fields greener than guacamole. Those farms that have shops offer the gamut of local produce: Brussels sprouts, organic eggs, strawberries and raspberries, every part of a pig, pre-plucked pheasants.

Farming hereabouts is intensive and, even in these difficult days, profitable. The villages – Stenton, Garvald, Gifford, East Linton – are within commuting distance of Edinburgh and of late have proved attractive to people, be they retired or stressed out or dreamers, who want to escape the clamour of life in an intemperate city. Come the 'Glorious' 12th of August, East Lothian plays host to shooting parties who have come from near and far intent on bagging grouse. Now the noise that punctures the silence is the 'pock-pock' of guns and the occasional yelp of an excitable dog. Countless grouse are slaughtered but then they are, too, all year round, as they insanely attempt against the odds to cross roads. An inventive cook could eat royally off the county's roadkill. Meanwhile, birds of prey – hawks, buzzards, owls ('cats with wings' as they've been described), sparrowhawks – those laziest of creatures, perch patiently atop telegraph poles, as if waiting for motorists to do their dirty work for them.

Described thus, the countryside of East Lothian and the life that it engenders would not seem markedly different from that experienced by those who lived a generation or two ago. Open in front of me as I write is George Scott-Moncrieff's book *The Lowlands of Scotland*. Among its many black and white plates are scenes I witness most weekends: roadside beeches, spectral and twisted like an arboreal interpretation of Munch's *Scream*; a hill stream, shallow and narrow, forging its course through spindly bracken; sheep voraciously grazing, like couch potatoes; a hedgerow-lined road with the broccoli-head of a forest at its end and the blank sea in the distance.

'East Lothian,' writes Scott-Moncrieff, 'is the heart of Lothian and one of the loveliest counties of the Lowlands. Its landscape lies in horizontal planes of colour: the ruddy twigs of stripped copses, green of grass, darker green of turnip and kale, dark and bright red ploughland. I suppose it is the rise and fall of the ground, neither too flat nor too broken, that makes the effect so marked. At harvest there are strokes of bronze-red wheat stubble: and earlier, stretches of mellowing grain. Towards Dunbar the earth is as red as the guts of man.'

But while elementally one may fool oneself that little has changed, that would be naive. As many of the diarists in this anthology are at pains to remind us, the countryside is in a constant state of evolution, some of which is natural and much of which is man-inspired. Even as Scott-Moncrieff was hymning East Lothian's easiness on the eye he must have been wincing at the unignorable, inharmonious, insensitive intrusion of Us. At the time he was writing, 1939, the bugbear was slag-heaps, the detritus of mining. In some places, he noted, there were 'Alps of red slag', welts and bruises designed, it would seem, to make a country lover's blood pressure balloon like the national debt. What is their counterpart today? The choice is various, rising on the Richter scale of irritation from ugly and unnecessary signage, the scattering of litter and the abandonment of caravans to the proliferation of wind farms, modern buildings the like of those in Slough which had John

Betjeman calling for the fall of 'friendly bombs', and the surrender of wild terrain to the game of golf.

In one's rage, one rails against all things new and modern. There is, though, even as fume emits from one's ears, the appreciation that nothing good ever lasts, that change is inevitable and that the countryside means different things to different people. One person's fallow field is another's potential landfill site or 'luxury' development. The countryside, it seems, is fair game for those who rarely visit it and care even less about it. It is just space to be filled and used, be it for another runway or a model village. Piece by piece, the jigsaw is filling up. Like lava, concrete spreads across land which, whether cultivated or not, is suffocated under its unyielding blanket. Nor, it would appear, is there much we can do about it, despite the creation of National Parks, the passing of legislation and the clout and claque of the Countryside Alliance. When I was a teenager, in the 1960s, the buzzword was 'greenbelt', a cordon around cities beyond which development was supposed to be forbidden. That has proved to be a pipedream, as acre after acre of what was once deemed sacrosanct has been swallowed in the maw of the bulldozer.

Of course, much countryside in Britain remains more or less unmolested. And, of course, too, much of it is as comely and rugged and serene as it ever was, a place where – on a good, inveterately inclement day – one could be far from the madding, shopping crowds. On a clear day from Bleak Law or Bullhope Law or Lowrans Law – 'law' being synonymous with 'hill' – you can see Edinburgh, 'well-set' as Auden said. To its east, at one o'clock, is the Bass Rock, whose lighthouse buildings, remarked Scott-Moncrieff, 'looked like something erected by an old seaman inside a bottle'. In fact, they were erected by Robert Louis Stevenson's uncle. The next landmark is teutonically sculptural, Torness nuclear power station, on the outskirts of Dunbar, set amidst some of the most fertile estate in Britain. Beside it is the landfill site where Edinburgh's waste is buried, a cement works and a barn the size of an aircraft hanger which houses a collection of avant-garde art.

Here it was in the eighteenth century that the geologist James Hutton studied the rocks on the foreshore and realised that they were detrital in origin, having been produced by erosion from the continents, deposited on the sea floor, transformed into stone by heat from below and then uplifted to form new continents. The cyclicity of such processes led him to envisage an Earth with 'no vestige of beginning and no prospect of an end'. Another former local resident was John Muir, the pioneer of American conservation, who argued successfully that Yosemite be granted National Park status, and after whom a nearby country park is named. Was Muir aware of Hutton? He surely was, but his knowledge of him, one suspects, was acquired belatedly, long after his family had emigrated from Dunbar to America.

For Muir, however, as for Hutton, East Lothian proved formative. 'When I was a boy in Scotland,' he wrote in his autobiography, 'I was fond of everything that was wild, and all my life I've been growing fonder and fonder of wild places and wild creatures. Fortunately around my native town of Dunbar, by the stormy North Sea, there was no lack of wildness, though most of the land lay in smooth cultivation. With red-blooded playmates, wild as myself, I loved to wander in the fields to hear the birds sing, and along the seashore to gaze and wonder at the shells and seaweeds, eels and crabs in the pools among the rocks when the tide was low; and best of all to watch the waves in awful storms thundering on the black headlands and craggy ruins of the old Dunbar Castle when the sea and the sky, the waves and the clouds, were mingled together as one. We never thought of playing truant, but after I was five or six years old I ran away to the seashore or the fields almost every Saturday, and every day in the school vacations except Sundays, though solemnly warned that I must play at home in the garden and back yard, lest I should learn to think bad thoughts and say bad words.'

Evidently, wildness, even in Muir's era, was under threat, something that needed to be sought, pursued, prized, cherished and nurtured. It is one of the threnetic themes of this book, in which diarists are continually intent on leaving behind a garrulous world where silence is increasingly difficult to find. Never truer were Thoreau's words: 'Men have become the tools of their tools.' However, in his book *The Wild Places*, Robert Macfarlane argues that there is more extant wildness than we sometimes think. 'It is easy to forget the physical presence of terrain,' he writes, 'that the countries we call England, Ireland, Scotland, Wales comprise more than 5,000 islands, 500 mountains and 300 rivers.'

One admires his optimism and would love to endorse it. But as Macfarlane himself acknowledges, his is an increasingly isolated voice. 'Time and again,' he notes, 'wildness has been declared dead in Britain and Ireland.' One of his doomsayers is John Fowles, one of the diarists who feature in this book. 'We are now, in hard fact, on the bleak threshold of losing much of the old landscape,' wrote Fowles. 'We have done unimaginably terrible things to our countryside. It is only here and there along our coasts and on the really high hills and mountains that the ancient richness of natural life is not yet in danger.'

Fowles's vision may strike some as extreme, even apocalyptic, but history appears to bear it out. His remarks, however, also reflect a change in attitude towards the countryside. For until relatively recently the countryside was there to be tamed, to be brought under our dominion, to become useful and profit-making, a resource to be exploited as we saw fit. Very few people considered it needed protection or conservation. Now there are myriad organisations, from the Campaign to Protect Rural England to the Open Spaces Society, the Council for National Parks to the Ramblers' Association, whose purposes overlap but who exist essentially to save the countryside from further urban invasion. It is, as Muir discovered in his heroic but vain attempt to foil the flooding of the Hetch Hetchy valley in Yosemite so that San Franciscans have an uninterrupted supply of water, an often hopeless, thankless task. Daily, man's needs come into conflict with those of the natural world, be it another mall, motorway or 'social' housing. Under-populated land is particularly vulnerable because it can offer little in the way of political leverage. Thus the majority's wishes almost always prevail. Down the centuries this has been dressed up variously. Some have called it improvement, others progress, still others modernisation. But call it what you will, it all amounts to much the same thing; the 'civilisation' of the countryside.

The fact is, as Rosemary Gibson describes in her book *The Scottish Countryside: Its Changing Face, 1700-2000*, that 'The rural landscape we see today is largely a man-made creation.' What's true of Scotland is undoubtedly the same for the rest of Britain. Three hundred years ago things were very different. 'Then,' writes Gibson, 'the landscape had a fragmented appearance, with numerous clusters of small farms scattered throughout. These were surrounded by narrow strips of cultivated ground in an otherwise bare landscape. Trees and hedges were scarce, but large areas of moorland and bog covered the countryside. There were few roads: many areas had only muddy tracks as a means of communication. But in the eighteenth and nineteenth centuries the appearance of the landscape changed dramatically.'

What happened was that agriculture was for many people no longer a viable means of making a living. Villages became depopulated, farms increased in size and farming was swiftly mechanised and industrial in scale. The consequences of this were far-reaching. By 1884, for example, Richard Jefferies, the son of a Wiltshire farmer and another of the diarists represented in the following pages, wrote, 'Now and again a finch, a starling or a sparrow would come to drink – athirst from the meadow or the corn-field – and start and almost entangle their wings in the bushes, so completely astonished that anyone should be there.'

This quote appears by way of an epigraph to Andrew O'Hagan's book *The End of British Farming*, which was published in 2001, the year of the last major outbreak of foot-and-mouth disease. Like O'Hagan, I wanted to see for myself the effects of foot-and-mouth on the countryside. As I travelled deep into the Scottish borders, from east to west, from Edinburgh towards Dumfries and Galloway, traffic thinned out until it became non-existent. There were empty roads for mile after mile. Entrances to farms and estates were taped off as if they were crime scenes and where admittance was essential there were mats sodden with disinfectant. Weirdly, given the circumstances, the fields were dense with sheep and cows which, of course, would be killed if found to be diseased. Occasionally one came across a pancaked badger or fox but to all intents and purposes the countryside had been closed off. No one was outdoors, no ramblers were on the hills, and in Gatehouse-of-Fleet, normally a magnet for tourists and day-trippers, you could have hit golf balls down the main street without fear of injuring anyone. Animals were being slaughtered in their hundreds of thousands and burnt in pyres. At the hotel in which I stayed, the only other guests were there because they were being paid to take part in the slaughter. 'Sheeping' was the euphemism they used to describe their ghastly task. Some of the men had come from the north-east of England for what was grim if comparatively well-paid work. The going rate was £18 for every sheep executed.

Nevertheless the government insisted that the worst was over. This outbreak of the disease had first been discovered at the end of February. By the beginning of March Scotland had its first case, which had been traced to a livestock dealer at Lockerbie in Dumfries and Galloway. Over the next couple of months more than 1.2 million animals were slaughtered in Scotland alone. As in the rest of the country, the disease was confronted by a rigorous stamping-out policy, which involved the wholesale slaughter of all animals on infected premises and all those regarded as 'dangerous contacts'. On the advice of the State Veterinary Service it was decided to impose a pre-emptive cull of all sheep within a radius of three kilometres of an infected farm. Later this was extended to cows.

The impact on the countryside was incalculable and traumatic. In a report on the outbreak, published in 2002 by the Royal Society of Edinburgh, VisitScotland – Scotland's national tourist agency – estimated that it had cost the tourism industry £200–250 million. That, though, did not take into account the lasting damage, be it psychological or economic. Once people stop going to a place it is difficult and expensive to persuade them to return. For the duration of foot-and-mouth the countryside was effectively closed and put in quarantine. It was like a place that had been evacuated or ethnically cleansed.

I spoke to Robin Spence, who farmed near Lockerbie. He said the waiting was the worst of it, watching the disease creep ever closer, praying against hope that your livestock would be spared. I thought of John Evelyn (another of the diarists represented in this book), writing not about a seventeenth-century outbreak of foot-and-mouth but its human equivalent, the Great Plague of 1665, in which people perished in their thousands and the shops stayed shut and the people remained at home, not knowing their fate, 'not knowing', as Evelyn put it, 'whose turne might be next'. In the event, Spence's herds and flocks did not escape and he lost more than 600 cattle and 700 sheep. Foot-and-mouth was diagnosed one day, a valuation – to compensate him for the loss of his animals – was arranged for eight o'clock the next morning, and an hour later the slaughter began. It went on until eleven o'clock that night. One could only imagine what it must have felt like to nurture recently born lambs and milk cows one day and then witness them being killed en masse the next. The animals were cremated and buried near his house and the pit was still smouldering two weeks later. You could see the smoke, he said, smell the flesh burning. He likened it to an anti-social barbecue.

But like the majority of farmers, Spence was determined to continue. Had he any option? His family had farmed in the area since 1947 and he had never considered doing anything else. It was a way of life; it was in the genes. You could tell by the way he talked and, despite everything that had happened, his attitude to life remained sunny. He was thirty-five years of age – young for a farmer these days – and unmarried. Many of his contemporaries who had been brought up on farms and were expected one day to step into their fathers' Wellington boots were increasingly seduced by urban delights, regular hours and creature comforts. The iPod generation were not attracted to cow dung and sheep dip. They saw the long hours their parents worked for low reward and determined to seek their fortunes elsewhere, away from mud-clogged byres, noxious smells and the edicts of Brussels-bound bureaucrats.

Five years later, on the anniversary of the foot-and-mouth outbreak, I returned to Dumfries and Galloway. Before heading off I called the editor of *Scottish Farmer* and asked how his magazine would be marking the occasion. There would be 'a token line', he said. In the aftermath of the outbreak, some farmers insisted that they'd had enough, that they would take the compensation and run, to who knows where. As it turned out, few did. Some used the government's money to diversify or try something new.

Dumfries and Galloway is one of those parts of Britain that it would not be unfair to call forgotten. Without a car, it is not easy to get around. (As John Fowles writes with feeling: 'The great folly of my life was not having learnt to drive.') Not without reason did John Buchan send Richard Hannay there when he wanted to make himself scarce. In those days trains were more frequent and stopped at more places. In the third-class carriage of a slow train Hannay encountered half a dozen hill farmers who were returning from the weekly market, including perhaps a forbear of Robin Spence, who puffed on their shag and clay pipes, 'their mouths full of prices' and their breaths 'highly flavoured with whisky'. At a station in the heart of a bog Hannay got off.

'It was a gorgeous spring evening,' wrote Buchan, 'with every hill showing as clear as cut amethyst. The air had the queer, rooty smell of bogs, but it was as fresh as mid-ocean, and it had the strangest effect on my spirits. I actually felt light-hearted. I might have been a boy out for a spring holiday tramp, instead of a man of thirty-seven very much wanted by the police . . . If you believe me, I swung along that road whistling. There was no plan of campaign in my head, only just to go on and on in this blessed, honest-smelling hill country, for every mile put me in a better humour with myself.'

Buchan's hymn was no hyperbole. The bosomy, velvet-green Galloway hills seem to stretch for ever, one folding gloriously into another like origami. The relative isolation of the region has bred a spirit of independence and inter-dependence, which is often the case in rural communities. Moreover, I was struck on my return by how unsentimental, pragmatic and adaptable farmers and others who live off the land tend to be. If stocking ostriches and llamas rather than sheep and pigs will keep the bank manager at bay, so be it. How the land is used may have changed but the land itself seemed impervious to this. Not so my own patch, I thought. Where once there were fields in which I picked leeks and gathered beetroot and turnip, and sat on summer's afternoons gorging on strawberries and raspberries, there are now houses, an industrial estate, schools and roads. And beside every perjink bungalow is a car which takes the family to the supermarket where local produce is highlighted as exotic, as once were Egyptian figs and Kenyan mangoes.

It is all part of our changing view of the countryside. The same month that I retraced my steps to Galloway, Clive Aslet, editor of *Country Life*, chronicled how things had moved on since the 1970s. Then, no newspaper worthy of the name would have been without an agricultural correspondent, and farming was regarded as a major industry. It also had its own ministry. In contrast, a few decades hence, 'agriculture was being treated as a sub-section of the countryside or environment brief'. Few people were employed on the land and concerns were growing about what farmers were doing in the countryside, with the increased use of pesticides, and about the welfare of animals. Farmers, formerly regarded with affection, had come routinely to be derided, like politicians or journalists. They were fat cats who'd got rich in the 1980s on European Union and other subsidies, in the process abusing the land of which they are caretakers. Any residual romantic notions about the countryside, a *Cider with Rosie* idyll, were obliterated with the advent of bovine spongiform encephalitis, or mad cow disease.

None of this was good news for rural Britain and for its sustaining industry, which was visibly shrinking and becoming more marginalised by the month. 'On the road to power,' reflected Aslet, 'Tony Blair, in white shirt and new shiny wellies, demonstrated his rural sympathies by visiting a farm in Bedfordshire.' He was rarely – if ever – seen on one thereafter. Farming may have been at the forefront of Prince Charles's mind, but it barely registered on Blair's radar, whose premiership will be remembered by country-dwellers for the banning of hunting while other pressing country matters, such as the lack of affordable housing for local people, the closure of rural pubs and post offices and the invisibility of public transport, went unremarked. To these Aslet added eyesores, such as wind farms and modern housing, which threatened to blight the landscape and make it less appealing to visitors.

What was true in 2006 is surely no less so today. But, as I found, it was not the whole story. For example, the owner of a guest-house in Gatehouse-of-Fleet whom I'd spoken to on my first visit reckoned that slowly but surely visitors were returning to the area. The annual Wigtown Show, a barometer of the community's spirit, was once again thriving. Meanwhile Robin Spence was gradually repopulating his 700 acres with livestock, though he was no longer interested in keeping sheep. Instead, he had 'ninety-odd' dairy cows and 650 fattening cattle. On the marriage front, however, there were 'no major developments'.

In hindsight, the foot-and-mouth crisis, horrible as it indubitably was, served to highlight many of the problems facing rural Britain. It may have been extreme but it was also illustrative of what the countryside and those who dwell in it have had to cope with down the centuries. Farming, more so than any other industry, is exposed to the vagaries of nature. In the past, when food was produced primarily for the table rather than the marketplace, the consequence of a bad harvest was hunger. The focus may have changed but the vagaries remain. The success of living in the countryside, much more so than in towns and cities, depends not only on what people do but on phenomena beyond their control. But, then, it was ever thus. That is why, as readers of this book will readily appreciate, the weather is of such predominant interest to country-dwellers. Indeed, the first sentence of the first entry, by the Rev. James Woodforde, is a description of 'a most dreadful Storm of Wind with Hail & Snow'. And so it continues, through the months and the seasons, across the decades and the centuries, day by day. Is there any nation on earth so obsessed with the weather? Does any other nation have quite so many weather connoisseurs?

Where country diarists are concerned, noting the weather is almost de rigueur. The template, if it may be called such, was drawn by Gilbert White, author of *The Natural History of Selborne* and *The Naturalist's Journal*. The latter, as White's biographer, Richard Mabey, has said, was prompted by the gift to White in 1767 of a set of printed forms described as *The Naturalist's Journal*. These were published by one Benjamin White and 'invented' by Daines Barrington, a prominent naturalist. Each page was designed to serve for a week and was divided 'horizontally into ten columns, for the recording of the wind, weather, plants first in flower and other details'. Another column was included for miscellaneous observations in which, Barrington said, 'it may also be proper to take notice of the common prognostics of the weather from animals, plants or hydroscopes, and compare them afterwards with the table of the weather, from which it may be perceived how far such prognostics can be relied upon . . . Many other particulars will daily offer themselves to the observer, when his attention to such points hath once become habitual, and from many such journals kept in different parts of the kingdom, perhaps the very best and accurate materials for a General Natural History of Great Britain may in time be expected, as well as many profitable improvements and discoveries.'

White took Barrington's advice to heart. Consequently, he produced a journal which is as fresh and interesting and illuminating today as it was when it was first written. The same may be said of many of the seventy or so diarists included in this anthology. Like diarists of other hues, the country species is as various as human beings. What binds them is their interest and concern for the countryside. Some, like White, like Dorothy Wordsworth and Roger Deakin, are noble amateur naturalists, for whom flora and fauna are the prime fascination. Others, such as Beatrix Potter, Thomas Turner, a village shopkeeper in eighteenth-century Sussex, and William Holland, are insatiable people-watchers, whose observations on the human comedy make engrossing reading. Still others, whose number includes Alan Clark, Sir Alec Guinness, Katherine Mansfield and Thomas Hardy, write colourful or humorous, emotional or descriptive diaries which just happen to be based in the country. We accompany Siegfried Sassoon on the hunting field, witness the killing of a badger through the eyes of Dearman Birchall, a nineteenth-century Gloucestershire squire, and learn from Francis Kilvert of an 'infallible' recipe for warming cold and wet feet on a journey. Collected together they offer a pointilliste-like portrait of the countryside over the past few centuries.

'What shall I write about?' asks the novelist Denton Welch. 'Shall I write about the bright morning with the sharp bird notes and the delicious spongy cooings of the pigeons on the roof of this house? Shall I write about the noises of the aeroplanes, the last flower on the wisteria that I can see mauve and pitiable out of my window? Shall I write about the war ending? Or of my breakfast of porridge, toast and marmalade and coffee? Or just about autumn. Waking up cold in the morning; coming back cold through the low blanket of mist by the waterfall last night – from the pub on Shipbourne Common, where Eric bought me a thimbleful of cherry brandy for three shillings, and we heard the loudmouthed woman holding forth on cubbing before breakfast.'

Welch, like so many diarists, needn't have bothered asking himself so many questions, for he knew the answers. Diarists create by accumulation, putting into print what they see and hear and think daily. As with previous anthologies with which the editor has been involved – *The Assassin's Cloak* and *The Secret Annexe* – the prime object in *The Country Diaries* has been readability. This is not an academic exercise, nor is intended for any other purpose than enjoyment. The book is arranged like a diary and, like a diary too, some days are fuller than others. Within each day entries are arranged chronologically. Some entries have been edited and a few have been translated into modern English. All of the diarists included have been published commercially, some in newspapers, whose country diaries offer a reflective haven in an otherwise clamorous world.

Not that one would like convey to readers the idea that what follows is in any way twee or soft-centred or naively romantic. On the contrary, as W.N.P. Barbellion, a naturalist on the staff of the Natural History Museum, was always eager to stress, the countryside and its contents are more robust than many think: 'Some folk don't like to walk over Bluebells or Buttercups or other flowers growing on the ground. But it is foolish to try to pamper Nature as if she were a sickly child. She is strong and can stand it. You can stamp on and crush a thousand flowers — they will all come up again next year.' Or so we must hope and trust.

# Acknowledgements

Anthologists are to literature what cuckoos and magpies are to ornithology. First thanks, therefore, must go to the diarists whose diaries I have plundered and the anthologists whose work I have piggybacked upon. The best places to unearth these gems are libraries, and the staff of three in particular – the National Library of Scotland, Edinburgh City Libraries and the University of Edinburgh Library – were especially helpful. I am grateful, too, to Canongate, my publisher, and in particular to Anya Serota who first floated the idea and Nick Davies who shepherded it into print. My copy editor, Annie Lee, was a model of enquiring efficiency and steely resolve. She may not have saved me from all the errors of my ways but because of her there are far fewer of them than there might have been. Any that remain, of course, are my fault entirely. I am also indebted to John Hinchcliffe whose illustrations are perfectly in tune with the text. Finally, and paramountly, a heartfelt thank you to Rosemary Goring, who has viewed this book's progress with the dispassionate air of a vet attending the prolonged birth of a calf and who, when push came to shove, was ready and eager to do her bit.

# JANUARY

# 1 January

1779 [Norfolk]

This morning very early about 1 o'clock a most dreadful Storm of Wind with Hail & Snow happened here and the Wind did not quite abait till the Evening. A little before 2 o'clock I got up, my bedsted rocking under me, and never in my life that I know of, did I remember the Wind so high or of so long continuance. I expected every Moment that some Part or other of my House must have been blown down, but blessed be God the whole stood, only a few Tiles displaced. My Servants also perceived their Bedsteds to shake. Thanks be to God that none of my People were hurt. My Chancel recd great Damage as did my Barn. The Leads from my Chancel were almost all blown up & smashed all to Pieces, the East Window also damaged but not greatly the North W Leads on the Top of the Church also, some of them blown up and ruffled, besides 2 Windows injured. The Clay on the North End of my Barn blown in and the West Side of the Roof, the Thatch, most all blown away, leaving many holes in it. The Damage sustained by me will amount I suppose to 50 pounds, if not more. However I thank God no Lives were lost that I hear of & I hope not. Mr Shadelows Barn, Michael Andrews's, with many others, all blown down. Numbers of Trees torn up by the Roots in many Places. In the Evening the Wind abated and was quite calm when I went to bed about 11 o'clock. Since what happened this morning, I prolonged the Letter that I designed to send to my Sister Pounsett to relate what had happened here by the Storm – And this Evening sent it by Mr Cary. A smart Frost this Evening. As the year begins rather unfortunately to me, hope the other Parts of it will be as propitious to me.

*James Woodforde*

## 1785 [Selborne, Hampshire]

Much snow on the ground. Ponds frozen-up & almost dry. Moles work: cocks crow. Ground soft under the snow. No field-fares seen; no wagtails. Ever-greens miserably scorched; even ivy, in warm aspects.

*Gilbert White*

## 1801 [Over Stowey, Salop]

Mr Amen called out of the barn to ring in the New Year, but the New Year has been *in* many hours ago. O Mr Amen, is this your method of proceding? Many things have been written in the newspapers pro and con the commencement of the New Century but nothing can be clearer to me than that the last century was all the preceding year in concluding. We were indeed in the year 1800 but that was not compleated before yesterday about twelve at night. The number ten being thus full and then we begin the number one of the New Century, but the year will not be compleated before twelve o'clock at night on 31 December next.

*William Holland*

## c.2000 [Walnut Tree Farm, Suffolk]

I am lying full length on my belly on frozen snow and frosty tussocks in the railway wood blowing like a dragon into the wigwam of fire at the core of a tangled blackthorn bonfire. I am clearing the blackthorn suckers that march out from the hedge like the army in *Macbeth*, the marching wood, threatening to overwhelm the whole wood in their dense spin thicket.

The technique is to get right down on the ground and go in with the triangular bow-saw at ground level, then grab the cut stems and drag the bushes away to the bonfire, which grows like a giant porcupine, bristling with spines that inflict a particular, unforgettable ache in the hands and thumbs of the woodman.

The bonfire just keeps working itself up to a sudden burst of wildly crackling, spitting flame, and burning a chimney up its centre. Then it dies down, frosting the twigs with fire but failing to ignite with any conviction because the wood is too fresh, too green and sappy. It is exhausting work, crawling at rabbit level through a blackthorn thicket and sawing through tough little trunks, You realise why blackthorn was used defensively as dead hedge by the Saxons; it is the true precursor of barbed wire.

I stumble back up the field for a tea-break to listen to myself on *Home Planet* on the radio and fall headlong in the snow by the shepherd's hut. Tracks everywhere in the snow, mostly rabbit, and a single bee orchid standing up with dried seeds in the snowy field.

A mauve, misty penumbra across the fields under a duck-egg sky and the glow of sunset. Everything very still and quiet.

*Roger Deakin*

## 2008 [Yorkshire]

A grey dark day and raining still, as it has been for the last week. Around four it eases off and we walk up by the lake. The waterfall at the top of the village is tumultuous, though the torrent has never been as powerful as it was in 1967 when (perhaps melodramatically) I envisaged the lake dam breaking and engulfing the whole village. The lake itself is always black and sinister, the farther cliff falling sheer into the water. It was once more exotically planted than with the pines that grow here now, as the Edwardian botanist Reginald Farrer used to sow the seeds he brought home from the Orient by firing them across the water into the cliff with a shotgun. The church clock is striking five when we turn back, the waterfall now illuminated under its own self-generated power, the same power that once lit the whole village, and I suppose one day might have to do so again.

*Alan Bennett*

# 2 January

## 1759 [East Hoathly, Sussex]

About 7.30 I went down to Mr Porter's, where I supped on some veal cutlets, 3 roasted chicken, a cold ham, sausages, a cold chicken pastry and tarts, in company with Mr and Mrs Coates, Jos. Fuller, Mr French and his wife, Mr Calverley, Tho. Fuller and his wife, Mrs Atkins and Mrs Eliz. Hicks. We played at brag in the even. My wife and I won 12d. which we gave to servants. We came home about 2.30 in the morn but I cannot say quite sober, that is, in regard to myself . . .

*Thomas Turner*

## 1996 [Essex House, Badminton]

Between Christmas and the New Year the weather has been record-breaking for arctic conditions. The cold really agonising. How lucky, I keep repeating to myself, that I am at home and not stranded in someone else's house, nor someone else in mine.

*James Lees-Milne*

# 3 January

## 1903 [Barnstaple, North Devon]

Am writing an essay on the life-history of insects and have abandoned the idea of writing on 'How Cats Spend their Time'.

*W.N.P. Barbellion*

## 2004 [Yorkshire]

Alan Bates dies on 27 December and we break the journey from Yorkshire at Derby in order to go to his funeral. It's at Bradbourne, a tiny village the taxi driver has never heard of, and he and his Asian colleagues have a map session before we eventually head off into the Derbyshire hills. The cab is old and draughty, it's beginning to snow and as we drive through this landscape of lost villages and frostbitten fields it gets more and more foggy and like a journey out of *Le Grand Meaulnes*.

It's all of an hour before we reach the church and everyone has gone in, the undertakers with a policeman looking on just shouldering the coffin. Since the bill is £40 I feel I need a receipt but while the driver ransacks his cab for a pad and pencil the policeman saunters over: 'The body is waiting to go in, sir.'

We make an undignified dash for the church where, hearing the door open, the congregation begin to rise, thinking we're the coffin, then sink back disappointed as, laden down with bags and both with backpacks on, we are ushered down the centre aisle to seats in the chancel. It looks like the most upstaging of showbiz entrances, the only consolation being that the deceased would have been the first to laugh.

*Alan Bennett*

# 4 January

1831 [Abbotsford, the Scottish Borders]
A base, gloomy day, and dispiriting in proportion. I walked out with Swanston [a forester] for about an hour: everything gloomy as the back of the chimney when there is no fire in it. My walk was a melancholy one, feeling myself weaker at every step and not very able to speak. This surely cannot be fancy, yet it looks something like it. If I knew but the extent at which my inability was like to stop, but every day is worse than another. I have trifled much time, too much; I must try to get afloat to-morrow, perhaps getting an amanuensis might spur me on, for one-half is nerves. It is a sad business though.

*Sir Walter Scott*

# 5 January

1701 [Wotton, Surrey]
The frost & Snow which so sudainly surpriz'd us, for a greater snow had scarse ben known to fall in one night: mealted away as sudainly by a gentle Thaw.

*John Evelyn*

## 1918 [Hogarth House, Richmond]

Then we took a tram to Kingston & had tea at Atkinsons, where one may have no more than a single bun. Everything is skimped now. Most of the butchers' shops are shut; the only open shop was besieged. You can't buy chocolates, or toffee; flowers cost so much that I have to pick leaves instead. We have cards for most foods. The only abundant shop windows are the drapers. Other shops parade tins, or cardboard boxes, doubtless empty. (This is an attempt at the concise, historic style.) Suddenly one has come to notice the war everywhere. I suppose there must be some undisturbed pockets of luxury somewhere still – up in Northumbrian or Cornish farm houses perhaps; but the general table is pretty bare. Papers, however, flourish, & by spending 6d we are supplied with enough to light a week's fires.

*Virginia Woolf*

## 1950 [Leigh-on-Sea, Essex]

A whim to go afar. To Canvey Island, up the sea-wall to Shell Haven [an oil refinery and storage depot]. A pale, cold, half-fine day; obscure blueness and insistent clouds, general bright blue-greyness, making in the morning the grass very green and the water grey and ruffled, an aqueous brightness everywhere. Later the weather settled into a cold, windy dullness. This part of Canvey isolated, overrun by rabbits. I meet a friendly man, with a red face, carrying an old sack bag with a bottle in it. One of the few country-men left. Then on into a wasteland of rubble-dumps, with to-and-fro lorries, cranes, wharves, distant oil-tanks. One or two houses deserted, forsaken; few birds. A strange part of the world. It seems so deserted in contrast with the oil-shipping atmosphere given by the tanks. I don't pass a soul. The creek here is wide, bleak and impersonal, another world from Old Leigh.

Past the oil-tanks home, they seem without men; past a white house set in a few shrubby trees, with one room lit on the top floor, past and around a deserted army camp, full of huts, towers and desuetude, back into the myriad-housed centre of Canvey. All bungalows and jerry-built, yet full of television aerials. The people, this centre, seem to ignore the desolation and harshness of the rest of the island east, with its hundreds of acres of grassland and marshy drains. Like the heart of the lettuce.

*John Fowles*

# 6 January

## 1802 [Over Stowey, Somerset]

Still snow, a vast quantity fell last night and now it continues to snow. Mr Amen snug at home tho' I have work for him in the barn. I see people moving about at the ends of long rusty guns, I fear mischief will be done. A brace of woodcocks and a goose brought me from Rich of Pepperill. I took the goose out of compassion for a large family but the woodcocks were immoderately dear, besides I have a woodcock and a hare and snipes in the house, and another to be brought today from another quarter. Master Morris put on boots that I gave him to walk in the snow. I told him I did not give them for that purpose, had they been old thick rusty boots, it would be another thing. What terrible weather this is for all kinds of birds, no food to be found anywhere and man, cruel man, adding to their calamity by hunting after their lives in every quarter, the whole region resounds with pops and explosions. Ann went off before dinner to her Father's, being Old Christmas Day when all the family are to meet, I like the plan very much and I find it much practised among the lower orders in this country. Betty, under the direction of Margaret managed the dinner which was sent up very neatly and we enjoyed ourselves.

*William Holland*

## 1997 [Yorkshire]

Ring Mr Redhead, the coal-merchant in Ingleton.

'Hello, Mr Redhead, this is Alan Bennett. I'm wanting some coal.'

'Goodness me! I am consorting with higher beings!'

Last time I rang Mr Redhead he said, 'Well, I don't care how celebrated you are, you'll never be a patch on your dad.' I remind him of this.

'That's correct and I reiterate it.'

*Alan Bennett*

# 7 January

## 1814 [Dorset]

The weather became so intensely severe, that the people of the house were busily employed in preparing puddings of the larks and other birds, which flocked into the house and shed, and were not only there, but even in the furze and on the shore, easily taken with the hand. I fired at 5 geese out of reach and shot a plover, which I lost (at night). Out sailing the whole day with a strong N.E. wind, and the severest cold I ever felt, and literally never saw a flock of wild fowl. Was all over Poole harbour, and very near Wareham, where, according to report of punters from that place, the same unheard-of scarcity prevailed. Such was the intensity of cold that I picked up pocketfuls of larks that had perished and fallen in the water, and on our return old Sturney and I had a hairbreadth escape of sharing the same fate, getting driven on a mud bank 2 miles from land; luckily, however, by throwing our ballast overboard &c. we got afloat just in time to save the tide.

*Colonel Peter Hawker*

## 1877 [Clyro, Radnorshire]

I went to the farmhouse of Dolfach on the hill to see the Holy Thorn there in blossom. The tree (a graft from the old Holy Thorn at Tibberton now cut down) bloomed on old Christmas Eve and there were 15 people watching round the tree to see it blow at midnight. I found old John Perry sitting at tea by the cheery firelight in the chimney corner. His kind daughter gave me a bit of spray off the Holy Thorn which was gathered from the tree at midnight, old Christmas Eve. She set great store by the spray and always gathered and kept a bit each year. The blossoms were not fully out and the leaves were scarcely unfolded but the daughter of the house assured me that the little white bud clusters would soon come out into full blow if put in soft water.

*Francis Kilvert*

## 1974 [Alderley Grange, Gloucestershire]

A. [his wife] is shocked that Olive Lloyd-Baker, that highly respectable county lady, lately High Sheriff of Gloucestershire, and dressed soberly and becomingly, has suddenly transformed herself. She now has short, closely cropped grey hair like a man, and wears a man's jacket, trousers and tie, in fact Radclyffe Hall rig. I say that her inhibitions of a lifetime have been released after seventy-one years because she has overlapped the age of permissiveness. She was always a secret lesbian and has now thrown her cap over the windmill.

*James Lees-Milne*

## 1991 [Wainfleet, Lincolnshire]

Never before have I found a rare bird so easy to observe. Only seconds after our arrival, and from several kilometres away, it stood out on these dark, sodden coastal fields like a miniature snowman. Snowy owl, the second largest owl in western Eurasia, is a truly magnificent creature. This bird, a male, was pure white apart from brown tips to some of the wing, mantle and tail feathers. Remaining immobile for long periods, the owls may easily be overlooked as just another pale rock. For the first hour of observation our bird was justifying the snowy's reputation for inertia. And for all its rarity and spectacular appearance, watching a completely stationary white object from several hundred metres away in the middle of a windswept field eventually began to pall. I was even tempted to abandon it briefly and follow a short-eared owl as it hunted along the field margin. Then suddenly all changed. The great white wings opened and it cruised off, swooping unsuccessfully at some panic-stricken partridge. Then, rather unexpectedly, he landed a few metres from a large hare. For a few comical seconds, the mammal (a potential prey species for the owl) seemed to blink at the pale apparition in disbelief, before beating a hasty retreat.

*Mark Cocker*

# 9 January

1768 [Selborne, Hampshire]
Lambs begin to fall. Nothing frozen in my cellar. Titmice pull straws from the eaves.

*Gilbert White*

# 10 January

1771 [Norfolk]
Brother John was greatly astonished by a Light this Evening as he came thro' Orchards, a Field by Ansford Church, which Light seemed to follow close behind him all the way through that Field & which he could not account for. I hope it is no Omen of Death in the Family. N.B. The Reflection of the snow I apprehend occasioned the Light that my Brother saw.

*James Woodforde*

1785 [Fyfield, Hampshire]
3 Herons feeding in the green wheat. Mr Lockston called and Mr and Mrs Lane drove over. Electricity by experiment, vast effect produced by me, by combing my hair.

*Henry White*

1824 [Halifax, West Yorkshire]
Washed & scaled my teeth with my penknife.

*Anne Lister*

1974 [Belmont, Lyme Regis]
I finish the article on subsidence in Lyme.

Our new card game is piquet, which I used to play with my father as a schoolboy. A very great game, far nobler and deeper and more enjoyable than the others we have tried. No better blend of skill and hazard.

Endless gales, three in the last week; one this morning was briefly the most savage for a long time. The branches of the old Italian cypress were bending like trout-rods. I will my trees to survive. And more rain this month already, it seems, than for the whole of January last year. I fear the ironies of existence: that my paper on subsidence will be met by reality at the bottom of the garden.

*John Fowles*

1980 [Sanna, Ardnamurchan]

How trusting-hungry are the small birds now! When I scattered crumbs at the garden gate this afternoon (later than usual for it was dusk and town-bred birds would have been well-filled to bed an hour before), a dozen sparrows hung precariously in the gusts, a bare yard or two from my hand. Though the gale thrust them constantly downwind, away from the source of food, still they persisted, flapping like little machines in an effort to keep pace with their own lives. At times they took the whirling nourishment on the wing.

*Alasdair Maclean*

## 11 January

1946 [Inverness-shire]

I have come from the closeness and intimacy of a country ceilidh, and ceilidhs in country districts have just enough interest to absorb me. When belated 'good nights' are said, I stand for a moment looking at the door that shuts me out from its inhabitants and cheer; I look at the great, clear, silent world stretching before me, and I am the most solitary being in existence, solitary only until I have walked far enough from the hospitable house to throw away its songs, its laughter, its intimacy from my mind. Then I cease being solitary and become immersed into the being of a moonlit, winter's night.

*Jessie Kesson*

# 12 January

## 1764 [Norfolk]

Breakfasted, supped &c. at Home. After Breakfast I rose upon Cream to my Curacy at Babcary about six Miles from hence, where I dined upon a Sheeps Heart that I carried there in my Pocket . . .

*James Woodforde*

## 1875 [Clyro, Radnorshire]

William Ferris told me to-day his reminiscences of the first train that ever came down the Great Western Railway. 'I was foddering,' he said, 'near the line. It was a hot day in May some 34 or 35 years ago, and I heard a roaring in the air. I looked up and thought there was a storm coming down from Christian Malford roaring in the tops of the trees, only the day was so fine and hot. Well, the roaring came nigher and nigher, then the train shot along and the dust did flee up.'

*Francis Kilvert*

## 1984 [Stromness, Orkney]

An old friend, George Maskell, from the west coast, arrived two evenings ago with a present of a pair of kippers. Nothing very remarkable about that, you may say; except that those kippers came from the place on earth most renowned for kippers, it's said.

It is a strange thing to say, but I haven't tasted a kipper for years. And why should that be, when kippers are among the tastiest food the sea produces – a rival to trout and smoked salmon?

The simple explanation is that in winter the kitchen window seizes up – the wood swells with rain – and so the smells of cooking must linger for a while. Of all the world's smells of cooking, fried kippers produce the richest oiliest longer-lasting smell (it reminds me of nothing so much as one of those Islay malts, that roll heavy and rich as peat-smoke about the tongue). So, after kippers, one can go about with the kipper-incense clinging for days, maybe, to the clothes. And right over the cooker is the pulley where the washing hangs – imagine putting kipper-penetrated newly-washed clothes back in the clothes cupboard!

*George Mackay Brown*

1997 [Saltwood Castle, Kent]

Lovely and enclosed by snow/fog. The M-way is silent, and one is reminded how peaceful, magical Saltwood could be transferred to a position in, say, Herefordshire, or the Welsh marches.

*Alan Clark*

## 13 January

1812 [Over Stowey, Somerset]

This morning was fine, a day rather mild for the time of the year. We had a good deal of bustle about a marriage. Old Savage Ware, past seventy, married to Jane Long, about sixty. Old Ware had lost his teeth and I had hard work to make him pronounce his words right. They were married out of the Poor House but kept their Revelling at Molly Weymouth's of the next door. The day afterwards they marched to a house of Ware's at Tyren. Ware, tho old, is a very laborious hearty workman. His children do not behave well to him and so he married.

*William Holland*

## 14 January

1977 [Combe Florey, Somerset]

Only 20 days after Christmas and our guests are beginning to leave for their various employments. It has been an expensive and debilitating business keeping them drunk enough to lose when I play them at ping-pong.

The season has been marred by ugly squabbles over the Stilton cheese – between those who prefer to scoop it out and those who say that the only sane or civilised approach is to slice it like Cheddar. I have no strong feelings on the matter, but this year I've noticed a sinister dogmatism and aggressiveness on the part of the slicers. Next year we had better order two Stiltons if we are to avoid bloodshed.

Or perhaps we shall have none. God knows what the future holds at a time when the overweening truculence of the workers is met by a middle class so hideously divided.

*Auberon Waugh*

# 15 January

### 1795 [Norfolk]

Got up this morning very bad indeed in the Gout in my right foot, could scarce bare to put him on the ground, and so it continued the whole Day and night, not free one Minute from violent pain. The Weather Most piercing, severe frost, with Wind & some Snow, the Wind from the East and very rough. We had some boiled Beef & a Hare rosted for dinner. I could eat but very little indeed for dinner to day. I had my bed warmed tonight & a fire in my bed-Room. I never was attacked so severe before in my life. Obliged to put on my great Shoe, lined with flannel. The Weather very much against me besides.

*James Woodforde*

### 1875 [Clyro, Radnorshire]

Speaking to the children at the school about the Collect for the 2nd Sunday after the Epiphany and God's peace I asked them what beautiful image and picture of peace we have in the xxxiii Psalm. 'The Good Shepherd,' said I, 'leading his sheep to − ?' 'To the slaughter,' said Frederick Herriman promptly. One day I asked the children to what animal is our Saviour compared in the Bible. Frank Matthews confidently held out his hand. 'To an ass,' he said.

*Francis Kilvert*

1973 [Belmont, Lyme Regis]

One dormouse nest, but empty. We have cleared part of the bank above the palm-tree this winter, and I'm afraid it must have been dislodged from there.

The *New Statesman* asked me to review novels last summer; and at last have taken up my counter-offer to do country books. The one they sent was worth waiting for: Ladurie's *Times of Feast, Times of Famine*, a remarkable and (unintentionally) poetic account of past climate and how it is detected. Extraordinary, the painstaking ingenuity of the methods used.

*John Fowles*

## 16 January

1755 [East Hoathly, Sussex]

This morning about 1 o'clock I had the misfortune to lose my little boy Peter, aged 21 weeks, 3 days. Paid for flour and other small things. At home all day. In the even read the 11th and 12th books of *Paradise Regained*, which I think is much inferior for the sublimity of style to *Paradise Lost*.

*Thomas Turner*

1871 [Clyro, Radnorshire]

Called on Lewis the policeman, who was in difficulty to know what to do with some Clyro boys who had been playing football on a Sunday.

*Francis Kilvert*

## 17 January

1697 [Wotton, Surrey]

The severe frost & weather not relenting, and freezing with snow, againe kept us from Church.

*John Evelyn*

1807 [Over Stowey, Somerset]

The weather is uncommonly mild for the season. Yesterday the Bell tolled and startled me in the morning. It was for Old Porter who (shocking to relate) had a child by his own daughter. I never heard of his illness before and I am sorry for this as I would certainly have called on him and spoken to him and prayed by him. He was ill once before and I attended him but he shocked me by his insensibility on speaking of the shocking crime he had been guilty of. He answered that he hoped God would forgive him. I replied that I hoped so too but that it was a crime of a most heinous Nature. There are others as bad as me he answered quick.

*William Holland*

1903 [Barnstaple, North Devon]

Went with L out catapult shooting. While walking down the road saw a Goldfinch, but very indistinctly – it might not have been one. Had some wonderful shots at a tree creeper in the hedge about a foot away from me. While near a stream, L spotted what he thought to be some Wild Duck and brought one down, hitting it right in the head. He is a splendid shot. We discovered on examining it that it was *not* a Wild Duck at all but an ordinary tame Wild Duck – a hen. We ran away, and to-night L tells me he saw the Farmer enter the poulterer's shop with the bird in his hand.

*W.N.P. Barbellion*

# 18 January

1825 [Upper Slaughter, Gloucestershire]

My mother's funeral at Chipping Norton. A most gloomy wet morning after a stormy night was congenial to the depression of my spirits. It was half past ten before we could reach the church. The service was performed by the curate, a vulgar unfeeling man: his careless manner, his uncouth pronunciation and coarse appearance were all forbidding. Crowds of curious spectators flocked round the coffin and vault; but all was curiosity, no sympathy was visible; most trying is this appearance of indifference and equally so the suppressed voices of the assistants as they lowered the coffin through the narrow mouth of the vault, grating against the top of the arch and at length - deposited beside the last inmate of the dark abode.

I cannot and ought not to lose sight of the blessings still reserved to me by a gracious Providence, an affectionate wife, a promising child, and ample provision of earthly comforts.

*F.E. Witts*

### 1969 [Belmont, Lyme Regis]

Tragedy at the bottom of the garden. We've had two or three days of violent gale and wind, to hurricane force at times. Just before six this evening the catamaran in the harbour broke adrift and to sea. The little lifeboat put out to bring it back; overturned; and one of the men, Robert Jeffard, known as Nimmer, was drowned. We didn't see it happen but went down at midnight to the Cobb and saw the battered lifeboat being trucked back. It wasn't, alas, a simple story of heroism. Jeffard and Roy Gollop, the fisherman, had a salvage interest in the 'cat'; and rang up the lifeboat secretary to ask if they could use the lifeboat. He foolishly said they could; so they did a stupid thing for a few pounds. We'd been watching the huge seas from the house all day, saying how no one could have lived out there in it. Now the whole of Lyme is angry and wants a scapegoat. But in a way it was a regional tragedy; the traditional greed of the inshore seaman, always on the scrounge, and West Country hatred of seeing a good penny roll down a drain.

*John Fowles*

## 19 January

### 1805 [Over Stowey, Somerset]

I walked into the garden and found a Robin Redbreast in my trap. I did not know before that they destroyed pease.

*William Holland*

# 20 January

### 1798 [Alfoxden, the Lake District]

The green paths down the hillsides are channels for streams. The young wheat is streaked by silver lines of water running between the ridges, the sheep are gathered together on the slopes. After the wet dark days, the country seems more populous. It peoples itself in the sunbeams. The garden, mimic of spring, is gay with flowers. The purple-starred hepatica spreads itself in the sun, and the clustering snow-drops put forth their white heads, at first upright, ribbed with green, and like a rosebud; when completely opened, hanging their heads downwards, but slowly lengthening their slender stems. The slanting woods of an unvarying brown, showing the light through the thin net-work of their upper boughs. Upon the highest ridge of that round hill covered with planted oaks, the shafts of the trees show in the light like columns of a ruin.

*Dorothy Wordsworth*

### 1922 [Gloucestershire]

Hunt, Kemble. Moderate day. Mare went beautifully.

*Siegfried Sassoon*

### 1936 [Ross & Cromarty]

Eventually we get to Tain and go to the little inn where we are received by a man in a kilt and given a dram. We walk across to the Town Hall, where there are the Provost, two ex-Provosts, and the local dominie. A good platform. The hall is amazingly full for such a night. The gallery is packed. The Provost makes a speech, and then I talk for 45 minutes. It goes very well indeed. Then we take the old boys round to the inn and have more drams. And then off we go into the night. Twenty-five miles to Dingwall skidding and slithering. The sound of water in the mist. Then the lighted hotel and the journalists in the lounge and warmth and sandwiches.

'How is the King?' is our first question. 'The 11.45 bulletin was bad. It said that His Majesty's life was moving peacefully to its close.' How strange!

That little hotel at Dingwall, the journalists, the heated room, beer, whisky, tobacco, and the snow whirling over the Highlands outside. And the passing of an epoch. I think back to that evening twenty-six years ago when I was having supper at the Carlton and the waiter came and turned out the lights: 'The King [Edward VII] is dead.'

*Harold Nicolson*

## 21 January

1830 [Upper Slaughter, Gloucestershire]

We had yesterday a very heavy fall of snow, accompanied with a very tempestuous wind which drifted the snow as it fell and so obstructed the roads. The fool-hardiest of travellers today was my neighbour Mr Dolphin who undertook to drive his coach and four from Lasborough, the seat of the Hon H. Moreton, five miles beyond Tetbury, a distance of 40 miles from Eyford. He had gone thither with his wife and her friend Miss Green on Tuesday with two female and three male domestics, to be ready to attend a ball given by Mr M. at Tetbury. He was entreated to stay, but my squire was a little wilful and started, with the addition of a couple of cart horses to force their way through the drifts in Lasborough Park. On the road through Tetbury, Cirencester, etc., he was more than once forced to put cart horses in requisition; no line of road can be more exposed. No carriage of any sort, cart or wagon had attempted to pass along. At times the drifts of snow were so deep, that the footboard in front of the box divided the snow like the prow of a vessel ploughing the waves; often the hind wheels were buried in the drifts, unable to revolve being entirely clogged with more snow, so the machine was dragged on bodily, rolling and pitching from side to side. Much credit ought to be given to my neighbour for consummate skill in the art which he professes best to understand, the art of coachmanship. Between 6 and 7 o'clock the cavalcade had reached the purlieus of Upper Slaughter but here their progress was inevitably stopped. To force their way through the drifts extending to the Cheltenham road, up the hill through my fields was beyond even Dolphin's skill and daring, and in a few minutes the whole party, coach, horses, servants etc., came to an anchor in my stable yard. I was summoned from my fireside.

Not small was the confusion in the dark. Poor Mrs D. half dead with fright and cold, hysterical, fainting, fearing, laughing, crying by turns; Miss Green more collected but sadly frightened. It was resolved that leaving the coach behind an attempt should be made to reach Eyford on foot. Wine and biscuits and the warmth of a good fire renovated the dropping strength and spirits of the ladies. The gala cloaks and muffs were left behind; my ladies equipped their friends in wraps of humbler pretensions but better calculated to face the inclemency of the night. We later learned with satisfaction the group had safely reached home.

F.E. Witts

# 22 January

### 1798 [Alfoxden, the Lake District]
Walked through the wood to Holford. The ivy twisting round the oaks like bristled serpents.

Dorothy Wordsworth

### 1822 [Halifax, West Yorkshire]
One of Mr Taylors (the young man) came at 7 this morning to destroy the old mare, Diamond. He stabbed her through the heart & she was dead in less than 5 minutes & buried immediately ... At 12, off in the gig to Halifax. Called at Isabella's washerwoman, then drove a little up Pellon Lane, then thro' the town ... Got home between 2 & 3 ... Tib drove from Halifax to Lightcliffe this morning. I really think I am as good, tho' not quite so stylish a driver as she. She ran us with the top against the wool sacks on a cart at the bottom of the Cunnery Lane & if all the horses had not been steady it might have been awkward. In spite of her not allowing herself to be ever frightened at anything, she was rather nervous after it.

Anne Lister

1984 [Combe Florey, Somerset]

When a couple in the Cornish village of Tywardreath, near St Austell, decide to show a little initiative and turn their semi-detached home into a massage parlour, they are immediately 'exposed' by a local reporter, raided by the police, prosecuted and forced to leave the neighbourhood.

The creep of a reporter is called Simon Heppenstall. I have already reported him to Friends of Massage. If he ever seeks employment in Fleet Street, he will be a marked man.

*Auberon Waugh*

# 23 January

1904 [Barnstaple, North Devon]

Went to meet the Stag hounds. Saw a hind in the stream at L with not a horse, hound, or man in sight. It looked quite unconcerned and did not seem to have been hunted. I tried to head it, but a confounded sheep-dog got there before me and drove it off in the wrong direction. I *was* mad, because if I had succeeded in heading it and there had been a kill, I should have got a slot. Got home at 6.30, after running and walking fifteen miles – tired out.

*W.N.P. Barbellion*

1927 [Knole, Kent]

Vita [Sackville-West] took me over the 4 acres building, which she loves: too little conscious beauty for my taste: smallish rooms looking on to buildings: no views: yet one or two things remain: Vita stalking in her Turkish dress, attended by small boys, down the gallery, wafting them on like some tall sailing ship – a sort of covey of noble English life: dogs walloping, children crowding, all very free and stately: & [a] cart bringing wood in to be sawn by the great circular saw. How do you see that? I asked Vita. She said she saw it as something that had gone on for hundreds of years. They had brought wood in from the Park to replenish the great fires like this for centuries: & her ancestresses had walked so on the snow with their great dogs bounding beside them. All the centuries seemed lit up, the past expressive, articulate;

not dumb & forgotten; but a crowd of people stood behind, not dead at all; not remarkable; fair faced, long limbed; affable; & so we reach the days of Elizabeth quite easily. After tea, looking for letters of Dryden's to show me, she tumbled out a love letter of Ld Dorsets (17th century) with a lock of his soft gold tinted hair which I held in my hand a moment. One had a sense of links fished up into the light which are usually submerged.

*Virginia Woolf*

### 1994 [Essex House, Badminton]

In the afternoon I walk to Worcester Lodge, an hour and a half. Not bad, considering my legs are now feeble. A fine afternoon with sun, with heralding of spring and definite whispering of Siren songs. Even at eighty-five I am disturbed, wanting to be off. In the garden a few aconites and snowdrops already out; and the goldfish, who should be hibernating at the bottom of the pool, are darting about.

*James Lees-Milne*

### 1999 [Saltwood Castle, Kent]

This morning incredibly frustrated trying to make cars respond. Batteries, carburettor needle sticking and petrol flood, damp terminals, etc etc. Quietly I went into the family garden and attacked fruiting bodies. A slightly petty piece in *The Times* by Matthew Parris attacking me for my 'love' of animals. This is the third time he has been unpleasant about me since I came back. Triggered, I suppose, by my – much acclaimed – Mandelson review. Essentially, all Parris is interested in is homosexual politics; the emancipation of homosexuals.

*Alan Clark*

## 24 January

### 1917 [Lewes, Sussex]

Went to view Dr Belcher's things. Nothing there I wanted. The squalor and heartlessness of sales. His hat box on the bed and 'lotted'. I remember Sunday mornings he, scrupulous in tall hat, and our little walks up the street after

church. Meanwhile, it's the coolest winter for 22 years they say. I can't sleep
or think. Brain and soul set solid in ice.

*Alice Dudeney*

### c.2000 [Walnut Tree Farm, Suffolk]

In the early sunshine, I strip to the waist, sit outside the kitchen doorstep
before a mirror propped up in a cane chair and cut my hair. It feels good,
even rejuvenating, to strip off the professor-like abundance of locks and feel
the sun on my skin.

*Roger Deakin*

## 25 January

### 1805 [Somerset]

I met today young Mackay who is come to see his sick father. This young
man is his son by a Negro Woman and has had from the father an excellent
education and is in Orders and has two Livings and is in good circumstances. Pity that he should suffer his father to suffer distress in his later
days, but he is so far from assisting him that in all his visits he is drawing
money from him and plundering him and I fear that poor Mrs Mackay will
be left without a shilling – I am not very partial to West Indians, especially
to your Negro Half Blood people.

*William Holland*

### 1906 [Farnham, Surrey]

Numerous tales are coming out, of attempts to coerce the labourers into
voting conservative. The Brewery men were all told how to vote, by the
chiefs. A district visitor (Miss Crump, I think) visiting her own tenants, told
them that if they supported the Liberal candidate, they could not be allowed
to stay in their cottages. Bide affirmed that he was going to bring his 100
men to vote for Brodrick. It is said that Charrington of Frensham Hill is
so overcome as to threaten that if he finds any man of his to have voted
for Cowan, that man will be immediately dismissed: further, he will deal no
more in Farnham: we are not to 'get the big loaf out of *him*'! At Waverley

Abbey, all the men had to wear Tory colours and were taken to the poll. But amongst themselves they said, of Brodrick, 'he's the feller as wants to interfere with our grub'; and they voted against him. They didn't talk so, though, when their master was by. (This is the tale of the wife of one of the men, who had spoken so to Miss Ketchell, Ann's lodger, in her shop.)

*George Sturt*

# 26 January

### 1784 [Norfolk]

I rejoiced much this morning on shooting an old Woodpecker, which has teized me a long Time in pulling out the Reed from my House. He had been often shot at by me and others, but never could be a match for him till this Morn'. For this last 3 Years in very cold Weather did he use to come here and destroy my Thatch. Many holes he has made this Year in the Roof, and as many before.

*James Woodforde*

### 1809 [Somerset]

In the evening I was called out to see two very bright stars very near each other. I viewed the stars through my telescope, they seemed very near each other and something similar in their faces tho one was brighter than the other. There seemed clearly and distinctly a black line round the surface of each with a luminous appearance beyond this ridge like a border and the middle had several black dots like writing in two or three lines across. They both had apparently some kind of dots or lines but the one was far more luminous than the other. My wife and I and all our people were out and I do not remember seeing such a thing before. I suppose our papers will be full of it tomorrow.

*William Holland*

### 1906 [Olton, Warwickshire]

The last few weeks, our own and our neighbours' gardens have been haunted by a very curious Robin. The whole of the upper plumage, which in ordinary

Robins is brown, shaded with olive green, is light silvery grey in this bird, so that when flying about it looks like a white bird with a scarlet breast. I hear that it was seen about here last summer, it is so conspicuous it is a wonder it has not fallen victim to somebody's gun.

*Edith Holden*

## 1978 [Stromness, Orkney]

I confess to a growing aversion, as I get older, to going out on winter's nights.

Round about the festive time, there was a cluster of invitations, all in the space of a few nights. Going by car to Kirkwall, in answer to one invitation, I observed with apprehension a large silver moth (a snowflake, to you unacquainted with our Norse habit of kennings), fluttering on to the car window and dying a watery death there. And I thought, supposing it is only the first of a billion silver moths, and we end up at 2 or 3 in the morning in some vast snow-drift near Maeshowe!

There was no need to worry. Such was the generosity of our Kirkwall hostess, we went home a merry car-ful: and the night was sweet and dark.

A few nights later, things looked more serious. A black half-gale, filled with sleet, was blowing athwart our road. We sat at another kind board, but outside the storm was getting wilder and wilder.

In other circumstances, I might have asked for a bed for the night; but with a Barleycorn glow inside one, one is ready to face anything . . . It was, I assure you, quite a thrilling drive home. From time to time the car was wrapped in a dense throbbing blizzard; that thinned out, and lightened; and showed the landscape under a new coating of snow. And there on the horizon another ink-black cloud swelled to engulf us. It was very exhilarating. (On an ordinary night I would have been a bit frightened!) I welcomed the labyrinth of lights under Brinkies Brae . . .

*George Mackay Brown*

## 1997 [Essex House, Badminton]

A beautiful day. In the early afternoon I drove along the lane from Badminton to Sopworth, left car on verge and walked through the village. Church locked, but Pevsner says nothing within. Nevertheless very pretty on summit over-looking a vast field. Graveyard full of wool merchants' tombs. Sopworth, two miles from Badminton as the crow flies, is in Wiltshire. I talked to an old lady with a spotted dog, who asked if I was 'a local man'. When I replied that I lived in Badminton, she expressed astonishment that I had walked all the way. I had to disabuse her. Ten years ago I would have done so, and back.

*James Lees-Milne*

## 27 January

1821 [Halifax, West Yorkshire]

Dawdling over my accounts & one thing or other. I had a balance of ninety pounds, twelve shillings & twopence three farthings, & now have seventy-four & one shilling & ninepence farthing. I am in a pretty prosperous way altogether . . . Letter from Miss Marsh (Micklegate, York). It seems they have been angry about [my] not taking William Cawood. He had 'walked here & back twice, 32 miles, & all for nothing, & from your cool manner of putting an end to the business, I am sure you could not have thought much about it, or your natural kindness would have softened the disappointment by some expression of concern.' Lord bless me! What could I do? I told the man how uncertain the thing was, that my uncle had not given warning to our present manservant, etc., & if he thought it worthwhile to inquire after such a place, as he must do after others, what was I to do? To pay him for his walking? Expressions of concern in such a case are mere nothings. I never thought of them, but where words of this sort are wanting I seldom say too much & often not enough.

*Anne Lister*

1823 [Dorset]

A sudden and general thaw, with a strong wind and an incessant pour of heavy rain. Nothing could be more novel or beautiful than the appearance of the harbour, which was one solid region of ice, with pyramids formed by the drifted snow, and frozen like glass; and on the thaw setting in the whole harbour appeared like a huge floating island as it was carried off by the fall of a high spring tide; and to see this huge movable body in motion with 14 wild swans sitting upon it, as it receded, and looking as if formed by nature for only inhabitants of such a wild region, gave one more the idea of a habitable country. Under an idea that every vagabond would eagerly seize the first day's shooting after the thaw, I, to be well to windward of the butterfly shooters, weathered the torrent of rain all day, and, by capital locks and good management, contrived to keep my gun dry for the five shots which I got. The geese were scattered in every direction, so that I could not bag more than 5 at a shot, and so drenching wet was the day that after the first half-hour not a dry stitch could be found to wipe out the pan of my gun, except the tail of my shirt, and while paddling to birds I had three inches of water under my stomach. I fairly brought home 17 geese. I took one very long shot at 8 swans, heard the shot strike them, and afterwards saw one leave the company and drop on the sea, where I dare not venture (about two miles to leeward), consequently had not the good fortune to bring one home. Wet all the evening, a west wind, and as mild as May.

*Colonel Peter Hawker*

# 28 January

## 1761 [Norfolk]

Peckham walked round the Parks for a Wager, this Morning; he walked round the Parks three Times in 26 Minutes, being 2 Mile & a Quarter. Williams & myself laid him a Crown that he did not do it in 30 Minutes, and we lost our Crown by four minutes. I owe Peckham for Walking 0.2.6. For Fruit 0.0.1. For Porter for Boteler & myself 0.0.2.

*James Woodforde*

## 1980 [Sanna, Ardnamurchan]

A sheep, an elderly ewe, was grazing round the perimeter of my garden today, thrusting her grey muzzle through the wire netting (uselessly large in mesh) and plucking away at the sacred herbage. I noticed this from the window where I was working and took violent exception, though I suppose no great harm was being done, if any was being done at all. However, I have been plagued recently by poaching livestock, eyeing my cultivation hungrily and probing its somewhat fragile defences.

So I flew to the door, hurled it open and rushed over to this poor creature. I was on top of her before she was aware of my coming, almost startling the life out of her. She wheeled to bolt, in her terror bending her body more sharply than her old joints could cope with. Away went her legs from under her and down she went, shoulder first to the ground, in an ungainly tangle.

No damage done. She was up immediately and off at a trot. Yet the incident depressed me. I had deprived a fellow creature of pride and dignity and woe to the man who does that! Of all possible sins against creation I believe that to be, in the eyes of nature, among the most serious. I returned to the house chastising myself bitterly and resolving to be more careful and more tolerant in future.

*Alasdair Maclean*


# 29 January

## 1800 [Somerset]

Met Forbes the surgeon going to kill a few patients. His horse has got the grease. Just as I was going to sit down to dinner a note came from Mrs Lewis of Cannington desiring me to go and bury a corpse at Holford. Twas not a very pleasant request at that time but Mrs Lewis had tried all the Clergymen around and her husband, who was formerly my Curate, is always ready when able to help anyone. I therefore took my glass of wine and mounted my horse defended from the rain and sleet by my thick Beaver. I was there before the corpse was ready.

*William Holland*


## 1837 [Oxfordshire]

We have had a great deal of snow today. This day for dinner had a part of a round of beef with potatos, cabbage and carrots, scimmerlads and bread pudding. For supper roast beef, pickle cabbage &c.&c. Had a Lady to dinner here today. The Lady's maid is taken very sick today: I sopose she has been eating to much or something of the kind. But she is very subject to sickness. Last summer, when we were coming home from Canterbury, she actually spewed all the way, a distance of sixty miles and not less time than eight hours. The people stared as we passed through the towns and villages as she couldent stop even then. It amused me very much to see how the country people stood stareing with their mouthes half open and half shut to see her pumping over the side of the carriage and me sitting by, quite unconserned, gnawing a piece of cake or some sandwiches or something or other, as her sickness did not spoil my apatite. It was very bad for her but I couldent do her any good as it was the motion of the carriage that caused her illness. I gave her something to drink every time we changed horses but no sooner than it was down than it came up again, and so the road from Canterbury to London was pretty well perfumed with Brandy, Rum, Shrub, wine and such stuff. She very soon recovered after she got home and was all the better for it after.

*William Tayler*

1876 [Slackfields Farm, Derbyshire]
*Foggy* Ploughing. Paid Daniels for petty manure.

*Henry Hill*

# 30 January

1999 [Saltwood Castle, Kent]
It is 11.30 a.m. on a grey January day. On the morning walk I looked up at the Mains (we walk around the moat now, in order to avoid contact between dogs and the public), said to Jane, 'For years all I wanted to do was get back through the bulkhead door that has no handle; now what I would like best is to settle at Saltwood, order my affairs, restore the Great Library and study, travel and drink good wine.'

*Alan Clark*

# 31 January

## 1776 [Selborne, Hampshire]

Below zero!! 32 deg. below the freezing point. At eleven it rose to 16½.
Rime. A most unusual degree of cold for S.E. England.

*Gilbert White*

## 1823 [Dorset]

A wet day, and as no jackanapes could get his gun off in the rain it was my
only chance; I therefore sallied out for one huge swan that had been the
target off the coast; and had become so wild that he could scarcely be looked
at: on my way out I fired a long shot and got 4 geese; soon after, as I
expected, we saw this huge bird, floating about in rough sea, and in a pour
of rain; I had two punts to manoeuvre on one side of him, while Reade
and I drifted down on the other; he sprung at about four hundred yards,
came luckily across my punt at about 75 yards, and down I fetched him,
like a cock pheasant, with the swivel gun. His fall was more like the para-
chute of an air balloon than a bird; he was shot quite dead; he weighed 21
lb, and measured 7 feet 8 inches from wing to wing, being the largest by
far of any I had killed.

*Colonel Peter Hawker*

# FEBRUARY

# 1 February

1760 [East Hoathly, Sussex]

*Friday* . . . In the even my wife went down to Mrs Atkins's to drink tea, and about 8.05 I went down, where we stayed and supped on some roast chicken, a cold ham, a hot boiled green tongue, a boiled leg of mutton, fried chaps, tarts, cold fine baked puddings etc. . . . We played at brag in the even and according to custom my wife and I lost 2s. 2½d. We came home about 2.20, very sober. My wife and I gave Mrs Atkins's servant 6d. each. How tired I am of those more-than-midnight revels; how inconsistent it is with the duty of a tradesman, for how is it possible for him to perform or pursue his business with vigour, industry and pleasure when the body must be disordered by the loss of sleep and perhaps the brain too by the too great a quantity of liquor which is often drunk at those times. And then, can a tradesman gaming have any palliation? No! It is impossible, though it's true we game more to pass away time than for thirst of gain, but what a way is it of spending that which is so valuable to mankind? Well may our great poet Mr [Edward] Young say 'When time turns a torment, then man turns a fool.' And suppose a game of cards innocent in itself, yet the consequences cannot be so if what is commonly called fortune should run against any one at play, that he lose more than his income will allow of. But supposing the person to lose can afford it without any ways in the least incommoding or straitening his circumstances; I say, suppose this case, it cannot be innocent because that sum which anyone can afford to lose he can at the same time afford to dispose of in any other way. Then that sum given away in charity must have been a better way in disposing of it. Therefore, if there is a better way to dispose of the money lost, losing it is not right, and then how oft are the passions moved in such a manner by a bad run of play, that the more warm of us

many times increase at that quality so much as to use oaths and execra-
tions not fit to be heard among Christians.

*Thomas Turner*

1827 [Somerset]

I find that my worthless tenant, Lewis, is determined to do all he can, under
the influence of Day, to annoy me.

I left my study after breakfast, with the intention of calling upon Hicks,
the Overseer. In my way, within two hundred yards of my own house, I
met Keel, my churchwarden, who immediately said, 'Hello! I was going to
call upon you, Mr Skinner, for I insist upon knowing who told you what
you told my wife yesterday, and frightened her out of her wits, namely, that
I had said you had been at Camerton long enough, and that we would strip
your gown from your shoulders?' I said I should not tell him who told me,
but I firmly believed it was true since his subsequent conduct was so insolent.
He replied, he would be d—d, but he would know! I said that his swearing
to his clergyman did not give me a better opinion of his veracity, neither
did the menacing attitude in which he put himself; if the farmers chose to
insult me in the manner they did of late, that I could not stir from my
house without experiencing some fresh aggravations, I could let the whole
of my tythe and have nothing further to say to them. 'Aye,' said he, 'you
may take mine to-morrow.' I said very well. I would after Lady Day; but in
the discharge of my duty at Church and when I was called upon to visit
the sick I would ever do my duty, so that there should be no fault to find
with me. 'Aye,' said he, 'but we won't come to Church.'

*John Skinner*

## 2 February

1946 [Inverness-shire]

The seasons bring change to the light and colour of water, just as they bring
change to the foliage of trees. A February river has the delicacy of a Botticelli
painting – nothing is hard or definite – the surrounding trees that glower

into the water's depths have neither the stark brown-ness of winter, the lime-greenness of spring, the overwhelming fullness of summer; they have blueness, the mist-blueness that is akin to dusk.

*Jessie Kesson*

# 3 February

1922 [Gloucestershire]
Hunt Minety.

'Riding past the post.' A grey south-westerly February morning. Hounds had been running 'quite nicely' for about ten minutes. The country 'deep but not holding' after the heavy rain of the past few days.

Horsemen were hustling on in scattered groups; the morning air was alive with the excitement of 'the chase', and the dull green landscape seemed to respond to the rousing cheer of the huntsman's voice as the hounds hit off the line again after a brief check. Away they streamed, throwing up little splashes of water as they raced across a half-flooded meadow.

My horse flew a fence with a watery ditch on the take-off side. 'How topping,' I thought, 'to be alive and well up in the hunt,' as I galloped along the sound turf of a green park. A young lady had fallen into the ditch behind me, but I had no intention of stopping to catch her loose horse. In the park I passed a square Queen Anne house with blank windows and smokeless chimneys; its formal garden with lawns and clipped yew-hedges sloped to a sunk fence. A stone statue stared at me as I galloped after the hounds.

And I thought of the eighteenth century and the couplets of Alexander Pope. I thought of the past, and I went on in a day-dream 'of other days than this'. I thought of conventional old-world ghosts, and a lover waiting by the sundial. But what did the sad-looking house think? I shall always remember that moment in the grey-green February morning, when I rode past the post. 'Hold up, horse!' I mumbled as we jumped the drop-fence into the lane.

*Siegfried Sassoon*

# 4 February

### 1769 [Selborne, Hampshire]

Fog, rain, sun, grey. Hedge sparrows sing vehemently.

*Gilbert White*

### 1798 [Alfoxden, the Lake District]

Walked a great part of the way to Stowey with Coleridge. The morning warm and sunny. The young lasses seen on the hill-tops, in the villages and roads, in their summer holiday clothes – pink petticoats and blue. Mothers with their children in arms, and the little ones that could just walk, tottering by their side. Midges or small flies spinning in the sunshine; the songs of the lark and the redbreast; daisies upon the turf; the hazels in blossom; honeysuckles budding. I saw one solitary strawberry flower under a hedge. The furze gay with blossom. The moss rubbed from the pailings by the sheep, that leave locks of wool, and the red marks with which they are spotted, upon the wood.

*Dorothy Wordsworth*

# 5 February

### 1790 [Norfolk]

My poor Cow rather better this morning, but not able to get up as yet, she having a Disorder which I never heard of before or any of our Somerset Friends. It is called Tail-shot, that is, a separation of some of the Joints of the Tail about a foot from the tip of the Tail, or rather the slipping of one Joint from another. It also makes all her Teeth quite loose in her head. The Cure, is to open that part of the Tail so slipt lengthways and put in an Onion boiled and some Salt, and bind it up with some coarse Tape.

*James Woodforde*

### 1802 [Grasmere, the Lake District]

After dinner I gathered mosses at Easedale. I saw before me sitting in the open field upon his Sack of Rags the old Ragman that I know. His coat

is of scarlet in a thousand patches. His Breeches knees were untied –
the breeches have been given him by some one. He has a round hat
pretty good, small crowned but large rimmed. When I came to him he
said Is there a brigg yonder that'll carry me ow'r t'watter? He seemed
half stupid.

*Dorothy Wordsworth*

## 1964 [Buckinghamshire]

Curious winter – every day for days now has been almost cloudless, the
weather like late March more than anything else. I did 'our' walk alone from
Wendover through Hampdenleaf Wood to Missenden. A cold wind, but out
of it, it was warm enough to sit and read. Not that I did, the only words I
had with me were this month's *Encounter*; as disastrously stuffy and silly a
number of it as I can remember . . .

But the country was very clean, very clear. Sad how the birds have gone,
after last winter's disaster [the winter of 1963 was the coldest in living
memory]. The corvidae and the blackbirds have come through well. Two or
three flocks of chaffinches, one at least a hundred strong. I heard greenfinches. One pair of great tits. One coal tit. But plenty of blue tits and,
surprisingly, marsh tits – I saw seven or eight. No long-tailed – they will
take years to recover. Plenty of hedge-sparrows. One nuthatch heard. But
no woodpeckers at all. No goldfinches. No larks. No pipits. No hawks. No
pigeons.

A cock bullfinch on top of a hawthorn bush, biting the buds, toppling
against the clear blue sky. An intense soft carmine against that intense soft
blue. Breathtaking, such moments.

I watched a man burn a field – a great bow-shaped sheet of orange flame
eating into the beige stubble, with the dim green-blue hills behind, the
white-grey smoke drifting up and the fiercely eager sound of the fire-crackle.
I could hear the sinister crepitation long after I had disappeared into the
trees.

In the deepest part of the woods, a hare.

I walked all day, saw hardly a soul. Then London at five o'clock in the
evening, all the people going home from work, the office blocks, the buses,

the neon lights, the urbanity of things. No other age but ours will know how strange the leap between this world and that world of the ageless winter trees.

*John Fowles*

# 6 February

1985 [Essex House, Badminton]
David and Caroline Beaufort [art dealer and his wife, owners of the Badminton estate] dined alone with us last night. I enjoy talking to David, who is a sensitive man underneath. Like John Evelyn, he has days when he sulks along the streets hoping to be unobserved. He had an awful experience hunting last Saturday. The 'antis' were out in full strength. He had to protect Princess Anne who was out. 'They' made the most disgusting remarks about her, which David could not repeat even to us. He tried to reason with some of the less objectionable 'antis'. One of them said to him, 'You ought not to be riding that horse, it ought to go free.' D. explained that the horse was comfortably stabled, fed twice a day, groomed, and enjoyed hunting even more than he did; that if 'let free', it would be dead in a week. He says that if this concerted group obstruction persists he will have to close down the hunt altogether. They trample the wheat, which the hunters carefully avoid.

*James Lees-Milne*

# 7 February

1878 [Dorset]
Father says that when there was a hanging at Dorchester in his boyhood it was carried out at one o'clock, it being the custom to wait until the mailcoach came in from London in case of a reprieve.

He says that at Puddletown Church, at the time of the old west-gallery violin, oboe and clarinet players, Tom Sherren (one of them) used to copy tunes during the sermon. So did my grandfather at Stinsford Church. Old

Squibb the parish clerk also used to stay up late at night helping my grandfather in his 'prick-noting', as he called it.

He says that William, son of Mr S— the Rector of W—, became the miller at O— Mill, and married a German woman whom he met at Puddletown Fair playing her tambourine. When her husband was gone to market she used to call in John Porter, who could play the fiddle, and lived near, and give him some gin, when she would beat the tambourine to his playing. She was a good-natured woman with blue eyes, brown hair, and a round face; rather slovenly. Her husband was a hot, hastly fellow, though you could hear by his speech that he was a better educated man than ordinary millers.

G.R.— (who is a humorist) showed me his fowl-house, which was built of old church-materials bought at Wellspring the builder's sale. R.'s chickens roost under the gilt-lettered Lord's Prayer and Creed, and the cock crows and flaps his wings against the Ten Commandments. It reminded me that I had seen these same Ten Commandments, Lord's Prayer and Creed, before, forming the sides of the stone-mason's shed in the same builder's yard, and that he had remarked casually that they did not prevent the workmen 'cussing and damning' the same as ever. It also reminded me of seeing the old font of — Church, Dorchester, in a garden used as flower-vase, the initials of ancient godparents and Churchwardens still eligible upon it. A comic business – church restoration.

*Thomas Hardy*

## 1917 [Weirleigh, Kent]

At home again – for the last time before I go back to the unmitigated hell of 'the spring offensive'.

A bright fire burning, Topper licking his paws in an armchair, two candles alight, the friendly books all round me on their shelves, and blue moonlight filtering through the white curtains from the dazzling white snow and clear stars outside, while the wind makes a little crooning in the chimneys, and the hall clock strikes ten. And poor old Mother quite cheerful. I am afraid she don't realise I am for France this month. And I was playing Morris dances and old English airs on the piano, so gay and full of green fields.

*Siegfried Sassoon*

# 8 February

1756 [East Hoathly, Sussex]

As I by experience find how much more conducive it is to my health, as well as pleasantness and serenity to my mind, to live in a low, moderate rate of diet, and as I know I shall never be able to comply therewith in so strict a manner as I should choose (by the unstable and over easiness of my temper), I think it therefore [right] (as it's a matter of so great importance to my health etc.) to draw up rules of proper regimen, which I do in manner and form following, and which, at all times when I am in health, I hope I shall always have the strictest regard to follow, as I think they are not inconsistent with either religion or morality: First, be it either in the summer or winter, to rise as early as I possibly can; that is, always to allow myself between 7 and 8 hours' sleep, or full 8, unless prevented on any particular or emergent occasion. 2ndly, to go to breakfast between the hours of 7 and 8 from Lady Day to St Michael, and from St Michael to Lady Day between the hours of 8 and 9. 3rdly, my breakfast to be always tea or coffee and never to exceed 4 dishes. If neither of those, half a pint of water or water gruel; and for eatables bread and cheese, bread and butter, light biscuit, buttered toast, or dry bread, and one morn in every week, dry bread only. 4thly, nothing more before dinner, and always to dine between the hours of 12 and 1 o'clock if at home. 5thly, my dinner to be meat, pudding, or any other thing of like nature, but always to have regard, if there is nothing but salt provision, to eat sparingly; and to eat plenty of any sort of garden stuff there is at table, together with plenty of bread and acids, if any, at table; and always to have the greatest regard to give white or fresh meats and pudding the preference before any sort of highly seasoned, salt, or very strong meat; and always one day in every respective week to eat no meat. 6thly, my drink at dinner to be always boiled water with a toast in it, or small beer, but water if I can have it, and never to drink anything stronger until after dinner. 7thly, if I drink tea at home or abroad to be small, green tea and not more than 4 dishes; and if I eat anything, not more than two ounces. 8thly, my supper never to be meat but weak broth, water gruel, milk pottage, bread and cheese, bread and bitter, apple-pie or some other sort of fruit pie, or some such light diet; my drink, water or small beer, and one night at least in every week to go to bed without any supper. 9thly, never to drink any sort of drams or spiritous liquors of what name or kind soever. 10thly, if I am at home, in company, or abroad, if there is nothing but strong beer, never to drink more than 4 glasses, one to toast the king's health, the 2nd to the royal family, the 3rd to all friends and the 4th to the pleasure of the company; if there is either wine or punch etc., never, upon any terms or persuasions whatever, to drink more than 8 glasses, nor each glass to hold or contain more than half a quarter of a pint, nor even so much if possibly to be avoided. 11thly, if I am constrained by extreme drought to drink between meals, that to be toast and water, small beer, or very small wine and water; to wit, ¼ pint of red or white wine to one pint of water. 12thly, never to drink any small or strong beer, winter or summer, without being warmed if possible. And lastly always to go to bed at or before ten o'clock when it can be done.

*Thomas Turner*

## 1870 [Clyro, Radnorshire]

From Wye Cliff to Pont Faen. Miss Child in great force. She showed me her clever drawings of horses and told me the adventures of the brown wood owl 'Ruth' which she took home from here last year. She wanted to call the owl 'Eve' but Mrs Bridge said it should be called 'Ruth'. She and her sister stranded in London at night went to London Bridge Hotel (having missed the last train) with little money and no luggage except the owl in the basket. The owl hooted all night in spite of their putting it up the chimney, before the looking glass, under the bedclothes, and in a circle of lighted candles which they hoped it would mistake for the sun. The owl went on hooting, upset the basket, got out and flew about the room. The chambermaid almost frightened to death dared not come inside the door. Miss Child asked the waiter to get some mice for 'Ruth' but none could be got.

*Francis Kilvert*

# 9 February

### 1802 [Grasmere, the Lake District]

A funeral came by of a poor woman who had drowned herself, some say because she was hard treated by her husband, others that he was a very decent respectable man and *she* but an indifferent wife. However this was she had only been married to him last Whitsuntide and had had very indifferent health ever since. She had got up in the night and drowned herself in the pond.

*Dorothy Wordsworth*

### c.2000 [Walnut Tree Farm, Suffolk]

The decline of the Church of England is a specially dangerous thing in rural areas. It means the vicars keep on changing every few years because there aren't enough of them to go round, and anyway the church no longer attracts the high quality of minds it once did. To make matters worse, each vicar has to look after a 'group' of parishes, so lacks the local knowledge and intimacy with the natural surroundings he or she would need to carry authority when pronouncing on conservation, questions of.

In earlier times a Gilbert White or a Parson Woodforde would have been quick to spot anything amiss with nature in the parish and to speak forth-rightly about it to any wrongdoers. Not any more. Worse, still, you have vicars who come in and cut down cedar trees in churchyards, or yews.

*Roger Deakin*

# 10 February

### 1987 [Bath]

Saw my first snowdrops this morning in Somerset Place. Still in unfolded stage, like pendulous, opalescent pearls, glistening with dew. Also the birth of a primrose. Couldn't believe it. Bent down, and there was the unmistakable leaf. Just a peep of pale yellow on the ground.

*James Lees-Milne*

# 11 February

1788 [Norfolk]

Nancy not being below Stairs this morning before the clock had done striking 10 forfeited – 0.0.6.

*James Woodforde*

1800 [Over Stowey, Somerset]

Little news in the paper. The intended Union with the potato headed Irishmen does not go on well. Saw Mr Cruckshanks the elder at the gate. He gave me a receipt for the Paddocks and I gave him one for the Tithe of Quantock. He seems very civil and gets old and a little stupid. People who live full and well get heavy and stupid sooner than Abstemious men. Heard of Mrs Morris's death this day whom we formerly knew by the name of Baker. A young woman and left six children – sad news indeed – mysterious are the dispensations of Providence.

*William Holland*

# 12 February

1878 [Dorset]

In a village near Yeovil about 100 years ago, there lived a dumb woman, well known to my informant's mother. One day the woman suddenly spoke and said:

'A cold winter, a forward spring,

A bloody summer, a dead King.'

She then dropped dead. The French Revolution followed immediately after.

*Thomas Hardy*

# 13 February

1870 [Clyro, Radnorshire]
Septuagesima Sunday, St Valentine's Eve

Preached at Clyro in the morning (Matthew xiv, 30). Very few people in Church, the weather fearful, violent deadly E. wind and the hardest frost we have had yet. Went to Bettws in the afternoon wrapped in two waist-coats, two coats, a muffler and a mackintosh, and was not at all too warm. Heard the Chapel bell pealing strongly for the second time since I have been here and when I got to the Chapel my beard moustaches and whiskers were so stiff with ice that I could hardly open my mouth and my beard was frozen to my mackintosh. There was a large christening party from Llwyn Gwilym. The baby was baptised in ice which was broken and swimming about the Font.

*Francis Kilvert*


1911 [Barnstaple, North Devon]
Feel like a piece of drawn threadwork, or an undeveloped negative, or a jelly fish on stilts, or a sloppy tadpole, or a weevil in a nut, or a spatchcocked eel. In other words and in short – ill.

*W.N.P. Barbellion*


# 14 February

1966 [Underhill Farm, Lyme Regis]
A morning as still as death, but a beautiful floating death, mist on the sea, first faint sunlight, a morning like a resurrection. I was at the bottom wall . . . Suddenly out of the light over the sea a faint soughing of wings, almost the whetting of a great scythe, louder and louder and moving westwards. For a few moments it seemed to fill the sky. I thought it must be some weird machine down on the Cobb but it moved over the sea well away from Lyme and down below me. Swans; and the sound magnified in some bizarre way. But the extraordinary thing is I never saw them, though I had

the Zeiss with me and visibility was good for at least two miles. Just the grey still sea and the winnowing wings.

*John Fowles*

## 15 February

1906 [Olton, Warwickshire]
Walking home from Solihull this afternoon I noticed a number of Gnats dancing in the bright sunshine. And I saw two little Shrew-Mice in different places on the bank, who darted quickly into their holes directly they saw me.

*Edith Holden*

## 16 February

1966 [Underhill Farm, Lyme Regis]
The linnets that haunt the garden (because I am a bad gardener and the fescue is rampant) with their fine Stravinsky-like songs and their ancient Chinese harp flight calls; the first pale, huge violets on the big 'step' down to the sea; finding a bed of moschatel in the woods; the wonderful owls that haunt our nights; a flock of fifty oystercatchers, black, white, coral-red against a pearl-grey sea; the grey-black depths in a watching rabbit's eyes – these things are poems in the language, and in a way to write poems in mine about them is not creative, but merely a matter of translation.

*John Fowles*

## 17 February

1661 [East Colne, Essex]
In the night it raind, the wind rose and was violent beyond measure, ov'turning a windmill at Colchester, wherein a youth kild, divers barnes, stables, outhouses, trees, rending divers dwellings; few escaped, my losse much, but

not like some others; God sanctifie all to us; throwing down stackes of chimneys, part of houses; the Lady Saltonstall kild in her bed, her house falling Whitehall twice on fire that day, some orchards almost ruind. Trees blown down within priory wall. Timber trees rent up in high standing woods; the winde was generall in England & Holland sea coast, but not in Scotland.

*Ralph Josselin*

1798 [Alfoxden, the Lake District]
A deep snow upon the ground. Wm and Coleridge walked to Mr Bartholemew's, and to Stowey. Wm returned and we walked through the wood into the Coombe to fetch some eggs. The sun shone bright and clear. A deep stillness in the thickest part of the wood, undisturbed except by the occasional dropping of the snow from the holly boughs; no other sound but that of water, and the slender notes of a redbreast, which sang at intervals on the outskirts of the southern side of the wood. There the bright green moss was bare at the roots of the trees, and the little birds were upon it. The whole appearance of the wood was enchanting; and each tree, taken singly, was beautiful. The branches of the hollies pendent with their white burden, but still sowing their bright red berries, and their glossy green leaves. The bare branches of the oaks thickened by the snow.

*Dorothy Wordsworth*

# 18 February

1925 [Wales]
Last night I was drunk – very drunk – and feel a little the better for it. The sherry and whisky I had ordered in Oxford came. Before dinner Gordon and I drank the sherry – which brought back a thousand sentimental associations. After dinner we took the whisky to Watson's room and I drank about half of it while Watson and Dean drank a quarter each. The result was that I was sick. I have not yet met Amy and am rather unwilling to do so. I think she will not report it to the proprietor Banks. The debauch has caused

something of a feud in the common-room – I must confess to finding Chaplin somewhat tiresome.

Today I have had a delightful afternoon and evening. I went to Rhyl for the afternoon and got permission to stay out to dinner. I bought a lot of things which I do not particularly want and spent most of the time in the hands of a most interesting barber who talked of phallic symbolism and the Gnostics. A lovely dinner and good wines and brandy. On Saturday I went to the Naples of the North with one of the ushers called Gordon and had dinner at the Grand Hotel. It was not very grand but there was some of the burgundy which I last drank on the regrettable evening when I went to the home of Lady Plunket – Clos de Vougeot 1911. A kind man took us home in an automatic carriage. No letter from Olivia, no shoes from Oxford, no money from anywhere.

On Sunday I started on an awful thing called week's duty. It means that I have no time at all from dawn to dusk so much to read a postcard or visit a water-closet. Already – today is Tuesday, Shrove Tuesday – my nerves are distraught. Yesterday I beat a charming boy called Clegg and kicked a hideous boy called Cooper and sent Cooke to the proprietor. Yesterday afternoon I had my first riding lesson and enjoyed it greatly. It is not an easy sport or a cheap one but most agreeable. No letter from Olivia. Yesterday in a history paper the boy Howarth wrote: 'In this year James II gave birth to a son but many people refused to believe it and said it had been brought to him in a hot water bottle.'

*Evelyn Waugh*

## 19 February

1716 [Oxfordshire]
This hath been such a severe Winter that the like hath not been known since the Year 1683. In some respects it exceeded that. For tho' the Frost did not last so long as it did at yt time, yet there was a much greater & deeper Snow. Indeed, it was the biggest Snow yt ever I knew: as it was also ye severest Frost yt ever I have been sensible of. It began on Monday,

Dec. 5th & continued 'till Friday, Febr. 10th following, which is almost ten weeks, before there was an intire Thaw. Indeed, it began to thaw two or three times, but then the Frost soon began again with more violence, & there was withall a very sharp & cold & high Wind for some Days. When it first began to thaw & afterwards to Freeze again, it made the ways extreme slippery & dangerous, & divers bad accidents happen'd thereupon.

Thomas Hearne

## 1771 [Norfolk]

My Father was brave & in very good Spirits this morning, but in the Evening was as bad as ever and talked very movingly to Sister Jane and me about his Funeral — And that he wanted to alter his Will, and mentioned the underwritten to me & Sister Jane, that he desired that his Maid (Eliz. Clothier) should have that House where Grace Stephens lives at present during her Life, and after her Life to go to Sister Jane, as well as all the other Poor Houses & Mrs Parrs House, and the Field called four Acres to her my Sister Jane: That Sister White has one hundred Pounds to make her equal to her Sister Clarke in Fortune: That I have all his Books and Book-Case in his Study: And that he would have no People invited to his Funeral to make a Show, but that he is carried to Ansford Church by six of his Poor Neighbours. Robin Francis & his Brother Thomas were mentioned and that they had half a Crown apiece — to be laid in the Vault where my Mother is by her Side. And that a little Monument be erected in the Side-Wall near the Vault in Memory of him & his Wife. My Poor Father is I think in much the same way as my Poor Mother was. Pray God Bless him & keep him, and give us all strength to bear so sore an Affliction as such a Separation must occasion, if it be thy divine Will to remove him from us. O God whenever such an Event happens take him to thyself, and give us Grace to follow his good Examples, that with him we may deserve to be Partakers of thy Heavenly Kingdom. Grant him O Lord an Easy and happy Exit. Better Parents no Children ever had than we have been blessed with — blessed be God for it — and make us more worthy than we are, for all thy goodness to us. Praise the Lord O my Soul, and forget not all his Benefits. Thou hast not dealt with us after our Sins, nor rewarded us according to our wickednesses. Praise thou the Lord O my Soul. I played at Back-Gammon with my Father in the Evening, it takes him in some degree of from thinking of his Pain I won 0.0.6. He went to bed before I went home being uneasy in his Bowels.

*James Woodforde*

## 20 February

1774 [Selborne, Hampshire]
The high wind last night blowed down a large old apple-tree in the orchard.

*Gilbert White*

## 21 February

1914 [Essex]
Pianoforte recital by F.M., at Frinton Hall last night in aid of Tendring Parish funds. Hall centrally heated, but draughty. Uncomfortable chairs. Rush-bottomed chair (cost about 3s.) for pianist. Old Broadwood baby grand. Pedal creaked. Rotten tone. Ladies of Frinton and of Tendring parishes in evening dress. Two parsons, who felt they must speechify afterwards. Pianist a man about 40, agreeable slightly curt smile. Ferocious look when he was playing often. Beethoven, Rameau, Chopin, Scarlatti, Debussy, Liszt, etc. Piano impossible. Intense, almost tragic sadness of provincial musical affairs, second-rate or tenth-rate under bad conditions.

*Arnold Bennett*

## 22 February

1872 [Binbrook Hall, nr Louth, Lincolnshire]
The panic among the labourers is somewhat waning; though a small riot took place in Horncastle last night. It originated in the pulling down of a stump orator by the police. His intention was to incite the labourers to

strike. It was an indiscretion to interfere with him. The mob made every use of loose brick for the purpose of destruction. The fray ended in broken windows, etc.

This evening I sold Mr Sawyer 7 Porket pigs, half-bred Berkshire, for £27.

*Cornelius Stovin*

### 1967 [Underhill Farm, Lyme Regis]

A fossil sponge – only an inch across – in a ball of flint. I chipped it open. I suppose it is ninety million years old; yet the slightest touch on the miniature pockets of tawny branches crumbles them. So fragile and yet so old.

*John Fowles*

### 1985 [Essex House, Badminton]

To church at Acton Turville at 9.30. The usual smattering of some half a dozen parishioners, and a young woman sitting in front of me whom I did not recognise, wearing a scarf which partly concealed her head. When we left the church she smiled at me, to which I responded. The Vicar told me she was Mrs X.; that she had never been to church before, but this was her third Sunday running, making him wonder if there was something wrong with her. When I told A. [Alvilde, his wife] she said that X. had recently started a wild affair with another woman, on learning of which Mrs X., in a towering rage, had kicked him in the balls.

*James Lees-Milne*

## 23 February

### 1758 [East Hoathly, Sussex]

This morn about 6 o'clock, just as my wife was gladly got to bed and had laid herself down to rest, we was awakened by Mrs Porter, who pretended she wanted some cream of tartar. But as soon as my wife got out of bed, she vowed she should come down, which she complied with and found she, Mr Porter, Mr Fuller and his wife with a lighted candle, part of a bottle of wine and a glass. Then the next thing in course must be to have me downstairs, which I being apprised of, fastened my door. But, however, upstairs they came and threatened as also attempted to break open my door, which I found they would do; so I therefore ordered the boys to open it. But as soon as ever it was open, they poured into my room, and as modesty forbid me to get out of my bed in the presence of women, so I refrained. But their immodesty permitted them to draw me out of bed (as the common phrase is) tipsy turvy. But, however, at the intercession of Mr Porter they permitted me to put on my breeches (though it was no more than to cast a veil over what undoubtedly they had before that time discovered); as also, instead of my clothes, they gave me time to put on my wife's petticoat. In this manner they made me dance with them without shoes or stockings until they had emptied their bottle of wine and also a bottle of my beer. They then contented themselves with sitting down to breakfast on a dish of coffee etc. They then obliged my wife to accompany them to Joseph Durrant's where they again breakfasted on tea etc. They then all adjoured to Mr Fuller's where they again breakfasted on tea, and there they also stayed and dined; and about 3.30 they all found their ways to their respective homes, beginning by that time to be a little serious, and in my opinion ashamed of their stupid enterprise, or drunken perambulation. Now let anyone but call in reason to his assistance and seriously reflect on what I have before recited, and they must I think join with me in thinking that the precepts delivered from the pulpit on Sundays by Mr Porter, though delivered with the greatest ardour, must lose a great deal of their efficacy by such examples. Myself and family at home dined on the remains of yesterday's dinner. Mr Jordan called on me but did not stay. Mr Elless and Joseph Fuller in the evening called in to ask me how I did after my fatigue and stayed and smoked a pipe with me. And so this ends the silliest frolic as I think I ever knew, and one that must cast an odium on Mr and Mrs P. and Mrs F. so long as it shall be remembered.

*Thomas Turner*

# 24 February

1947 [Middle Orchard, Kent]

Today is the coldest day of all; frost feathers, flowers, ferns all over the windows, giving a dim clouded light inside; my pen frozen, so that I could not write with it or fill it.

Then broadest sunlight pouring on to me in bed, warm, melting the frost flowers so that a steam goes up, waving, wreathing its shadow across the page as I write. I have a lot to do.

*Denton Welch*

# 25 February

c.2003 [South of England]

On sallow bushes in damp places, flowers like silvery buttons are coming out along the twigs. These are the male catkins, which will turn from silver to gold, since they will be covered before long with little flecks of bright yellow pollen. The 'pussy willow' twigs, as they are often called, are broken off and carried in church processions on Palm Sunday, the last Sunday before Easter. As the catkins are starting to appear so early, it must be hoped that there will still be some left by then. The stringy, green female catkins appear at the same time as the golden pollen, and are fertilised with the help of the wind. Early bees and other insects also come to the sallow catkins.

*Derwent May*

# 26 February

1878 [Clyro, Radnorshire]

At 10 a.m. went on the box of Miss Newton's brougham to the reopening of Mansel Grange Church after a good restoration. More than 25 clergy in surplices. The Bishop preached in the morning, the Archdeacon, Lord Saye and Sele in the afternoon. It was difficult to say what was the worse sermon. The former was a screed, the latter a rigmarole, but the rigmarole was more appropriate and more to the purpose than the screed.

*Francis Kilvert*

## 27 February

1755 [East Hoathly, Sussex]

At home all day; wrote out bills. In the Lewes newspaper of the 24th think the following worthy of memorandum: 'York, Feb 11 – At the adjournment of the Quarter Sessions for this city and county thereof, James Monkman of New Buildens, near Sutton-on-the-Forest, yeoman, was convicted of regratings contrary to statute 5 and 6 King Edward VI. The fact was that he bought 6 chickens in open market in the city at 6d. each and immediately after sold them again in the same manner at 7½d. each; for which offence he forfeited the value of the goods, received sentence of 2 months' imprisonment and was accordingly committed to the city gaol. By the above-mentioned statute the punishment for 2nd offence of forestalling, engrossing or regrating is a forfeiture of double the value of the goods and six months' imprisonment; and for the 3rd offence the offender loses all his goods, must stand in a pillory and be imprisoned during the King's pleasure.'

*Thomas Turner*

## 28 February

1879 [Clyro, Radnorshire]

Walking in the garden in the evening I discovered that the intense frost of the last month had caused a slip and settlement of the rail on the terrace walk and caused the wall supporting the terrace to bulge dangerously. A large slice of the Vicarage river bank just below the hydraulic ram has slipped into the river, the churchyard wall has bulged, Brobury Churchyard wall has been thrown down by the frost, the walls all over the place have been strained and shaken, the plaster is peeling and shelling off the house and conservatory, and the steps from the upper to the lower garden are in ruins. This is the work of the frost of 1878–1879.

*Francis Kilvert*

## 29 February

1876 [Slackfields Farm, Derbyshire]
*Mild*. Sent turnip pulper to Derby for new teeth and repairs. Two loads of manure from G. Greaves. Paid Mr Parker, Kilburn for manure.

*Henry Hill*

2001 [Hickling, Norfolk]
In broad daylight it sat atop the clean-cut slabs of loam in the middle of the field. It gnawed at a hunk of sugar beet, while its back, full and rounded like a flexed bicep, was hunched against me as if in disdain. Through the telescope I could see the eyes glint like black marbles. Most disgusting of all was the tail – a scaly wire with a gross swelling at its base.

What is it about rats that we find so repellent? Despite the fact that they are carriers of disease – 50–70 per cent of brown rats in England are thought to be infected with leptospirosis – they are fastidiously clean animals, constantly grooming themselves. Individuals such as this one live in the countryside, no more a nuisance than the rabbits occupying the same hedgerow. They breed prolifically and attack human produce, but then so do mice.

Britain actually owes the brown rats a huge debt, because when they arrived from Asia in the early eighteenth century they displaced the black rat, whose fleas had been the vector of bubonic plague. The black rat was far more of a town-dwelling species and dependent upon human food. The effect of this predation could be devastating. In the winter of 1685 black rats came ashore on the Hebridean island of North Rona from a ship-wreck and soon found their way into the islanders' food stores. In the spring the clan chief's steward came ashore to find the last surviving woman on the rocky beach. The entire population had starved to death.

*Mark Cocker*

# MARCH

# 1 March

1785 [Fyfield, Hampshire]
Servants at ye farm, many of them ill. Carters and plough boys with rheumatism, and one has quite lost ye use of his limbs owing it is supposed to the great severity of ye weather.

*Henry White*

1886 [Sawrey, the Lake District]
Rather heavy snow. There has been a most singular nuisance going on since Christmas about Manchester. A gang of young men calling themselves *Spring-heeled Jacks* have been going about in the dusk frightening people. They wore india-rubber dresses which would puff at will to a great size, horns, a lantern and springs in their boots.

One jumped right over a cab in the Eccles Road, nearly frightening the gentleman inside out of his wits. One poor girl in Swinton Lane had a fit. They were cowardly bullies, also thieves, for they took money. Some say they are Medical Students from Owens College, and it is not impossible I am afraid.

They were bad to catch, but the authorities sent some detectives. One of these met a *Jack* who demanded his money or his life. The detective pretended to be frightened and get out money, but instead he produced some handcuffs and caught him. Another was captured on a Sunday evening by some young men who beat him soundly, and then discovered he was an acquaintance. One was in the next garden to *Hopefield* a fortnight since.

The maids durst not stir out a step in the evening, which, my Aunt remarked, was well.

*Beatrix Potter*

# 2 March

### 1886 [Bowden Hall, Gloucester]

Davis, the cowman, caught and killed a fine badger. It was sleeping in a corner under the manger at the stalls. He was feeding the cows and stuck his foot into its rump, and beat it on the head. They are getting rare. I do not remember one being caught here before though we have often found their holes in the wood. They are not in the least destructive of anything one wishes to preserve. We had it stuffed at a cost of 20/- and put into what the taxidermist called a menacing attitude.

*Dearman Birchall*

### 1968 [Underhill Farm, Lyme Regis]

A barn owl has suddenly appeared. It comes in daylight and flies about all the yards, up round the studio, sits on the wall, watching me. The first I have seen here, so it seems more than a bird. An omen. We spent half an hour yesterday watching that white heart-shaped face, with the curious trickles of blood from the inner corners of the beautiful brown-black eyes down beside the beak (actually rust-red feathers). Really a very beautiful and gravely comic creature, and not in the least ominous. When it hawks, like a huge buff moth. The huge head, all symbolic weeping heart, is what makes it grotesque; and over those neat white trews.

*John Fowles*

# 3 March

### 1756 [East Hoathly, Sussex]

In the even I was sent for down to Halland. Accordingly about 7 o'clock I called on Tho. Davy, and we went down. When I came, I found that it was Ann Smith had sent for me to ask my advice in the following affair, as she tells it, to wit: About 8 years ago she kept the house of Tho. Baker in the parish of Waldron, who, being an elderly man, and at the same time in all probability might have a feeble insurrection of an unruly member which might prompt him to make his addresses to her, as she says he did; and as he found his affection slighted, and understanding she was indebted to Mr Venner of the same parish the sum of £2 7s. 0d., and as a means, as he simply imagined, to ingratiate himself in her favour, he (as she solemnly avers) went and paid the same without her knowledge or orders; and, when he had so done, never offered to make any drawback in her wages when she left him, though she says he often told her he had paid it; and when she went away, she went and asked Mr Venner whether she owed him anything, who answered, 'No!' So it is plain Baker had paid the money. But as Baker is now in low circumstances (though still a single person), he has lately made a demand of the same, notwithstanding it has been near 8 years since, and (as she says) never pretended to have any demand on her before, and she always looked upon it as a free gift. Now my advice was as this, to wit: if what she repeated to me was true and that he actually paid it without her knowledge and designed it as a free gift to her without any proviso to the contrary, I thought she was not obliged to pay it, only as change in circumstances and gratitude should always oblige everyone to return favours where they have received any. But if it was any ways by her orders he paid it, or she was to outset it in her wages or to make him any other gratuity and did not, I thought in justice she ought to pay him.

*Thomas Turner*

# 4 March

## 1836 [Ansford Inn, nr Bristol]
Left Clifton after our week's sojourn there (my first week as a wife!!), and drove with our own horses in the open carriage through Bristol on our road to Stafford. Passed through the villages of Whitchurch, Pensford, Clutton, Farrington Gurney, Ston Easton to Old Down Inn, being 19 miles. There we remained 2 hours, and after then drove on to Shepton Mallet, a dirty assize town, and on to Ansford Inn which is very clean and comfortable (13 miles). The road was very hilly and dirty the whole way, and we passed through some pretty districts.

*Emily Smith*

# 5 March

## 1776 [Norfolk]

At one o'clock to day as a Leg of Mutton was rosting by the Kitchen Fire, a very dreadful Fire happened in the Chimney, It played above the Tunn near 2 Yards and very fiercely, I thought the whole House would have been in Flames every Moment, but the Wind being very high and to the South-West, blowed the Flame a quite contrary way to the Thatch, which blessed be God prevented the whole House from it &c. Our Cary & Ansford Friends were very good indeed & came to our Assistance in a very little Time, and brought Cary Engine with them, and by the Blessing and mercy of God in about 2 Hours it was happily extinguished, and for which Great Goodness O Lord, to whom I return my most unfeigned thanks and ever make me O Lord ever thankful & mindful for this so great a Deliverance to me and all in this House. My poor Sister was terribly frightened indeed. Thomas one of Ansford Inn Servants was the most active man in it, he was up to the Tun in a Minute and was the Man that threw down the first Pail of Water down it and many more were thrown down immediately, after that we got some wet Ruggs, & Whirn-Sheets & Blanketts and threw down the Chimney and covered over the Tunn upon top quite close, put out the Fire below, stopped up the Bottom also as close as we could, then continued pouring Water thro' the Wall in the Poining End. A Hole was made thro' the Ceiling also in the Kitchen Chamber to examine above, and all was safe – Robin Francis, James Lintern, our Boy, Jasorn Cock with many others very active indeed. Mr Willm Burge Junr came himself & sent all his Workmen immediately, James Clarke's Man & Richard, My Uncle's, Mr Whites & Perrys and many others came immediately, all Ansford & Cary almost came, and none but was greatly alarmed. My Uncle sent down some Cyder in Pails to the People & we gave them more – I offered a Guinea to the People upon the House, but they would not take it, Mr Burge would not suffer it. I don't know what we should have done was it not for our very kind & good Friends. It alarmed me very much indeed all the Day after I could eat no Meat all the Day or scarce anything else. Mr White sent us down some Victuals. It happened entirely for want of having the Chimney swept, it had not been swept for above a twelvemonth not since Christmas twelve-month. It is amazing that Mr Pounsett should neglect it so long, very wrong of him indeed only to save one Sixpence. Sister Clarke, Miss Patty Clarke, Sister White and Mr James Clarke supped & spent the Evening with us. Brother Heighes & Richard Clarke spent part of the Afternoon with us. Poor Patty Clarke was greatly alarmed as was Sister Clarke & Nancy Woodforde who were at it. I did not go to Bed till two in the morning to Night and every thing I thank God was safe before that. N.B. Washing Week – all the Cloaths out a drying when the Fire happened.

*James Woodforde*

## 6 March

1783 [Norfolk]

The first thing I was informed of when I came down stairs, was, that my Stable had been broken up, in the Night and that there was stolen out of it, a Hatchet, a Hook, a Bridle, and a pair of hedging Gloves of Bens. There was seen Yesterday a Couple of idle Fellows passing and repassing my House, I saw them once go by, one of them was in a long blue Coat, the other in a brown one. They came in at the back Window of the Stable, which they cut away, to wrench it open with a large stick wch was found just by, they left behind them a Pr of Sheep Sheers broke directly in the middle – They also took Bens Cart Whip, which they left on the Muck-heap. I think myself well of, in having so few things stolen as there were so many in the Stable and in the Corn Room. I sent for Harry Dunnell to mend the Window and to John Spaule to make some new iron work for the same, all which were done by Evening and all right again. Harry Dunnell dined with our Folks and for his work to day I gave him 0.1.0. There were several Stables in the Parish broke into besides mine last night, Peachmans, Bucks, Widow Pratts, Manns and Forsters – and several things stolen. Nancy was very much alarmed on hearing the above. [The two men were caught for another offence and sentenced to three years in prison.]

*James Woodforde*

1910 [Barnstaple, North Devon]

The facts are undeniable: Life is pain. No sophistry can win me over to any other view. And yet years ago I set out so hopefully and healthfully – what are birds' eggs to me *now*? My ambition is enormous but vague. I am too distributed in my abilities to achieve distinction.

*W.N.P. Barbellion*

# 7 *March*

1788 [Fyfield, Kent]

Informer against the people in this and neighbouring village for selling Spirits without a Licence. Convicted of perjury at Winchester Assizes and sentenced to be transported to Botany Bay for 7 years.

*Henry White*

1911 [Barnstaple, North Devon]

How the beastly mob loves a tragedy! The sudden death of the Bank Manager is simply thrilling the town and the newspapers sell like hot cakes. Scarcely before the body is cold the coincidence of his death on the anniversary of his birth is discussed in every household; every one tells everybody else where they saw him last – 'he looked all right then.' The policeman and the housemaid, the Mayor and the Town Clerk, the cabman and the billposter, stand and discuss the deceased gentleman's last words or what the widow's left with. 'Ah well, it is very sad,' they remark to one another with no emotion and continue on their way.

*W.N.P. Barbellion*

# 8 *March*

1780 [Norfolk]

We were very quere after Dinner to day, having but a plain Dinner, viz. some hash Mutton, a plain Sewet Pudding and a couple of Rabbitts rosted.

Sam made me rather angry at Dinner when I asked Sister Clarke if she would have the Outside of the Pudding or the first Cut of it, upon which Sam said, I hope you will not, Madam, for you know that I always give the outside to the Dogs.

*James Woodforde*

# 9 March

1987 [Essex House, Badminton]
During the night, deep snow fell on dry ground. Woke up to see cedar trees weighted down. Had to brush snow from doorsteps; mail and paper late and warning of bad roads. So postponed driving to Bath. Took two dogs to the The Slates. A thick, light carpet of snow, unwalked on, virginal. The dogs adored it. Was surprised on looking at the snow that it does not lie smooth, in spite of there being no wind today. It lies with faint marks as of a net having covered it. Walked to the flagstaff. A gorgeous morning. Far warmer than yesterday. The sky ice blue; figures of riders down the lanes like silhouettes in the distance. The west front of the wall to Park Piece swathed in snow. None the far side. All snow disappeared by afternoon.

*James Lees-Milne*

# 10 March

1853 [Penjerrick, Cornwall]
As we turned the corner of a lane during our walk, a man and a bull came in sight; the former crying out, 'Ladies, save yourselves as you can!' the latter scudding onwards slowly but furiously. I jumped aside on a little hedge, but thought the depth below rather too great — about nine or ten feet; but the man cried 'Jump!' and I jumped. To the horror of all, the bull jumped after me. My fall stunned me, so that I knew nothing of my terrible neighbour, whose deep autograph may now be seen quite close to my little one. He thought me dead, and only gazed without any attempt at touching me,

though pacing round, pawing and snorting, and thus we were for about twenty minutes. The man, a kind soul but no hero, stood on the hedge above, charging me from time to time not to move. Indeed, my first recollection is of his friendly voice. And so I lay still, wondering how much was reality and how much dream; and when I tried to think of my situation, I pronounced it too dreadful to be true, and certainly a dream. Then I contemplated a drop of blood and a lump of mud, which looked very real indeed, and I thought it very imprudent in any man to make me lie in a pool – it would surely give me rheumatism. I longed to peep at the bull, but was afraid to venture on such a movement. Then I thought, I shall probably be killed in a few minutes, how is it that I am not taking it more solemnly? I tried to do so, seeking rather for preparation for death than restoration to life. Then I checked myself with the thought, It's only a dream, so it's really quite profane to treat it in this way; and so I went on oscillating. There was, however, a rest in the dear will of God which I love to remember; also a sense of the simplicity of my condition – nothing to do to involve others in suffering, only to endure what was laid upon me. To me the time did not seem nearly so long as they say it was: at length the drover, having found some bullocks, drove them into the field, and my bull, after a good deal of hesitation, went off to his own species. Then they had a laugh at me that I stayed to pick up some oranges I had dropped before taking the man's hand and being pulled up the hedge; but in all this I acted as a somnambulist, with only fitful gleams of consciousness and memory.

*Caroline Fox*

# 11 March

1775 [Selborne, Hampshire]
Vast rain. This rain must occasion great floods. The truffle-hunter came this morning, & took a few truffles: he complains that those fungi never abound in wet winters, & springs.

*Gilbert White*

1998 [Weardale, Durham]

The wind carved patterns in the snow that fell overnight, lifting it over walls and dumping it in rippled, undulating drifts that buried footpaths and filled ditches. Tracks were everywhere: a squirrel's footprints crossing a bridge over a stream, a fox along the edge of a plantation, a smaller mammal – perhaps a stoat – leaving an indistinct trail in the deep snow. One set of rabbit tracks stopped at a brown, snow-spattered mound in the middle of the path. As we approached it lumbered painfully under a gate and into a field: a rabbit, almost blind with myxomatosis, its head swollen and its joints stiff. It shuffled a few yards, then hunched in the shelter of the wall.

*Phil Gates*

## 12 March

1916 [Lewes, Sussex]

At night armed with a hat pin and a bottle of brine went down the garden in the dark with my electric torch and caught two (*only* two) slugs glutting themselves with Crown Imperials. I shall go down every night.

*Alice Dudeney*

## 13 March

1906 [Olton, Warwickshire]

Another heavy fall of snow in the night. The cold has almost silenced the birds this morning. Numbers of them came onto the lawn to be fed; the Starlings and Cock Chaffinches look especially gay just now in their spring coats.

*Edith Holden*

1946 [Inverness-shire]

The only humans that are truly close to spring are the harrower and the early sower. All the farm-workers from grieve to orra-loon bend over the clipper in the neep-park for one hundred and thirty kye are still in their winter feed. When the neep-park is bereft of its labourers, the carts rumble past my door, their great loads of straw swaying precariously. 'Howin' neeps', 'plantin' tatties', 'liftin' tatties', 'hairst' – these are the well-known 'rush' times in a country dweller's year. Yet there is no season in that life that can be taped off as a 'slack' season. Nor do country dwellers ever give the impression of haste; they take each day and its work in the slow, dignified stride with which the earth sends them.

*Jessie Kesson*

## 14 March

### 1802 [Grasmere, the Lake District]

William had slept badly – he got up at 9 o'clock, but before he rose he had finished the Beggar Boys – and while we were at Breakfast that is (for I had breakfasted) he, with his Basin of Broth before him untouched and a little plate of Bread and butter he wrote the Poem to a Butterfly! He ate not a morsel, nor put on his stockings but sate with his shirt neck unbuttoned, and his waistcoat open while he did it. The thought first came upon him as we were talking about the pleasure we both always feel at the sight of a Butterfly. I told him I used to chase them a little but that I was afraid of brushing the dust off their wings, and did not catch them. He told me how they used to kill all the white ones when he went to school because they were Frenchmen.

*Dorothy Wordsworth*

## 15 March

### 1799 [Tewkesbury]

I began my tour through England and Scotland; the lovely weather continuing, such as the oldest man alive has not seen before, for January, February, and half of March . . . I preached in Mr Stephen's orchard to far more than his church would have contained. And it was no inconvenience either to me or them, as it was a mild, still evening.

*John Wesley*

1802 [Grasmere, the Lake District]

A sailor who was travelling from Liverpool to Whitehaven called; he was faint and pale when he knocked at the door – a young man very well dressed. We sate by the kitchen fire talking with him for 2 hours. He told us most interesting stories of his life. His name was Isaac Chapel – he had been at sea since he was 15 years old. He was by trade a sail-maker. His last voyage was to the Coast of Guinea. He had been on board a slave ship, the captain's name Maxwell, where one man had been killed, a boy put to lodge with the pigs and was half-eaten, one boy set to watch in the hot sun till he dropped down dead. He had been cast away in North America and had travelled 30 days among the Indians, where he had been well treated. He had twice swum from a King's ship in the night and escaped; he said he would rather be in hell than be pressed. He was now going to wait in England to appear against Captain Maxwell. 'O he's a rascal, Sir, he ought to be put in the papers!' The poor man had not been in bed since Friday night. He left Liverpool at 2 o'clock on Saturday morning. He had called at a farm house to beg victuals and had been refused. The woman said she would give him nothing. 'Won't you? Then I can't help it.'

*Dorothy Wordsworth*

# 16 March

1785 [Norfolk]

Dr Thorne called here this morning – He has been inoculating John Gooch and whole Family. Nancy complained very much this morning of the Wind in her Stomach – I desired her to drink some strong Beer after Dinner instead of Wine, which she did and was better after it – She was much oppressed by Hysteric wind before – She also by my desire had some Milk for breakfast and is to continue it. Neighbour Clarkes Wife and Family as well as can be expected. It is a good kind of small Pox they have.

*James Woodforde*

1870 [Clyro, Radnorshire]
I ate so much I could hardly walk and saw stars.

*Francis Kilvert*

*c.*2000 [Walnut Tree Farm, Suffolk]
Yesterday it turned mild for the first time in ages and last night I found a
newt crossing the kitchen floor at some speed. On Sunday night I saw frogs
and toads crossing the road, and another one on the common at Mellis. At
Thrandeston, where there's a notable frog pond on the village green, two
people were fixing up a road sign with a crossed-out frog on it, and this
morning the first toads are in full voice beside the moat.

*Roger Deakin*

## 17 March

1906 [Barnstaple, North Devon]
Woke up this morning covered with spots, chest inflamed, and bad cough.
H carted me down from the attic to the Lower Bedroom, and when the
Dr came he confirmed the general opinion that I had measles. It is simply
disgusting, I have somewhere near 10,000 spots on me.

*W.N.P. Barbellion*

## 18 March

1802 [Grasmere, the Lake District]
I went through the fields, and sate ½ an hour afraid to pass a Cow. The
Cow looked at me and I looked at the Cow and whenever I stirred the
Cow gave over eating.

*Dorothy Wordsworth*

1829 [Abbotsford, the Scottish Borders]
The day was showery but not unpleasant – soft dropping rains, attended by
mild atmosphere, that spoke of birds in their seasons. and a chirping of birds

that had a touch of Spring in it. I had the patience to get fully wet, and the grace to be thankful for it.

*Sir Walter Scott*

# 19 March

1942 [Jersey]
Worked in greenhouse, took Chrysanth. cuttings, etc. Joy [a friend] phoned to thank for the eggs we sent. Hens have laid well this week and mother has been able to spare eggs to many friends. People in town don't see eggs!

*Nan Le Ruez*

# 20 March

1803 [Somerset]
Very mild and the day turned out tolerable. Rode to Asholt, not many at Church. Came back, few at Church here in the afternoon. That Villain Porter had the impudence to come there, it disconcerted me much. His own daughter confesses herself to be with child by him. Oh Abominable Villain. I will punish him if there is any law to be had.

*William Holland*

# 21 March

1672 [Lamport, Northamptonshire]
A gentleman named Feilding went into his barn and took an ear of corn into his mouth and by chance the beard of it stuck under his tongue so that he could not get it out. He did not trouble much about it, but after five or six hours it became troublesome, and after thirteen or fourteen hours the wound turned septic and he died.

*Thomas Isham (aged 16)*

1756 [East Hoathly, Sussex]
*Sunday* I was at home all day, but not at church. Oh fie! no just reason for not being there . . .

*Thomas Turner*

# 22 March

1800 [Somerset]
Robert called me down rather early to see the horse's leg dressed. 'Tis a nasty wound quite to the bone. Robert has cleaned it and puts on a precipitate plaster. He wishes me to send for the farrier but I have no opinion of a country farrier, they always pretend a great deal of knowledge and know nothing about the matter. I am generally my own farrier by the aid of Bartlett and generally succeed. At Stowey met Mr Symes the Lawyer. He told me that Mrs Parrot has bought off her prosecutor. Alas, alas that money should be able to screen a person from Justice in this Kingdom so remarkable for good laws and uncorrupted Judges. She was accused of stealing lace out of a shop in Bath, is a person of considerable fortune and has a poor Jerry Sneak of a husband who adheres to her through all difficulties.

*William Holland*

# 23 March

1931 [New Forest]
The smell of the earth? Yes, we've got it now, and the tang of wet leaves and bracken under a thin diaphanous mist that enhances the colours close at hand, and drops a light veil over the distance. Larches rise from a floor of glowing orange fern and soft brown needles and stand ghostlike and shadowy and grey, just dimmed by mist, each drooping branch and twig encrusted with grey lichen. The sloping field beyond the wood has a bloom on it like dew. In the brown and purple hedges catkins have shaken loose and changed to gold. Low clouds hem us in, with just a line of light on

the horizon. Looking back, you see the sloping field now has pale sunlight breaking over it. A magpie crosses the path. The tail feathers of a jay make a pied streak as it disappears among the bushes. In the shallow pool among the furze bushes, where the frog spawn lay is now a congested mass of small black tadpoles.

*Janet Case*

### 1975 [Belmont, Lyme Regis]

A thump on the study window, a frantic dashing of wings, a tit squawking for dear life; and I am staring at a fine sparrowhawk, tawny and slate-blue, perched on the balcony rail just two feet outside the glass door. He caught nothing, except me.

*John Fowles*

## 24 March

### 1932 [Perth]

I'm afraid these bairn-rhymes [poems in Scots] which I write from time to time must appear rather formidable for a child – yet what can one do? Even grown-ups in Scotland are children so far as their native tongue is concerned. All of us must wade through the vocabulary if we are to regain our lost heritage. If the schools were interested that would be the most fitting field in which to sow the Word. There are signs that the Educational Authorities are beginning to realise that Scots is turning in its grave. Let them hurry on and dig it up.

*William Soutar*

## 25 March

### 1769 [Selborne, Hampshire]

Frogs croak: spawn abounds.

*Gilbert White*

# 26 March

### 1826 [Abbotsford, the Scottish Borders]

Here is a disagreeable morning, snowing and hailing, with gleams of bright sunshine between, and all the ground white, and all the air frozen. I don't like this jumbling of weather. It is ungenial, and gives chilblains. Besides, with its whiteness, and its coldness, and its glister, it resembles that most disagreeable of all things, a vain, cold, empty, beautiful woman, who has neither head nor heart, but only features like a doll.

*Sir Walter Scott*

### 1870 [Clyro, Radnorshire]

A delicious day upon Clyro Hill. It was sunny and warm under the sheltering bank and woods of Wern Vawr and pleasant walking along the low road to the old farm house with its large projecting and high-gabled porch. There was a stir about the house and yard. They had killed a fat stall-fed heifer yesterday and a party of people much interested in the matter, among them old Jones and his wife, were busy cutting up the carcase in the barn. A man went to and from the barn to the house with huge joints of beef having first weighed them on the great steelyard which hangs at the barn door. In the house Mrs Jones of New Building an old daughter of the house was engaged in the kitchen taking up joints from where the man had laid them and carrying them into an inner room or larder to put salt on them. By the fire sat a young woman who hid her face and did not look up. She had a baby lying across her lap.

*Francis Kilvert*

### 1926 [Buckinghamshire]

Today I have been entertaining Young – the lecher from Denbighshire. He came on a marvellous bicycle – a Sunbeam. We lunched at the Bell and went to see the children at football. He fell in love with R—. I fell down rather painfully trying to take the corner up to the speed-hill. I am very much tired tonight.

Yesterday I went to a point-to-point meeting at Kimble and lost £4 which I can very ill afford.

We had a party at the Bell. We got drunk. When we were all in bed David and Babe and Eliza arrived with a car full of Charleston records from London.

*Evelyn Waugh*

### 1975 [Belmont, Lyme Regis]

We wake up to snow; not very thick, and it thaws by midday, but it remains, especially after a phenomenally mild winter, vilely cold.

*John Fowles*

## 27 March

### 1802 [Grasmere, the Lake District]

A divine morning. At Breakfast Wm wrote part of an ode. Mr Olliff [a local farmer] sent the dung and Wm went to work in the garden. We sate all day in the orchard.

*Dorothy Wordsworth*

### 1985 [Essex House, Badminton]

Maundy Thursday, and a day of mourning indeed. I telephoned Riley the vet who suggested I bring Honey [his whippet] at 6.30. What with Easter on our heels, A. [Alvilde, his wife] agreed I should take her today – better than further delay and the agony of watching her decline. Riley a saintly man, who bore with my bitter tears which I could not control. I sat in the waiting room with Honey, stroking her neck and ears without daring to look at her. For her it was no worse a visit than many previous ones. Riley came in with syringe in hand and gave her a prick which she did not even feel. In five minutes she was asleep, having lain herself on the floor. I apologised for my emotion. He said it was normal and right and he felt the same over his own dogs' demise. When it was clear she was unconscious, he said, 'You may go now. Just give her a pat.' I did so and kissed her little head and bolted. This was pre-arranged, for then he would despatch her. A. had gone to Communion in my absence; when she returned, we both shamelessly wept. I said the piteous thing about dogs was their innocence. She said it was their implicit trust in us. Whatever it be, they wring the heart. I felt remorseful over my occasional irritation with Honey, who did have some tiresome habits – not coming in when put out last thing, and other sillinesses. Remorseful about the times I was angry with her and smacked her. *Eheu*, I grieve and am miserable. She was good, good, good, devoid of malice and spite. My companion for over a decade who, until she became incontinent, slept on my bed at nights. The hell of it all.

*James Lees-Milne*

## 28 March

1765 [East Hoathly, Sussex]
In the afternoon rode over to Chiddingly, to pay my charmer, or intended wife or sweetheart or whatever other name may be more proper, a visit at her father's where I drank tea, in company with their family and Miss Ann Thatcher. I supped there on some rasures of bacon. It being an excessive wet and windy night I had the opportunity, sure I should say the pleasure, or perhaps some might say the unspeakable happiness, to sit up with Molly Hicks, or my charmer, all night. I came home at forty minutes past five in the morning – I must not say fatigued; no, no, that could not be; it could be only a little sleepy for want of rest. Well to be sure, she is a most clever girl; but however, to be serious in the affair, I certainly esteem the girl, and think she appears worthy of my esteem.

*Thomas Turner*

## 29 March

1777 [Norfolk]
Andrews the Smuggler brought me this Night about 11 o'clock a Bagg of Hyson Tea 6 Pd Weight, He frightned us a little by whistling under the

Parlour Window just as we were going to bed. I gave him some Geneva and paid him for the Tea at 10/6 Per Pd – 3.3.0.

*James Woodforde*

## 1870 [Clyro, Radnorshire]

Home at 6, dressed for dinner. At 6.30 Charles with the mail phaeton and the two mares, grey and bay, dashed up to the door in grand style. I was ready and away we went to the Vicarage to pick up the Vicar who took the reins. At Peter's Pool we overtook and passed at dashing pace the Clyro Court brougham with one horse wherein were the Squire and Mr Frank Guise the recorder of Hereford bound like ourselves for dinner at Oakfield. It was refreshing to see the Vicar's stylish equipage driven by himself with two servants behind, dashing past the small humble turn-out of the Squire, rather reversing the usual order of things.

*Francis Kilvert*

## 1973 [Belmont, Lyme Regis]

First chaffchaffs singing.

*John Fowles*

# 30 March

## 1787 [Selborne, Hampshire]

Chaffinches pull off the blossoms of the polyanths, which are beautifully variegated.

*Gilbert White*

## 1876 [Slackfields Farm, Derbyshire]

*Fine.* Wet night. Chain harrowing Birches.

*Henry Hill*

# 31 March

## 1977 [Belmont, Lyme Regis]

My fifty-first birthday. Not good. I feel a growing depression; emptiness, staleness, boredom, after the last six months of work on the novel. Now it is dead, a corpse and its attendant vultures. I suppose I need a holiday, but Eliz is totally absorbed in getting the Branscombe shop ready. Anna [his step-daughter] is here to help her, Doris comes at the weekend. She and Anna are the two faces I see for a few hours each evening. I work in the garden a bit, but do not enjoy it. The garden, yes, still, always; but the work seems meaningless.

The great folly of my life was not having learnt to drive. I have days here when I feel imprisoned. No one comes here, I go nowhere. I can't even share the excitements of the book, since we tacitly exclude all that from our life. And that odd, old lack of ever having any intelligent discussion about anything with anyone. My tattle, the Branscombe tattle, book sale telephone-calls with London. Television is a great relief, egotropic, at night. And stumbling my way through some Bach scores I bought recently on the recorder; one I love, I begin to master it a little, the Andante from the Italian Concerto.

A call from Lois Wallace [his agent] in New York. *Daniel Martin* will be the Book of the Month Club's October main choice. A few minutes later Ned Bradford [his American publisher] was on the line from Boston, with the same news. I did sound warmer to him, liking him so much better. He said the price was $305,000, the highest they have ever got for a novel; and that they were now hoping for half a million for the paperback rights.

*John Fowles*

## 1980 [Ardnamurchan]

Last night, in a house in Kilchoan, I watched willy-nilly, a 'Highland' programme on television. I was trapped and could not well make my escape. All present but me enjoyed the programme thoroughly; all were Highlanders; all believed themselves to be watching something authentically native. The room was crowded and I was the only scowler there. I was a small oasis of gloom in a desert of delight.

The star performer on this programme was the celebrated Mr X, a singer of popular songs in a pseudo-Gaelic vein and a man, I assure you, more admired in these parts than was the great Maighstir Alasdair in his prime, when he sheltered from the redcoats in the caves of Arisaig, in the desolation that followed Culloden, with his pockets empty and the poetry burning a hole in his mind. My solitary groan when he flashed into view was lost in a chorus of 'oohs' and 'ahs'. He was robed in the full Balmoral fig, the dress that never was on land or sea. He was Tailor-and-Cutter beautiful, an exquisite. O not a *sgian dhu* nor a grouse-foot brooch was out of place about him. His stockings were as unwrinkled as his brow. His hair reflected the studio lights as brightly as his toe-caps.

He sang and he glittered and he clutched the microphone to his mouth like a child with a lollipop. He swayed from the knees. He shimmered and he shimmied.

I thought of my grandfather, in the dungarees and the Burns-and-Laird Line guernsey, the seaboots and the flat cloth cap of all his days. I remember him standing in the peat-bog, in the true Highlands, heaving the newly-cut sods up on to the bank, his palms plated with callouses, an old-master network of ingrained dirt. And round about him the reality of his life sucked and squelched . . .

My stomach turns. Away with all this tartanry, this obscene and irrelevant clutter of sporrans and gewgaws! Whatever legitimacy it might have had — and it had precious little — has become so tainted a man must needs be lacking in pride and honour and a sense of the absurd to countenance it.

*Alasdair Maclean*

1991 [Saltwood Castle, Kent]
Easter Sunday

The special moisture in the spring air — if not the foggy inland — with the sun lightly obscured, but a luminous promise. We went to Communion this morning. I enjoy it now because of the opening prayer, whose significance (as with so much now) I never before appreciated. '. . . to whom all hearts are open, all desires known, and from whom no secrets are hid . . .'

*Alan Clark*

# APRIL

# 1 April

1764 [Norfolk]
There was an Eclipse of the Sun this Morning about nine o'clock, but it was nothing to what was expected by most People.

*James Woodforde*

c.2003 [South of England]
The 'dawn' chorus is now in full voice long before sunrise. The ringing notes of the song thrushes usually break the silence when it is still pitch dark, and great tits, blackbirds and wrens soon follow. Most of them stop singing to look for food as soon as it is light enough for them to see the insects and spiders that they need, but they will start up again later in the morning. Where there are lighted gardens, robins sing both night and day, and are often mistaken for nightingales.

*Derwent May*

# 2 April

1903 [Barnstaple, North Devon]
I was glad yesterday to see the egg season so well in. I shall have to get blow-pipes and egg drills. Spring has really arrived and even the grasshoppers are beginning to stridulate, yet Burke describes these little creatures as being 'loud and troublesome' and the chirp unpleasant. Like Samuel Johnson he must have preferred brick walls to green hedges. Many people go for a walk and yet are unable to admire Nature simply because their power of observation is untrained. Of course some are not suited to the study at all and do not trouble themselves about it. In that case they should not talk of what

they do not understand . . . I might have noticed that I have used the term 'Study of Nature'. But it cannot be called a *study*. It is a pastime of sheer delight, with naught but beautiful dreams and lovely thoughts, where we are urged forward by the fact that we are in God's world which He made for us to be our comfort in time of trouble . . . Language cannot express the joy and happy forgetfulness during a ramble in the country. I do not mean that all the ins and outs and exact knowledge of a naturalist are necessary to produce such delight, but merely the common objects – Sun, Thrush, Grasshopper, Primrose and Dew.

*W.N.P. Barbellion*

# 3 April

1784 [Selborne, Hampshire]
The crocus's are full blown, & would make a fine show, if the sun would shine warm. The ever-green-trees are not injured, as about London. On this day *a nightingale* was heard at Bramshot!

*Gilbert White*

# 4 April

1649 [Essex]
Dry, windie, indifferently cleare in the nights very cold, and much given to frosts . . . good to purge the aire, and to prevent infection, the small poxe is about in the country . . . oh lord watch over mee and mine.

*Ralph Josselin*

1876 [Slackfields Farm, Derbyshire]
*Fine* Ploughing headlands in Barn Slackfield. Fetched nine gallons gas tar from Belper @ 2d. 3 bus. peas from Mr F. Hawkins.

*Henry Hill*

# 5 April

1790

Here I met with one of the most extraordinary phenomena that I ever saw, or heard of: – Mr Sellers has in his yard a large Newfoundland dog, and an old raven. These have fallen deeply in love with each other, and never desire to be apart. The bird has learned the bark of the dog, so that few can distinguish them. She is inconsolable when he goes out; and, if he stays out a day or two, she will get up all the bones and scraps she can, and hoard them up for him till he comes back.

*John Wesley*

1870 [Clyro, Radnorshire]

The day broke cloudless after a sharp frost. Up early and went to Cae Mawr to breakfast, at 8 o'clock. Drove to Hay in Morrell's carriage. We drove on to Llanigon village and sent the carriage back. Walked up by the Church and took the field path to see Cilonw Farm.

Down the pretty steep winding lane we went skirting the Honddu. Across the valley at the mouth of a great dreadful dingle stood the ruins of the house which was swept away while the people were dancing, by an avalanche of snow or a torrent of snow water let loose by a sudden thaw. A young man who was coming up from Llanthony to join the party was saved by his greyhound unaccountably hanging behind, whining and running back so as to entice his master home again. I had not seen Capel y Ffin for 4 years but I remembered the place perfectly, the old chapel short stout and boxy with its little bell turret (the whole building reminded one of an owl), the quiet peaceful chapel yard shaded by the seven great solemn yews, the chapel house, a farm house over the way, and the Great Honddu brook crossing the road and crossed in turn by the stone foot bridge. Before the chapel house door by the brookside a buxom comely wholesome girl with fair hair, rosy face, blue eyes and fair clear skin stood washing at a tub in the sunshine, up to the elbows of her round white lusty arms in soapsuds. We asked her how far it was to the place where the monks were building their monastery. 'Oh,' she said, smiling kindly and stopping her washing for a moment to direct us. 'Oh none just. Please to go over the brook and up the lane.' Two tramps were lounging against the bridge lighting their pipes and said to each other when we had passed, 'They are only going to see the monks.'

*Francis Kilvert*

# 6 April

1929 [New Forest]
Ice in the morning, a burning sun by noon, and what the ground is asking for is good, soft rain. No wonder the flowers are stunted as well as late. It is still a case of *looking* for primroses and wood anemones. No plenties yet. Only the wild daffodils that are never long of stalk are making as brave a show as ever with their crowds of yellow heads in a sea of blue-green leaves. It is a blessed lot to live in daffodil country. Sometimes you see a line of larger daffodils running straight part way across a field, marking where once a cottage garden lay – perhaps a cottage held on a three-lives' tenancy, which at the last was left to moulder into dust. So, too, a yew tree will mark a forgotten cottage site. They like a yew beside the cottage door.

*Janet Case*

# 7 April

1826 [Abbotsford, the Scottish Borders]
Made out my morning's task; at one drove to Chiefswood, and walked home by the Rhymer's Glen, Mars Lee, and Haxell Cleugh. Took me three hours. The heath gets somewhat heavier every year – but never mind, I like it altogether as well as the day I could tread it best. My plantations are getting all into green leaf, especially the larches, if theirs may be called leaves, which are only a sort of hair, and from the number of birds drawn to these wastes, I may congratulate myself on having literally made the desert to sing. As I

returned, there was, in the phraseology of that most precise of prigs in a white collarless coat and *chapeau bas*, Mister Commissary Ramsay – 'a rather dense inspissation of rain'. Deil care.

*Sir Walter Scott*

# 8 April

### 1922 [Wiltshire]

To-day has been a case of putting the clock back eight years. My preliminary sensations were similar to those which I experienced eight years ago when I last rode a hunt race; similar, as far as I can remember, to all the other twenty races I rode in during a normal young 'sportsman's' bump-round on his cherished quadruped. After the delicious thrills of keyed-up nervousness, he mounts with the utmost deliberation, and the mare is led out of the paddock. People consult their race-cards as we pass – 'No 8, Mr S. Sassoon's Lady Jill'.

The starter drops his flag. We're off. There are only four horses in the race. They jump the first two fences in a bunch. The next is the water. I do the wrong thing, through lack of 'dash', and allow two horses to go at it immediately in front of me. It is what racing-folk call 'getting blinded'. But Lady Jill jumps it beautifully and clears the hedge and twelve feet of water with plenty to spare. Now I settle down to ride the race astutely. Two horses drop behind and remain there. (Both fell and finished a long way behind.) The other is a big-striding grey, ridden by his owner, a genial, middle-aged, hard-bitten man (who is also the Inspector of Drains for the Swindon District). We go on together, and my mare gets too close to the fifth fence ('meets it wrong'), a big fence on a bank, with a ditch on the near side. She swerves to the right, and gets over with a scramble. Probably I rode her at it badly. (Lucky not to fall.) I allow the grey to go on a length or two in front, and so we cross half-a-dozen fences. Then we meet a couple of very wet and holding fields, and I hold the mare together very carefully, waiting till we get on sound turf again. She is hitting the fences and showing signs of distress, but I am confident that she can gallop away from the grey when I 'ask her the question'. At last we land in the long meadow; turn sharp to the right, 'cut off a corner' and come up on the inside in the approved style. There are only three more fences. The mare gets level with her leisurely-striding opponent. She goes a length in front. But the grey passes her again, and I shake her up for a real effort; the situation is becoming critical. Stride by stride, I realise the mare is 'beat'. The damned grey canters on with his deceptive stride, and wins by more lengths than I care to count. (The judge gave it as twenty but it was less.)

As I jump the last fence someone shouts 'Good old Sig!' But good old Sig exclaims 'Damnation!' in subdued tones, and his heart is rent by bitter angry disappointment. Anyhow I rode her all right to the end. 'Caught her by the head and sat still', but that was no consolation in the hour of defeat.

*Siegfried Sassoon*

# 9 April

1789 [Selborne, Hampshire]
Brimstone butter-fly. The tortoise comes out. Dog violets blow. Summer like.

*Gilbert White*

1818 [Somerset]
My wife was very busy indoors with Betty and they wiped and cleaned every book and made it very neat and clean. A very tedious business and it had not been done before these two years past tho my wife used to have cleaned off dust &cc every year. Govett who lives in the Rectory sent to borrow a Willy full of coal. Tho the man is a Methodist and is separated from his wife and keeps a woman in the house and I have no intercourse with him yet I did not chuse to refuse him such a thing and so let him have it. He must have a tolerable good opinion of my Liberality to venture to ask me such a favour, seeing that we do not speak to each other.

*William Holland*

1933 [Antrobus, Cheshire]

Flowers are opening rather before their time, and there was a red campion in bloom near Northwich on April 15th. On Saturday we visited an unspoilt Cheshire valley where primroses still grow in great profusion, and there we found several cowslips and many scores of bluebells fully open. Blackthorns, which were already in flower on March 26th, were a mass of blossom.

Our pleasure was somewhat marred by the activities of a harpy with a trowel and several large paper bags for the primrose plants. Expostulation was useless. The primroses were wanted for 'the border', though why plants in full flower should be dug up when a sixpenny packet of polyanthus seed would do the job so much better is difficult to understand.

*A. W. Boyd*

# 10 April

1836 [Stafford]

Reginald [her husband] spoke from the pulpit of the people's constantly coming into church after the beginning of the service. Thunder and lightning. In the afternoon the boys of the Sunday School sit up by the altar to keep them in better view and order as to their conduct.

*Emily Smith*

# 11 April

1794 [Norfolk]

One of my Greyhounds, young Fly, got to Betty Cary's this morning and ran away with a Shoulder of Mutton undressed & eat it all up. They made great lamentation & work about it. I had the Greyhound hanged in the Evening.

*James Woodforde*

# 12 April

1770 [Stove, Orkney]
A very fine dry day all day my 3 Plewghs in the Pow & the Shortland Sown
the Clay Sheed & harrowed it one Plewgh furrowing the havest pl:d Land
& in the Wt Sheed planted the Ministes Potatoes my men Evening & Morg
in the Ware
    NE

*Patrick Fea*

# 13 April

1872 [Clyro, Radnorshire]
The two old women Hannah Jones and Sarah Probert were both lying in
bed and groaning horribly. I gave them some money and their cries and
groans suddenly ceased.

*Francis Kilvert*

1995 [Hampshire]
This is the eleventh day of sunshine; anyway in the south. Cherry blossom
is softly brilliant and heart-touching. A lot of my time is spent assisting
indignant bumble-bees trapped behind window-panes: their bigness, noisiness
and silliness is somehow appealing.

*Alec Guinness*

# 14 April

1776 [Norfolk]
Very much fatigued & hurried this morning by hearing that my Brother
John had a Fall from his Horse in the Night coming from Evercreech &
was found senseless about 1 in the morning a little below the turnpike. He
has cut his Face much & much bruised inwardly, but no Bone broke –

thank God he was not killed. He was bled & put to bed about 3 in the morning. In the Afternoon I went down to see him and he was up & below Stairs at Dinner but in Pain. I did not expect to see him so well as he was. I hope this will caution him from riding when merry – he has had many Falls before but none so bad as this.

*James Woodforde*

# 15 April

### 1778 [Norfolk]

Brewed a vessell of strong Beer to day. My two large Piggs, by drinking some Beer grounds – taking out of 3 Barrells to day, got so amazingly drunk by it, That they were not able to stand and appeared like dead things almost. I never saw Piggs so drunk in my life – I slit their Ears for them without feeling.

*James Woodforde*

### 1802 [Grasmere, the Lake District]

It was a threatening misty morning – but mild. We set off after dinner from Eusemere . . . When we were in the woods beyond Gowbarrow park we saw a few daffodils close to the water side. We fancied that the lake had floated the seeds ashore and that the little colony had so sprung up. But as we went along there more and yet more and at last under the boughs of the trees, we saw that there was a long belt of them along the shore, about the breadth of a country turnpike road. I never saw daffodils so beautiful they grew among the mossy stones about and about them, some rested their heads upon these stones as on a pillow for weariness and the rest tossed and reeled and danced and seemed as if they verily laughed with the wind that blew upon them over the lake, they looked so gay ever glancing ever changing. This wind blew directly over the lake to them. There was here and there a little knot and a few stragglers a few yards higher up but they were so few as not to disturb the simplicity and unity and life of that one busy highway. We rested again and again.

*Dorothy Wordsworth*

1968 [Underhill Farm, Lyme Regis]
Working on this last [his novel, *The French Lieutenant's Woman*], a small spider
stepped on to the page I was correcting – it turned out to be a rarity,
*Scytodes thoracica* no less, a young one. Adults must be living in the workroom,
as it is an indoor spider. *Scytodes* has the most ingenious of all arachnoid
hunting systems. It captures its prey *retiarius* fashion, squirting a microscopic
jet of 'glue' from its jaws and oscillating its head at the same time to produce
a zigzag 'hose' effect. The victim is gullivered to the ground.

*John Fowles*


# 16 April


1778 [Norfolk]
My 2 Piggs are still unable to walk yet, but they are better than they were
Yesterday. They tumble about the Yard & can by no means stand at all steady
yet. In the Afternoon my 2 Piggs were tolerably sober.

*James Woodforde*


# 17 April


1816 [Over Stowey, Somerset]
A fine open mild morning. I rode out and called on many of my Old and
Poor Parishioners and I found at last Old George Adams at the end of a
long lane in Cockercombe. He is 86 and came out at last, weak with a long
beard. I gave him some of the Sacrament Money. God Bless you said he I
have no one but you and Madam to look after me. I answered you have
your own family, son and daughter. He shook his head and replied, looking
steadfastly at me, they are best off who can help themselves. Then I called
on the Old Colonel as they call him. He is 87 if not eight. He has got two
houses so I did not give him any money but he may have something to eat
and drink if he sends for it. He has been a shrewd man in his day. Then I
called on Rich who lately lived at Ely Green, he kept a Publick House, got

rich by it and took a little himself so that he and his wife look dropsical and blodded but he was a relation of the late Mr Rich of Crosse who gave him a little estate so now he means to live soberly and moderately and repent of his sins he told me. I enquired of the health of both of them and had some Parish news of him and understood the Whites were coming to Plainsfield again. After speaking a word or two others I returned home and Mrs Sealy came in to drink tea. We had a brewing this morning. Mr Luke managed the whole business.

*William Holland*

1949 [Sissinghurst, Kent]
After sunset I climb up to pull down the flag. There is a great red glow in the west and the whole of Kent lies below me bathed in golden light. The garden looks so rich from the eminence; masses of blossom and daffodils among the dark of the yews. It truly is a most beautiful garden – so varied, so calm, so enclosed. It is a garden I should envy much if it belonged to someone else.

*Harold Nicolson*

# 18 April

1952 [Keswick, the Lake District]
The sun strikes warmly on the south-east facing wall of the kitchen garden at the farm and uncurls the fronds of the spleenwort and wall rue. Halfway up is a deep recess, about four feet long, floored with Borrowdale stone, made to take the skeps used by beekeepers not so long ago. It is empty now and hives are used instead, but the bees' ways never change. My hives face the morning sun and the bees are soon afield. By half past eight they are on the gooseberry flowers, and as the sun rises higher their contented hum spreads to the willows at the garden's edge and the gorse on the hill. I have been spring-cleaning the hives, and when the roof and wooden walls are taken away the brood chamber is moved, the floor brushed clean, and all made neat. In the brood chamber the busy workers are tending the young

bees as they come from the cells. Comparatively few are hatching as yet and the other cells are filled with pollen, which, with nectar or sugar syrup, will constitute their food. There is the lemon yellow of pussy-willow pollen, the dull yellow of gorse, the delicate green of bat willow, and, perhaps the most striking of all, the deep-red orange pollen of the purple crocuses – a fair and glowing record of hard work and a promise of summer's plenty.

*Enid J. Wilson*

# 19 April

**1921 [Gloucestershire]**
Walked three miles out of Gloucester and up a gorse-clad hill, and back over some lush green meadows. A lovely morning; apple-blossom; and a peacock in a farm-yard, shaking out his tail feathers, and turning to face me with an array of eyes and barbaric dignity.

*Siegfried Sassoon*

# 20 April

**1826 [Abbotsford, the Scottish Borders]**
The day was so tempting that I went out with Tom Purdie to cut some trees, the rather that my task was very well advanced. He led me into the wood, as the blind King of Bohemia was led by his four knights into the thick of the battle at Agincourt or Crecy, and then, like the old King, 'I struck good strokes more than one,' which is manly exercise.

*Sir Walter Scott*

**1874 [Surrey]**
Young elmleaves lash and lip the sprays. This has been a very beautiful day – fields about us deep green lighted underneath with white daisies, yellower fresh green of leaves above which bathes the skirts of the elms, and their tops are touched and worded with leaf too . . . Blue shadows fell all up the

meadow at sunset and then standing at the far Park corner my eye was struck by such a sense of green in the tufts and pashes of grass, with purple shadow thrown back in the black mould behind them, as I do not remember ever to have been exceeded in looking at green grass.

*Gerard Manley Hopkins*

## 21 April

1903 [Barnstaple, North Devon]
S and I have made a little hut in the woods out of a large natural hole in the ground by a big tree. We have pulled down branches all around it and stuck in upright sticks as a paling. We are training ivy to grow over the sticks. We smoke 'Pioneer' cigarettes here and hide the packets in a hole under the roots of the tree. It's like a sort of cupboard.

*W.N.P. Barbellion*

## 22 April

1836 [Stafford]
Execution of our pig which had been bought and fattening since 26 March, nearly a month and weighing 7 score lbs. Was at the school for a long time. Oh Lord, bless me with heavenly illumination and knowledge to be able to teach these little ones. Bought counterpane, and blankets etc. for the servants' bed.

*Emily Smith*

## 23 April

1783 [Fyfield, Hampshire]
Parish accounts settled and amounted to more than last year by —. 13 rates gathered again. Many antient people now on ye book.

*Henry White*

1906 [Olton, Warwickshire]

Bright and cold. Saw two live vipers which had been brought in from the moor; one of them was more than two feet long. The gentleman who had captured them handled them quite fearlessly, he held up one by the back of the neck and forcing its mouth open with a stick, he showed me the two little pink fangs in the upper jaw. When on the ground they reared themselves up and hissed, and struck repeatedly at a walking stick placed in front of them.

*Edith Holden*

# 24 April

1937 [Antrobus, Cheshire]

A solitary house-martin was flying with hundreds of sand-martins and swallows over the mere on April 19th, the very day on which I saw my first last year. It is strange that house-martins and swallows, birds so near akin and so much alike in their ways, should really have so little in common; they feed together, but migrate at different times and do not compete for nesting-sites.

In a wayside pit within a few feet of the highway a pair of the mute swans have built their nest. They are so tame that one will sit on her eggs and the other beside the nest while they feed on the bread that is thrown to them by children from a cottage hard-by. One day a second and older cob (or male bird) appeared, severely thrashed and ducked the young cob, and drove him off to stand disconsolately on the road. Triangular dramas meet with little sympathy among our country folk, and next day the interloper was driven off by a farmer and made to walk miles along the high road away from the nest. When next I rode down the lane the original cob was hiding behind a hedge, but the pen, his mate, sat stolidly on her eggs. On the following day they were once more living side by side, to the relief of my scandalised neighbours, whose visits to the 'pictures' are too few to have accustomed them to such goings on.

*A. W. Boyd*

1948 [Crouch, Kent]

Four nights ago, with the moon pouring down and the nightingale singing and stopping, singing and stopping unaccountably, I suddenly heard another sound. I thought it was a laugh from some woman in the lane. I imagined her wandering round the fields with her lover after leaving the pub. I heard it again and then again. It was no laugh but extravagant sobbing. It rang out, drowning the nightingale, dirtying the night. I ran into Eric's room and told him. He came into my room and we sat by the open french door. The sobbing was a mechanical repetition of notes falling in a scale from high to low. The light was on in the bungalow through the apple trees. The weeping came from there, where a Hungarian lives with his English wife. They are young, newly married in September or October. There was no hint of comforting, reasoning from the husband, no word from the woman, just the hard boo-hoo crying, louder than any other crying I have ever heard, then the sudden ceasing, the light flicked off and nothing. The nightingale streamed on, the wind grew colder, and the moon milked itself into the grass's hair.

*Denton Welch*

## 25 April

1829 [Abbotsford, the Scottish Borders]

Maxpopple [Scott's cousin, William Scott] dined and slept here with four of his family, much amused with what they heard and saw. By good fortune a ventriloquist and partial juggler came in and we had him in the library after dinner. He was a half-starved wretched-looking creature, who seemed to have eat more fire than bread. So I caused him to [be] well stuff'd, and gave him a guinea rather to his poverty than to skill.

*Sir Walter Scott*

# 26 April

## 1887 [Goring-on-Sea, Sussex]

Chiffchaff! Rather a sad song. Sunny day, some rain. Snow early morning at 5 o'clock.

*Richard Jefferies*

## 1994 [Cheshire]

At last the spring butterflies have started to appear, not in any great quantity, but individuals have been tempted out by the few sunny days we have had. Temperatures haven't matched the sunshine, with the weather still coming from the north and west, but at least the combination of the wind and sun has gone some way to drying out the fields which have been soaked for so long. On a visit to my butterfly-recording patch on 13 April, I was welcomed by the sight of a small tortoiseshell, a peacock and a comma – only one of each but it was a start. Later in the day I saw a member of the fourth family of our winter hibernating species, the brimstone, flying strongly and purposefully along a roadside hedge. This is a familiar sight in spring, when brimstones will wander over large areas looking for the sole feed plant for this year's offspring – the buckthorn. In our area this will be the alder buckthorn, which is an uncommon plant locally – I know of only three sites around the valley. Three days later I watched two of these bright yellow insects feeding on the nectar from a group of primroses which grew on the steep embankment of a stretch of woodland. The brimstone is an important pollinator of wild primroses, and as each long tongue reached down the flower tube to find the nectar, so pollen would become attached and be carried to the next receptive plant. Although the sun has brought the butterflies out, the winds have been from the wrong direction to encourage much bird migration. Nevertheless, the urge to reach their breeding territories has seen the arrival of two willow-warblers and a black cap on 15 April, and several wheatears on passage. No doubt the same urge led to the departure of siskins who had wintered in the garden and were last seen at the nut baskets on 10 April.

*J.M. Thompson*

# 27 April

### 1775 [Selborne, Hampshire]

Early tulips blow. A pair of house-martins appear, & frequent the nest at the end of the house; a single one also wants to go in. These must be of the family bred there last year. The nest was built last summer. The martins throw the rubbish out of their nest. Bank-martins abound on short-heath: they come full as soon as the house-swallow. Two swans inhabit Oakhanger-ponds: they came of themselves in winter with three more. Pulled down many old House-martins nests; they were full of rubbish, & the exuviae of the hippobosca hirundinis in the pupa state. These insects obtain so much sometimes in y(ir) nests, as to render the place insupportable to the young, & oblige them to throw themselves on the ground. The case is the same sometimes with young swifts.

*Gilbert White*

### 1812 [Somerset]

I was surprised to see women carrying heath from Quantock almost half naked, they generally put all the rags they have on on the occasion as they find the Heath to tear their peticoats. One woman seemed to have nothing but a flannel peticoat on. I could not see what was the matter but while I passed by she sat down and two others put a large bundle of heather on her to cover. I took no notice but went on yet thought they should have been further removed from the side of the road. The day not quite so cold on the Hill as the time before.

*William Holland*

### 1826 [Abbotsford, the Scottish Borders]

This is one of those abominable April mornings which deserve the name of *Sans Cullotides*, as being cold, beggarly, coarse, savage and intrusive. The earth lies an inch deep with snow, to the confusion of the worshippers of Flora. It is this uncertainty in April, and the descent of snow and frost when one thinks themselves clear of them, and that after fine encouraging weather, that destroys our Scottish fruit and flowers. It is as imprudent to attach yourself to flowers in Scotland as to a caged bird; the cat, sooner or later, snaps one up, and these – *Sans Cullotides* – annihilate the other. It was but yesterday I was admiring the glorious flourish of the pears and apricots, and now hath come the killing frost.

*Sir Walter Scott*

## 28 April

1804 [Somerset]
I heard the Cuckow for the first time this year on this very day.

*William Holland*

## 29 April

1946 [Inverness-shire]
There are two places I love to visit in search of April. One is a high hill-slope nine miles west of Inverness. It is curious – up there where one is surrounded by crags, deep gulleys, and all the sterner stuff that goes to make a hill – to find Spring so profuse, and green, and gentle . . .

The second place to which I go in search of April is a Morayshire wood. It spreads squarely solid for five miles on each side of the North Road. It is my conception of an absolute wood. Thick, dark oak trees emphasise its solidity: even in Spring they remain heavy and shaggy. You could explore this wood for a life-time without exhausting its revelations. One moment you are in the heart of the wood; a few stops and you find yourself on the heights of a disused quarry; and, when this happens, if you have sensitivity, you know that all history lies in those great, moss-covered boulders, and shaggy, old trees, and that kings and wars are but incidents.

*Jessie Kesson*

# 30 April

1870 [Clyro, Radnorshire]
May Eve, Saturday
This evening being May Eve I ought to have put some birch and wittan (mountain ash) over the door to keep out the 'old witch'. But I was too lazy to go out and get it. Let us hope the old witch will not come in during the night. The young witches are welcome.

*Francis Kilvert*

c.2000 [Walnut Tree Farm, Suffolk]
Yesterday, the wind changed. It went round from the north-east to south-west, and at last four swallows appeared over the house. I heard them first, then saw them flying and twittering round and round above the garden. The quince blossomed its pale pink peony flowers, the apple tree came into flower, and the cuckoo flowers on the lawn and out on the wide windswept sea of the common were in full pale mauve flower.

I have been eating the young dandelions, the fresh, sharp, tasty new sorrel leaves, land cress and white campion leaves, which John Evelyn recommends in his herbal. Those swallows and their magic wand brought all the waving sea of cow-parsley outside my north window effervescing into a white froth of flower. The ash tree filled with goldfinches pecking at its flowers – fascinated by them – and greenfinches flitted along the hedges like English parrots.

*Roger Deakin*

# MAY

# 1 May

**1783 [Fyfield, Hampshire]**

Trouts begin to come up ye brook in pursuit of minnows, about 200 minnows were caught, nearly as good to eat as gudgeons.

*Henry White*

**1802 [Grasmere, the Lake District]**

Heard the cuckow today this first of May.

*Dorothy Wordsworth*

# 2 May

**1782 [Selborne, Hampshire]**

Two swifts at Nore Hill passed me by at a steady rate towards this village as if they were just arrived.

*Gilbert White*

**1926 [New Forest]**

There is no denying our nightingale is something of a failure. For three years the delight to an ex-Londoner of hearing those poignant notes piercing the night admitted of no criticism. But this year we are beginning to let ourselves be just. He raps out those single notes so quickly and mechanically, running up to six or eight at a time, then passes to his jug-jugs, and from that to a tentative warble – a mere snatch. After this tuning up one waits expectant for the real song to begin. But it never does begin. There is a pause, and then the same thing happens. You may lie and listen from your bed for an hour or more, and he achieves nothing more sustained or passionate than that – and never has done.

*Janet Case*

# 3 May

## 1993 [The Lake District]

Old men with walking sticks, young children in gym shoes and even babies cocooned in fathers' rucksacks were on top of Catbells the other day and, in their dozens, wandering along the lazy ridge to High Spy. It was a perfect day for idling on the tops – warm and sunny, barely a breath of wind and matchless views to far horizons. The last drifts of snow were still clinging to the tops of Helvellyn and later, from High Spy, we saw the last white hand-kerchiefs of winter on Great Gable. Catbells has always seemed, to me, a family hill for enthusiasts of all ages but mostly for children; it was, I recall, my daughter's first 'mountain', ticked off at the age of two and a half. A pretty name for a child's mountain – the hill where Beatrix Potter's Mrs Tiggy-Winkle had some of her adventures, finally disappearing through a door some-where Newlands way. And from the top, this bright afternoon, Keswick looked a fairy town in a magic landscape and Derwentwater, spread out below us like a pond, ringed with wooded fells and dotted with enchanted islands with white yachts becalmed as if floating butterflies, an exciting place for youthful adventure. We had to dawdle; there was so much to see and admire – the lovely, unspoiled Vale of Newlands and every step of the routes up Robinson and Hindscarth, the crumpled ram's-horn shape of the summit of Causey Pike and its exciting ridge, the crowded woodlands and crags of Borrowdale with sixty years of adventurous memories and, straight ahead a glimpse of the highest land in England. Two jet aircraft streaked, and in a sudden crash of sound, through the Jaws of Borrowdale below on our left and a pair of ravens, as always up here, performed aerobatics for us high about the perch of High Spy. We came down by Hause Gate, past the memorial seat for Hugh Walpole, who lived in the lovely house, today carpeted with daffodils, on the lower slope of the fell looking out across the lake. Each morning, after breakfast, he would cross the lawn to his big library over the garage and write quickly, often describing scenes he could see from his windows, so that many of his heroes strode these grassy slopes or ran up through the bracken and the heather to watch the sun setting behind Grasmere.

*A. Harry Griffin*

# 4 May

### 1866 [Oxfordshire]

Fine. Alone in Powder Hill wood. Elms far off have that flaky look now but nearer the web of springing green with long curls moulds off the skeleton of the branches. Fields pinned with daisies. Buds of apple blossoms look like nails of blood. Some ashes are out. I reckon the spring is at least a fortnight later than last year for on Shakespere's birthday, April 21, it being the tercentenary, Ilbert crowned a bust of Shakespere with bluebells and put it in his window, and they are not plentiful yet.

*Gerard Manley Hopkins*

### 1924 [Lewes, Sussex]

Mr Gale to tea smelling abominably of mothball.

*Alice Dudeney*

# 5 May

### 1946 [Inverness-shire]

The vivid green of the corn parks contrasts strangely with the insipid whiteish-green of the neighbouring hay-fields. All the farm labour is concentrated in the neep park. A curious scene to witness. One tractor-lad sows the manure, another tractor follows in his wake to open the drills – and lastly a solitary horse walks slowly into its undisputed own, pulling the turnip-sower. In front of this mechanised busyness the manual labourers, who can never quite be replaced, clear the park of weeds. For, like all things that are produced from the soil, there's a lot mair tae neeps that just the atein' o' them!

*Jessie Kesson*

# 6 May

## 1783 [Norfolk]

Cobb the Rat-Catcher dined with our Folks to day. We caught and killed about 3 Dozen of Rats in the Barn before Dinner to day – 3 old female Rats with their young ones – 2 old dog Rats and some half grown.

*James Woodforde*

## 1870 [Clyro, Radnorshire]

I set off for Newchurch again, my second visit there this week.

When I got on to the open of the Little Mountain the lapwings were wheeling about the hill by the score, hurtling and rustling with their wings, squirling and wailing, tumbling and lurching on every side, very much disturbed, anxious and jealous about their nests. As I entered the fold of Gilfach y rheol, Janet issued from the house door and rushed across the yard and turning the corner of the wain-house I found the two younger ladies assisting at the castration of the lambs, catching and holding the poor little beasts and standing by whilst the operation was performed, seeming to enjoy the spectacle. It was the first time I had seen clergyman's daughters helping to castrate lambs or witnessing that operation and it rather gave me a turn of disgust at first. But I made allowance for them and considered in how rough a way the poor children have been brought up, so they thought no harm of it, and I forgave them. I am glad however that Emmeline was not present, and Sarah was of course out of the way. Matilda was struggling in a pen with a large stout white lamb, and when she had mastered him and got him well between her legs and knees I ventured to ask where her father was. She signified by a nod and a word that he was advancing behind me, and turning I saw him crossing the yard with his usual outstretched hand and cordial welcome. I don't think the elder members of the family quite expected that the young ladies would be caught by a morning caller castrating lambs, and probably they would have selected some other occupation for them had they foreseen the coming of a guest. However they carried it off uncommonly well.

*Francis Kilvert*

# 7 May

1945 [Yorkshire]
VE Day

They had no wireless in the cottage where I had supper, so I didn't hear the nine o'clock news. Walking back to camp afterwards, the first sign of anything unusual that I noticed was a string of small triangular flags being hoisted up across the road by some workmen. The flags appeared quite suddenly out of the leaf-laden boughs of a chestnut, crossed a patch of sago-coloured sky, and disappeared into the dark foliage of another tree. They looked surprised to be there. They were not new flags. They had flapped for a jubilee and a coronation and numerous local festivals, and now they seemed to be getting a little tired of it all. They were faded and grubby and washed-out-looking. They hung languidly in the bluish evening air. The workmen tapped away at the trees and thrust ladders up into the ripe foliage, bringing down showers of leaves and a snow of pink and white blossom. Further on there was a cottage with two Union Jacks thrust out from the window-sill. They hung down stiffly to attention. Against the mellow sun-bleached texture of the stone their strident colours looked ridiculous, and because they were there on purpose to disturb the quiet and familiar contours they gave a feeling of uneasiness. From there onwards all the little cottages were sprouting flags.

There was no one about to see them, and no very clear reason how they came to be there. Menacing each other across the lane with their shrill colours they were like a flock of rare and fabulous birds which had alighted suddenly and without warning, clinging to chimney pots, window-sills and door posts. They were of many different sizes and shapes and attitudes corresponding partly to the income levels of their owners, and partly to a certain capriciousness which they seemed to acquire on their own. Some of them, having been unfurled, had hitched themselves up again shyly over the poles. Others had a narrow strip of wood fastened along the extreme edge, so that they were forced to suffer the maximum exposure. The large houses had older flags sewn together from pieces of silk with white painted poles and sometimes a gold tassel. The cottages all had new flags; little pieces of calico dyed with raw-looking colours. When it rained they would run.

On the dung-crusted door of a stable a V had been made with red, white and blue ribbon, and inside the V, hurriedly chalked as an afterthought, a red E. In the little window of the grocer's was a newspaper cutting of the Prime Minister. It was stuck on the window with four large pieces of brown tape like a police notice. In the window that has bird seed and bottles of sauce was a gold frame with a reproduced oil-painting of two exceedingly mild and dignified lions, and in the bottom left-hand corner the word 'PEARS'. In front there was a photograph of the Royal Family in sepia, with the word 'CORONATION' underneath and a round circle of rust from a drawing-pin. All the familiar and reliable things had suddenly disclosed a secret and unsuspected threat, though it would be impossible to say exactly what it was they threatened. But when the last house was passed and there were only fields and hedges and ditches frothing with tall white cow-parsley, there was a feeling of relief and reassurance.

*Keith Vaughan*

# 8 May

1906 [Barnstaple, North Devon]
On interviewing my old friend Dr H—, found I had chicken pox. This instead of being a Diary of a Naturalist's observations will be one of infectious diseases.

*W.N.P. Barbellion*

1949 [East Anglia]
Pay surreptitious visit to blackbird's nest discovered in ivy garden wall a week ago, and find three eggs in it. Retailing this to Rosemary (born a 'townee') at tea, she enquires blankly how I knew it was a blackbird's the first time if there weren't any eggs?

Any country bumpkin, myself included, can answer that, I tell her promptly. Blackbirds always build their nests of dried grass, about six inches in diameter, and three or so deep, and reinforce it with a mud lining, which in turn is lined with more dried grass. Thrushes commence in the same way, but stop when the mud wall is completed. The chaffinch's nest, perhaps one-quarter the size, is made of lichen and moss, horsehair and sheepswool, blended by the most superb craftsmanship into one enchanting whole. Wrens favour moss with a warm, preferably horsehair, lining, and are one of the few species to add a roof, the entrance being a round hole on the nest side. Swans build a solitary sedge pile on river banks or in willow belts. Herons, contrary to what one might expect, build their yard-wide stick-and-grass nests in trees, and dwell in colonies, like rooks. Sandmartins, also colonists, have miniature rabbit burrows in sand and gravel pits, with a few shreds of grass at the end of them. Kingfishers, individualists like the swans, choose earth, clay, or sandy banks near rivers, emulate the sandmartins by using tunnels, but make the actual nest by the simple but unlovable method of regurgitating the bones of the fish they swallow. Housemartins and swallows both use mud-scales lined with feathers, the latter favouring saucer-shaped nests, the former preferring a style somewhat like the wrens. House-sparrows are untidy as the martins are houseproud, a jumbled bundle of feathers and straw passing for a nest unless they dispossess the housemartins, as they not infrequently do.

Am quite prepared to enlarge on the architectural habits of woodpeckers, moorhens, wild ducks, robins, 'yellow-hammers' and blue-tits, 'pee-wits' and skylarks, turtle-doves and pigeons, the warbler tribe and anything else she fancies. But deduce from Rosemary's dazed expression that it's time to change the subject, so hastily enquire after health of other occupants of married quarters at R.A.F. Station, Eastmere, instead.

*Elizabeth M. Harland*

# 9 May

1968 [Underhill Farm, Lyme Regis]
Three o'clock of a sunny afternoon, and a fox below the window. A very large one, and bold. It looked round, then went on its buoyant lope-walk along the sheds and down into the upper yard. No animal has quite such an air of vicious, savage independence about it; I think the more humorous

aspects of the fox mythology – its trick, its cunning – have something to do with the tail. Quite why such a long tail was thought necessary by evolution is a mystery; for it's certainly blinded man to the animal's nature.

*John Fowles*

### 1992 [Saltwood Castle, Kent]

I have been wrestling with the lawn in the Inner Bailey. We bought a new ATCO and it cuts crazily well so that even a half stripe needs its large plastic bag emptying. But the lawn remains obstinate – resistant to striping and with ridged 'bare marks'. The garden is relentless in its demands on time. Not only is the lawn like the Forth Bridge, it needs restarting as soon as you finish, but there is scything of nettles and use of the tractor in the arboretum and the wood, and a few 'artist's' touches in the Garden House.

*Alan Clark*

## 10 May

### 1906 [Olton, Warwickshire]

Saw a dead Hedge-hog curled up by the roadside.

*Edith Holden*

## 11 May

### 1876 [Slackfields Farm, Derbyshire]

*Very dry and cold.* Working ground for potatoes.

*Henry Hill*

### 1996 [Hampshire]

A glossy young crow tried to get into the house yesterday, perhaps a dozen or more times. He either bashed himself at the windows or fluttered against them or, perched on a balcony railing, peered in while squawking. Maybe he caught his reflection in the glass and thought it was a mate. This morning, far too early, he was at it again but 'as the day goes on' (BBC weather forecast) he seems to be tiring. He's going to be a bloody nuisance if he keeps it up.

*Alec Guinness*

# 12 May

1800 [Somerset]
There is a fire downstairs in the parlour which should not be at this time of year. Lent the great horse to the Clerk to bring some potatoes, this will not do, to keep a horse for the whole Parish. In going to bed I stepped into the brew house and found it full of faggots for washing. I grew very angry and insisted on some being thrown out lest they should set the house on fire.

*William Holland*

# 13 May

1917 [Chapelwood Manor, Sussex]
This notebook began not many miles from Arras in the bloody month of April, when guns began to bellow. And now my disciplined wanderings have sent me to a very pleasant country house, where perfect good taste prevails, and nobody sleeps in the clothes he wore last week and this.

It is a grey-timbered and many-gabled house, built twelve years ago. Dark yew-hedges and formal gardens are round it. And its windows look across Sussex toward Lewes and Beachy Head – all woods and sloping meadows and hedges in their young green, and growing wheat, with clumps of daffodils in the field beyond the gardens.

Sleepless, I am waiting for the dawn and the first English birds I have heard sing their maytime madrigals since 1915. The gables of the house begin to show distinct against a clear, starry sky. Cocks are crowing; an owl hooting away in the woods; and the busy clock ticks on the mantelpiece. I feel as if I were soon to get up and dress for a cub-hunt – swallow my cocoa and boiled eggs, and then hear the tramp of horses' feet trampling the gravel outside.

All this is a long way from Arras and the battles. I am back in the years before battles were invented or Rolls of Honour thought about at all. As I lie on my bed with a yellow-shaded electric lamp shining (on my pink pyjamas) I can see the sky through the open, uncurtained window. The sky is a wonderful deep-blue colour, as I see it. When I turn out the light the window is a patch of greyish white on the darkness, with tree-tops standing up, very shadowy and still. It is the quietest of mornings; not a breath of wind.

I hear a cuckoo – a long way off. Then a blackbird goes scolding along the garden trees. Soon the chorus will begin. Put out the light.

*Siegfried Sassoon*

1996 [Hampshire]

The crow came banging at the window again. I drove him away with wild gestures and now I feel horribly mean. In the past hour I have learned he is probably half tame. A local garage had befriended a crow and he disappeared a few days go. What to do? He would be impossible to catch to redeliver to his old stomping ground.

*Alec Guinness*

# 14 May

1800 [Grasmere, the Lake District]

A young woman begged at the door – she had come from Manchester on Sunday morn with two shillings and a slip of paper which she supposed was a Bank note – it was a cheat. She had buried her husband and three children within a year and a half – all in one grave – burying very dear – paupers all put in one place – 20 shillings paid for as much ground as will bury a man – a stone to be put over it or the right will be lost – 11/6 each time the ground is opened.

*Dorothy Wordsworth*

### 1866 [Oxfordshire]

Chestnuts in bloom. The blooms are, as one feels, not straight but the tips bent inwards: then being thrown in some cases forwards, a good deal out of the upright, the curved type is easily seen in multiplicity which in one might be unnoticed. A brown tulip is a noble flower, the curves and close folding of the petals delightful. Anothers thick furry black. Young copper beech leaves seen against the sky pale brown with rosy blush along the ribs of each leaf. Solomon's seal.

*Gerard Manley Hopkins*

### 1911 [Barnstaple, North Devon]

I hate living in this little town. If someone dies, he is sure to be someone you had a joke with the night before. A suicide – ten to one – implicates your bosom friend, or else the man in the bookshop cut him down. There have been three deaths since I came home – I knew them all. It depresses me. The town seems a mortuary with all these dead bodies lying in it. Lucky for you, if you're a fat, rubicund, unimaginative physician.

*W.N.P. Barbellion*

## 15 May

### 1836 [Wareham, Dorset]

Went to the Sunday School. Mr Edward Banks did duty at Wareham church in the morning. Dear Reggy preached for the Church Missionary Society. Not £6 collected owing to the eclipse (annular) of the sun.

*Emily Smith*

# 16 May

1974 [Belmont, Lyme Regis]
Sitting on the bench in the cistus walk, I see an ant crawling up my trouser-leg; then realise it isn't an ant, but a spider — and later, under the microscope, that it is the very rare ant-mimic jumping-spider, *Synageles venator*. Locket and Millidge [authors of *British Spiders*] report it only from 'a few coastal sandhills' and 'in one Huntingdonshire fen'. Its resemblance to a small black ant is indeed remarkable, and probably isn't as rare as they say. But I was delighted to discover it.

*John Fowles*

# 17 May

1916 [Lewes, Sussex]
I gave Esther [her maid] notice, because out of sheer venom knowing I will not wash my face in anything but rain water (hence my indisputably lovely skin!) she had emptied the tub saying the rain water 'stunk!'

*Alice Dudeney*

# 18 May

1701 [Wotton, Surrey]
After an extraordinary drouth, God sent very plentifull showers, the wind coming West & South.

*John Evelyn*

1837 [Oxfordshire]
This is a very busy day as we are going to have a party this evening something larger than usual. We had four to dinner and about fifty or sixty in the evening. The plan of manageing these parties are thus: — there are two

men besides myself, one opened the door and let the Company in, I shewed them into a parlour where there was three maidservants to make tea and give it to them and take off their cloaks and bonnets, and the other man shewed them up into the drawingroom and gave in their names as lowd as he can bawl in the drawingroom. There is very good singing and music in their way. After they have been here some time, we carrey them up some refreshments on trays and hand about amongst them. This is all kinds of sweet cakes and biscuits, lemonade, ashet, negros, orangade and many other pleasent drinks but the best is the different kinds of ices. This is stuff made of ice pounded, mixed with cream, and juce of strawberrey, some of apricot and oranges – in short, there are many different kinds. It's quite as cold as eating ice alone. It's eat out of glass saucers with a spoon. It's from ten to sixteen shillings a quart, it depends on what fruit it's made of. The company comes jeneraly about ten or eleven o'clock and stays until one or two in the morning. Sweet hearting matches are very often made up at these parties.

*William Tayler*

# 19 May

1760 [East Hoathly, Sussex]
This day was played in the park a cricket match between an eleven whose names were John in this parish and an eleven of any other name, which I suppose was won by the latter with ease . . .

*Thomas Turner*

1800 [Grasmere, the Lake District]
Sauntered a good deal in the garden, bound carpets, mended old clothes. Read Timon of Athens. Dried linen. Molly weeded the turnips, John stuck the peas.

*Dorothy Wordsworth*

# 20 May

### 1757 [East Hoathly, Sussex]

This day went down to Mr Porter's to inform them that the livery lace was not come, when I think Mrs Porter treated me with as much imperious and scornful usage as had she been what I think she is, that is, more of a Turk or infidel than a Christian, and I an abject slave. N.B. If Mrs Porter is neither Turk nor infidel, I am sure her behaviour is not Christian, or at least not like that of a clergyman's wife.

*Thomas Turner*

### 1828 [Sussex]

I set out for Brighton this morning in a light coach, which performed the distance in six hours – otherwise the journey was uncomfortable. Three women, the very specimens of womankind, – I mean trumpery, – a child who was sick, but afterwards looked and smiled, and was the only thing like company. The road is pleasant enough till it gets into the Wealds of Sussex, a huge succession of green downs which sweep along the sea-coast for many miles. Brighton seems grown twice as large since 1815. It is a city of loiterers and invalids – a Vanity Fair for pipers, dancing of bears, and for the feats of Mr Punch.

*Sir Walter Scott*

# 21 May

### 1768 [Selborne, Hampshire]

*Lanius minor ruffus*, red-backed butcher-bird, shot near the village. Its gizzard was full of the legs & parts of beetles.

*Gilbert White*

# 22 May

1988 [Belmont, Lyme Regis]

I garden all afternoon in the silence, sun and wind. The garden defeats me; what does one do? We think the house might make £300,000 now; but the most miserable places now in Lyme fetch up to £200,000. None of them begin to equal Belmont. I do not want to leave this area, for all its faults in town terms; petty politicking Lyme, hellish Seaton.

*John Fowles*

# 23 May

1652 [Bromley, nr London]

The morning growing excessively hot, I sent my footman some hours before, and so rod negligently, under favour of the shade, 'til being now come to within three miles of Bromley, at a place calld the procession Oake, started out two Cutt-throats, and striking with their long staves at the horse, taking hold of the reignes, threw me down, and immediately tooke my sword, and haled me into a deepe Thickett, some quarter of a mile from the high-way, where they might securely rob me, as they soone did; what they got of mony was not considerable, but they tooke two rings, the one an emrald with diamonds, an [Onyx], and a pair of boucles set with rubies and diamonds which were of value, and after all, barbarously bound my hands behind me, and my feete, having before pull'd off my bootes: and then set up against an Oake, with most bloudy threatnings to cutt my throat, if I offred to crie out, or make any noise, for that they should be within hearing, I not being the person they looked for: I told them, if they had not basely surpriz'd me, they should not have made so easy a prize, and that it should teach me hereafter never to ride neere an hedge; since had I ben in the mid way, they durst not have adventur'd on me, at which they cock'd their pistols and told me they had long guns too, and were 14 companions, which all were lies: I begg'd for my Onyx and told them it being engraven with my armes, would betray them, but nothing prevaild: My horse bridle they slipt, and search'd the saddle which they likewise pull'd off, but let the horse alone to graze, and then turning againe bridld him, and tied him to a Tree, yet so as he might graze, and so left me bound: The reason they tooke not my horse, was I suppose, because he was mark'd, and cropt on both Eares, and well known on that roade, and these rogues were lusty foote padders, as they are cald: Well, being left in this manner, grievously was I tormented with the flies, the ants, and the sunn, so as I sweate intollerably, nor little was my anxiety how I should get loose in that solitary place, where I could neither heare or see any creature but my poore horse and a few sheepe stragling in the Coppse; til after neere two houres attempting I got my hands to turne paulme to paulme, whereas before they were tied back to back, and then I stuck a greate while ere' I could slip the cord over my wrist to my thumb, which at last I did, and then being quite loose soone unbound my feete, and so saddling my horse, and roaming a while about, I at last perceiv'd a dust to rise, and soone after heard the rattling of a Cart, towards which I made, and by the help of two Country fellows that were driving it, got downe a steepe bank, into the highway againe; but could heare nothing of the Villains: So I rod to Colonel Blounts house a great justiciarie of the times, who sent out hugh and Crie immediately.

*John Evelyn*

## 1997 [Wayland Wood, Norfolk]

In a region famous for its diversity of landscape, Norfolk is surprisingly poor in woodland. One notable exception, however, is Wayland, the inspiration for the old folk story, *Babes in the Wood*. Although it would now be very difficult for anyone to get lost in Wayland's meagre thirty-four hectares, what it lacks in size, it makes up for in age.

Currently managed by the Norfolk Wildlife Trust as a nature reserve, the area was a working wood for more than a thousand years, utilised for its crops of hazel, ash and oak. The Domesday Book indicated its importance even in the eleventh century, when the surrounding area drew its name from the wood. The word 'Wayland' further enshrines its antiquity since the second portion derives from the old Norse *lúndr*, meaning grove or sacred grove.

As well as being able to see and smell this immense past, one can also hear it. Mature woods like Wayland hold the greatest densities of breeding birds. Come here as dawn breaks and their songs pour forth with as much impact as the light itself. This dawn chorus offers me a sense of connection not only through time but also across geographical space, because as I stand surrounded by the melodies of blackbirds and thrushes and warblers, I try to recall how these species are actually singing nationwide. In fact the dawn chorus is continent-wide, passing every spring day in a great cycle around the northern hemisphere. As the day bursts open in North America and then Asia, Europe and North Africa, so the birds renew in waves their vocal statements about territory and sexual potency.

*Mark Cocker*

## 24 May

1685 [Wotton, Surrey]
We had hitherto not any raine for many monethes, insomuch as the Caterpillar had already devoured all the Winter fruite through the whole land, and even killed severall greate and old trees; such two Winters, and Summers I had never known.

*John Evelyn*

1785 [Selborne, Hampshire]
Swifts copulate in the air, as they flie.

*Gilbert White*

## 25 May

c.2000 [Walnut Tree Farm, Suffolk]
Today there is a frog in my woodpile in the vegetable garden. I swim two lengths in the moat. It is 15/16°C and the water is clear after recent rains. Cold, but not impossible. The ladder seems to lose a rung each year. Time, perhaps, to make a replacement. I'm also considering building a new landing

deck for the front pond, to take the place of what used to be a fishing plat-form for the village children, before parents stopped allowing their offspring out into the countryside alone.

*Roger Deakin*

## 26 May

### 1925 [Lewes, Sussex]

The chief event of the day has been that Edgar the tortoise having been caught 3 times eating 1. pansies; 2 ranunculus; 3. pinks, got translated to the Brack Mount. I stood on a kitchen chair and put him over the wall and watched him go – rather sad! But he just could *not* be borne with any longer.

*Alice Dudeney*

### 1979 [Combe Florey, Somerset]

Back in Somerset for the weekend I find all the roads are lined with broken-down cars and caravans caught by the petrol famine. One man offers me his wife and two daughters in exchange for five gallons of petrol; when I offer him a pint of methylated spirits for one of his daughters he bursts into tears.

Eventually, of course, these stranded holidaymakers – many of them from Birmingham, Solihull and Wolverhampton – will end up being fed to the pigs. Before their final moment of truth, they should be allowed a little glimpse of how much they are hated.

*Auberon Waugh*

## 27 May

### 1971 [Belmont House, Lyme Regis]

The Whitsun madness: traffic all night. One casualty was a hedgehog outside our gate. It filled me with anger. I thought it was the larger of the two I give bread and milk to every night. But they were there again.

*John Fowles*

# 28 May

### 1802 [Grasmere, the Lake District]

I was much better than yesterday, though poorly. William tired himself with hammering at a passage … We sate in the orchard. The sky cloudy the air sweet and cool. The young Bullfinches in their party coloured Raiment bustle about the Blossoms and poize themselves like Wire-dancers or tumblers, shaking the twigs and dancing off the Blossoms. There is yet one primrose in the garden. The stitchwort is fading. The wild columbines are coming into beauty. The vetches are in abundance, Blossoming and seeding. That pretty little waxy-looking Dial-like yellow flower, the speedwell, and some others whose names I do not yet know. In the garden we have lilies and many other flowers. The scarlet Beans are up in crowds. It is now between 8 and nine o'clock. It has rained sweetly for two hours and a half – the air is very mild. The heckberry blossoms are dropping off fast, almost gone – barberries are in beauty – snowballs coming forward – May roses blooming.

*Dorothy Wordsworth*


### 1870 [Clyro, Radnorshire]

Charles while driving me over told me of the charge brought against Brewer by Janet, late kitchenmaid at Clyro Vicarage, accusing him of being the father of her child. Janet wrote to him at Clyro, making the charge, as soon as the child was born, and poor Mrs Brewer opened the letter, read it, and sent it on to her husband. I am told she is nearly heartbroken. Poor child. Charles fears the charge is too well founded. I was thunderstruck. I always thought so well of Brewer and believed him to be such a very different man.

*Francis Kilvert*

# 29 May

1915 [Buckinghamshire]

Some folk don't like to walk over Bluebells or Buttercups or other flowers growing on the ground. But it is foolish to try to pamper Nature as if she were a sickly child. She is strong and can stand it. You can stamp on and crush a thousand flowers – they will all come up again next year.

*W.N.P. Barbellion*

# 30 May

1800 [Grasmere, the Lake District]

As I came past Rydale in the morning I saw a Heron swimming with only its neck out of water – it beat and struggled amongst the water when it flew away and was long in getting loose.

*Dorothy Wordsworth*

1925 [Lewes, Sussex]

Was telling Charlotte about Edgar when she said calmly: 'But I can see a tortoise on the Brack Mount now,' and there was poor Edgar halfway across the stony bit on his way back to us. So touched that I got the steps, climbed on to the Brack Mount and brought him home. He instantly made for some young asters! Got a wooden box, and knocked the bottom out and put some wire on top to make him a little cage.

*Alice Dudeney*

# 31 May

1756 [East Hoathly, Sussex]

Saw in the Lewes newspaper of this day that on Saturday there was several explosions heard in the bowels of the earth like an earthquake in the parishes of Waldron and Hellingly, as also by one person in this parish . . .

*Thomas Turner*

1792 [Lincolnshire]

At 3 o'clock I left Grantham, mount the hill to Gunnerby village, where appear'd something like a feast, which I love to see, or to hear the squeak of a fiddle; and allways look about for a cricket-match, or Fives playing: for little recreation have the poor, and but a short summer.

*John Byng*

1800 [Somerset]

My little boy is not very well, has taken Rhubard, he is cutting teeth. No potatoes to be got at Bridgewater, what will become of us. Robert went to William Hill and procured a few but he staid long, for which I gave him a jubation. He is, with all his surliness and taciturnity, at times as great a gossip as any old woman in the Parish.

*William Holland*

# JUNE

# 1 June

## 1785 [Norfolk]

Mr and Mrs Custance called here about 11 o'clock and took Nancy with them in their Coach to go to Norwich. They would have taken me up also but I preferred going on horseback, about 12 therefore, I went to Norwich and took Briton with me, and we got there about 2 o'clock – but was wet getting thither. About 3 o'clock this Afternoon a violent Tempest arose at Norwich in the North East, very loud Thunder with strong white Lightening with heavy Rain – which lasted about an Hour – immediately after which Mr Deckers Balloon with Decker himself in a boat annexed to it, ascended from Quantrells Gardens and very majestically. It was out of Sight in about 10 Minutes, but appeared again on his Descent. It went in a South East Direction – I saw it from Brecondale Hill, and it went almost over my Head. Mr and Mrs Custance and Nancy were at Mackay's Gardens. They saw it also very plain from thence. A vast Concourse of People were assembled to see it. It was rather unfortunate that the Weather proved so unfavourable – but added greatly to the Courage of Decker that he ascended so very soon after the Tempest. It also bursted twice before he ascended in it, upon the filling it, if it had not, a Girl about 14 was to have went with him in it – but after so much Gas had been let out – it would not carry both. Mr Du Quesne was there and in the Gardens. Mrs Thorne, Mrs Davy and Captain Thorne overtook me going to Norwich just by the Turnpike – I parted with them just by St Giles's Gate and saw nothing more of them afterwards – They were wet as well as we on the Road – I put up my Horses at the Woolpack. The Tempest happened as I was on Brecondale Hill. I went directly to a red House adjoining, and was very kindly asked to walk in to a Parlour, which I accepted – Whilst I was there I found that I was got into Mrs Thornes Brothers, Mr Thos Agges. I saw a very pretty

Quaker there, a young Woman. After I returned from seeing the Balloon –
I went to a Perfumers Shop in the Jaymarket by name Amyot and bought
some Essence of Jessamine, Lavender, Bergamot for all which I paid 0.2.0.
I then called at Priests, there saw Du Quesne, but neither eat or drank there
– For some Amber Grease, Oil of Time, Lavender, and Spermaceti pd 0.2.3.
After that I mounted my Mare and set of for Weston – got home about 8
o'clock this Evening and then dined, supped and slept in the Old House –
Nancy was home about an Hour before me – very much tired. We were
very wet coming home this Evening. At Norwich for 1 half Pint of Porter
and gave the Maid 0.3. Mr and Mrs Custance, Nancy, myself, and in short all
that went to see the Baloon were highly pleased. We were all sorry that the
Weather was so bad for it. Decker however has gained great Credit by it.

*James Woodforde*

## 1908 [Barnstaple, North Devon]

Went to L Sessions. After the Court rose, I transcribed my notes quickly
and walked out to the famous Valley of Rocks which Southey described as
the ribs of the old Earth poking through. At the bottom of one of the hills
saw a snake, a Red Viper. Put my boot on him quickly so that he couldn't
get away and then recognised him as a specimen of what I consider to be
the fourth species of British Serpent – *Vipera rubra*. The difficulty was to
know how to secure him. This species is more ferocious than the ordinary
*V. bera* and I did not like the idea of putting my hand down to seize him
by the neck. I stood some time with my foot so firmly pressed down on
its back that my leg ached and I began to wonder if I had been bitten. I
held on and presently hailed a baker's cart coming along the road. The man
got out and ran across the grass to where I stood. I showed him what I had
beneath my boot and he produced a piece of string which I fastened round
the snake's tail and so gently hauled the little brute up. It already appeared
moribund, but I squashed its head on the grass with my heel to make certain.
After parting with the baker, to whom all thanks be given, I remember that
Adders are tenacious of life and so I continue to wallop him against a stone.
As he was lifeless I wrapped him in paper and put him in my pocket –
though to make assurance doubly sure I left the string on and let its end

hang out over my pocket. So home by a two hours' railway journey with the Adder in the pocket of my overcoat and the overcoat on the rack over my head. Settled down to the reading of a book on Spinoza's *Ethics*. At home it proved to be quite alive, and, on being pulled out by the string, coiled up on the drawing-room floor and hissed in fury, to my infinite surprise. Finished him off with the poker and so spoilt the skin.

*W.N.P. Barbellion*

# 2 June

### 1802 [Grasmere, the Lake District]

In the morning we observed that the scarlet Beans were drooping in the leaves in great numbers owing, we guess, to an insect. We sate a while in the orchard – then we went to the old carpenter's about the hurdles. Yesterday an old man called, a grey-headed man, above 70 years of age. He said he had been a soldier, that his wife and children had died in Jamaica. He had a Beggar's wallet over his shoulders, a coat of shreds and patches altogether of a drab colour – he was tall and though his body was bent he had the look of one used to have been upright. I talked a while with him, and then gave him a piece of cold Bacon and a penny. Said he, 'You're a fine woman!' I could not help smiling. I suppose he meant 'You're a kind woman'.

*Dorothy Wordsworth*

### 1915 [Buckinghamshire]

Farmer Whaley is a funny old man with a soft pious voice. When he feeds the Fowls, he sucks in a gentle, caressing noise between his lips for all the world as if he fed them because he loved them, and not because he wants to fatten them up for killing. His daughter, Lucy, aged 22, loves all the animals of the farm and they all love her; the Cows stand monumentally still while she strokes them down the blaze or affectionately waggles their dewlaps. This morning, she walked up to the little Calf in the farmyard scarcely a fortnight old which started to 'back' in a funny way, spraddling out its legs and lowering its head. Miss Lucy laughed merrily and cried,

'Ah! you funny little thing,' and went off on her own way to feed the Fowls who all raced to the gate as soon as they heard her footsteps. She brought in two double-yoked Ducks' eggs for us to see and marvel at. In the breakfast room stands a stuffed Collie dog in a glass case. I'd as soon embalm my grandmother and keep her on the sideboard.

*W.N.P. Barbellion*

1962 [Sissinghurst, Kent]
It is a lovely morning. I get up early and walk around the garden. V. [Vita Sackville-West, his wife] is asleep, and I do not disturb her. Glen [the Labrador] dances on the lawn with his brother, Brandy. I breakfast with Niggs [his son], and then I force myself to do my review of the composite book, *Companion to Homer*. I finish it about 12.30, and start reading the newspaper. Ursula is with Vita. At about 1.5 she observes that Vita is breathing heavily, and then suddenly is silent. She dies without fear or self-reproach at 1.15. Ursula comes to tell me. I pick some of her favourite flowers and lay them on the bed.

*Harold Nicolson*

1986 [Essex House, Badminton]
Here we are, Midsummer nearly reached, a filthy weather. The occasional fitfully sunny day, then greyness and rain again. Twice heard the cuckoo this year. The heron steals our fish, and left one so pitted with bites it had to be destroyed.

*James Lees-Milne*

# 3 June

1802 [Grasmere, the Lake District]
Yesterday morning William walked as far as the Swan with Aggy Fisher. She was going to attend upon Goan's dying Infant. She said, 'There are many heavier crosses to bear than the death of an Infant', and went on 'There was a woman in this vale who buried 4 grown-up children in one year, and

I have heard her say when many years were gone by that she had more pleasure in thinking of those 4 than her living Children, for as Children get up and have families of their own their duty to their parents *"wears out and weakens"*. She could trip lightly by the graves of those who died when they were young, with a light step, as she went to Church on a Sunday.'

*Dorothy Wordsworth*

### 1871 [Clyro, Radnorshire]
Mrs Griffiths told me that a few days ago a man named Evans kicked his wife to death at Rhulen. He kicked her bosom black and her breasts mortified.

*Francis Kilvert*

### 1935 [Perth]
A blackbird whistling in the rain: He must be the Caruso of the tribe – I could have listened to him for hours the interplay of notes was so varied, defiant, witty, confident, merry, bold – anything but melancholy. Just when it was almost too late I thought I'd note down his wurlywas – but found it well nigh impossible to catch the sound and transpose the syllables at the moment: one would have to listen for a long time – but here is the rough and ready transcription: chickee-chickee-chee: ti-ti-ti-titty-titty: chittie-cheea: tweeto-tweeto-tweeto: what-ya-doin', what-ya-doin': hullo-hullo-hullo: chejoey-chejoey-what-what-what: gee-up, gee-up, hoo-hoo-hoo; get away, get away, you would, you would, you would, would you?: hoi-hoi-hoi – have a look at me . . . Well – you are worth looking at, too.

*William Soutar*

## 4 June

### 1776 [Norfolk]
My Tooth pained me all night, got up a little after 5 this morning and sent for one Reeves a Man who draws Teeth in this Parish and about 7 he came and drew my Tooth but shockingly bad indeed, he broke away a great Piece of my Gum and broke one of the Fangs of the Tooth it gave me exquisite

Pain all the Day after and my Face swelled prodigiously in the Evening & much Pain. Very bad in much Pain the whole Day long. Gave the old Man that drew it however 0.2.6. He is too old I think to draw Teeth, can't see very well.

*James Woodforde*

## 1875 [Clyro, Radnorshire]

Mrs Vincent told me that her husband had not suffered so much lately from the pressure of water upon his heart which had been sensibly relieved by the water running out of his heels.

*Francis Kilvert*

# 5 June

## 1907 [Barnstaple, North Devon]

A half hour of to-day I spent in a punt under a copper beech out of the pouring rain listening to Lady —'s gamekeeper at A talking about beasts and local politics – just after a visit of inspection to the Heronry in the firs on the island in the middle of the Lake. It was delightful to hear him describing a Heron killing an Eel with 'a dap on the niddick', helping out the figure with a pat on the nape of his thick bull neck.

*W.N.P. Barbelllion*

## 1946 [Inverness-shire]

I am not a naturalist, I only know that each day I take a near cut through the fields to the town. My near cut has taken on the aspect of a beaten track. The track owes its origins to sentiment. I made it for myself. Daisies, which lose their whiteness when the sun shines fully on the fields to take on the sheen of silver, are so profuse that each step of mine cuts down the lives of these rightful owners. Hence my track. By destroying a few I preserve the multitude. When the sun has gone, I return to find the field curiously empty, the daisies have gathered their immensities of whiteness into curled, rose balls.

*Jessie Kesson*

# 6 June

## 1909 [Lundy Island]

Out egg-collecting with the Lighthouse Keepers. They walk about the cliffs as surefooted as cats, and feed their dogs on birds' eggs collected in a little bag at the end of a long pole. One dog ate three right off in as many minutes, putting his teeth through and cracking the shell, then lapping up the contents.

*W.N.P. Barbellion*

## 1970 [Belmont, Lyme Regis]

A cocktail party at Maisie Forrester's in Ware Lane; the assembled upper middle class (in Lyme terms) of the town. They really are the dullest and most abominably retarded community one can imagine; there is a bizarre air of being besieged about them. A constant harking back to the past: who lived in which house, how long their family has had associations with Lyme. It's how the pecking order is established. Of course they are intensely suspicious of us. We are interlopers – even though most of such people have only lived here a year or two longer.

The one tolerable person is the old actress Maisie herself, her face rouged and made up so that she looks like a stout old geisha, or a distinguished brothel madame. She's good; salty, with style. A credit to the humanising power of theatre.

The encounter made Eliz [his wife] rage against Lyme; I get away by retreating into my ornithological self. I find such people agreeably clear-cut, both specifically and behaviourally.

*John Fowles*

## c.2000 [Walnut Tree Farm, Suffolk]

Outside my study window there are tits, a little family of four or five, all diligently pecking off the aphids on a rose. The perfect gardeners, so much better than a spray.

*Roger Deakin*

# 7 *June*

## 1932 [Perth]

Gardeners here putting in flowers in the plot of ground outside my window. Old Mr McQueen the 'boss' along supervising. It is a sad sight to watch an old man trying to keep a little plot for himself in the busy garden of the world. The strong young men are turning over the earth and he is standing as a presiding spirit – but the pose is too much for him, and soon he is sitting on a barrow and fumbling for a pipe ... If we dig down far enough into the mind of man I think we ought to discover that sexual shame is an attribute of fear; and a similar fear is responsible for the cringing element in religion – fear of the 'mystery'; and this is the negative or blasphemous attitude to life, the antipole to the creative which is born of wonder.

*William Soutar*

# 8 *June*

## 1980 [Combe Florey]

Somerset is enthralled by reports in the *Daily Telegraph* of a blackmail trial at Exeter Crown Court involving well-known Taunton personalities. One of them died of a heart attack when his former lady-love allegedly demanded £8,000 for some letters. Only the *Daily Telegraph* reveals the true nature of his fancy, which was for knicker-sniffing.

The man concerned, who was a popular lecturer at Taunton Polytechnic, retired policeman and fairly well-known author of legal textbooks, is referred to as Mr X. It is a strangely appropriate name under the circumstances, because he could be anyone. Nearly all the Old Age Pensioners of West Somerset, as I happen to know, indulge in this harmless but controversial pastime.

The saddest aspect is how ashamed they are when found out. If the Church of England is too timid to speak out, Cardinal Vass should announce that any elderly person or 'old dear' who has a loving, stable and joyous relationship with any particular article of underwear is welcome to bring it to the weekly People's Community Service and Love Feast, where Father O'Bubblegum will bless their relationship with all proper solemnity.

*Auberon Waugh*

# 9 June

1800 [Grasmere, the Lake District]
In the morning W cut down the winter cherry tree. I sowed French Beans and weeded. A coronetted Landau went by when we were sitting upon the sodded wall. The ladies (evidently Tourists) turned an eye of interest upon our little garden and cottage. We went to R. Newton's [inn] for pike-floats and went round to Mr Gell's Boat and on to the Lake to fish. We caught nothing – it was extremely cold. The Reeds and Bullrushes or Bullpipes of a tender soft green, making a plain whose surface moved with the wind. The reeds not yet tall. The lake clear to the Bottom, but saw no fish. In the evening I stuck peas, watered the garden and planted Brocoli. Did not go for a walk for it was very cold. A poor Girl came to beg who had no work at home and was going in search of it to Kendal. She slept in Mr Benson's Lathe [barn], and went off after Breakfast in the morning with 7p and a letter to the Mayor of Kendal.

*Dorothy Wordsworth*

# 10 June

1802 [Grasmere, the Lake District]
Coleridge came in with a sack-full of Books, etc. and a Branch of mountain ash. He had been attacked by a cow. He came over by Grisdale. A furious wind. Mr Simpson drank tea. William very poorly – we went to bed latish. I slept in sitting room.

*Dorothy Wordsworth*

# 11 June

1976 [Combe Florey, Somerset]

The roads of West Somerset are jammed as never before with caravans from Birmingham and the West Midlands. Their horrible occupants only come down here to search for a place where they can go to the lavatory free. Then they return to Birmingham, boasting in their hideous flat voices about how much money they have saved.

I don't suppose many of the brutes can read, but anybody who wants a good book for the holidays is recommended to try a new publication from the Church Information Office: *The Churchyard Handbook* (CIO, £2.40).

It laments the passing of that ancient literary form, the epitaph, suggesting that many of the tombstones put up nowadays dedicated to 'Mum' or 'Dad' or 'Ginger' would be more suitable for a dog cemetery than for the resting place of Christians.

The trouble is that people can afford tombstones nowadays who have no business to be remembered at all. Few of these repulsive creatures in caravans are Christians, I imagine, but I would happily spend the rest of my days composing epitaphs for them in exchange for a suitable fee:

> He had a shit on Gwennap Head,
> It cost him nothing. Now he's dead.

> He left a turd on Porlock Hill
> As he lies here, it lies there still.

*Auberon Waugh*

# 12 June

1755 [East Hoathly, Sussex]

At home all day. In the afternoon Tho. Cornwell beat me at cricket; lost 6d. Paid Halland gardener 12d. for two gallons of gooseberries. Found in

*The History of England* that England was first divided into counties, parishes etc. in King Alfred's reign, about the year 890 . . .

*Thomas Turner*

### 1874 [Clyro, Radnorshire]

Bathing yesterday and to-day. Yesterday the sea was very calm but the wind has changed to the East and this morning a rough and troublesome sea came tumbling into the bay and plunging in foam upon the shore. The bay was full of white horses. At Shanklin one has to adopt the detestable custom of bathing in drawers. If ladies don't like to see men naked why don't they keep away from the sight? To-day I had a pair of drawers given me which I could not keep on. The rough waves stripped them off and tore them round my ankles. While thus fettered I was seized and flung down by a heavy sea which retreating suddenly left me naked on the sharp shingle from which I rose streaming with blood. After this I took the wretched and dangerous rag off and of course there were some ladies looking on as I came up out of the water.

*Francis Kilvert*

## 13 June

### 1703 [Wotton, Surrey]

The raines have ben so greate, continual & unseasonable, as have hardly ben known in the memory of any alive; The weather now neere Midsomer cold & so Wet, as theatens a famine, after our murmuring at the Cheapnesse of Corne.

*John Evelyn*

### 1866 [Oxfordshire]

Grace of willow bushes with their sprays shooting over and reversed in water.

*Gerard Manley Hopkins*

# 14 June

1792 [Selborne, Hampshire]
Mr Burbey has got eleven martins nests under the eaves of his old shop.

*Gilbert White*

# 15 June

1949 [East Anglia]
To furniture sale at Carrow, itch to possess having been thoroughly aroused on view day, but determined to bid only for carpet we really need for Hillingsett Lodge drawing-room, and not for numerous things I should merely love to own. Struck, as usual, by forlorn appearance of the various 'effects', which, like words removed from their context, have lost much of their stature and meaning. Lot 467 draws near . . . nearer . . . and is cast upon the table, and I promptly join the bidders. Have previously agreed with Adam [her husband] on what seems to us stupendous-colossal price. But with horrid rapidity the bidding gallops to our limit, hesitates a fraction, like a horse in two minds about refusing a fence, then is over and away, leaving me very much an also-ran. Before setting out, have made most elaborate plans for triumphal homecoming with carpet, measuring up back of car, wondering if I shall take trailer, or entrust precious purchase to furniture removers at sale. Cannot help recalling, as go home empty-handed, historic occasion when male-parent departed on salmon-fishing jaunt loaded with frail baskets and full of instructions to us to be on lookout for every parcel post, only to return at end of holiday with baskets full of rock plants.

*Elizabeth M. Harland*

# 16 June

## 1675 [Kent]

Here I saw two strange sights to me. One was Deal Beach, reaching from the South Foreland almost to the North Foreland; and is nothing else but as it were a very great bank of stones and flints and shells of fishes: higher than the smooth sands by many fathoms and very broad, being daily augmented by the sea: and is so clear and void of sand or dust that the inhabitants (slighting the green grass which is close by it) do spread their linen on those stones to dry and whiten: which also lie so loose that you tread up to the ankles every step you go: yet on this bank stands the town of Deal. The other thing which was strange to me was that, in all places else wherever I yet was, the chiefest care of the neat housewife was to keep their rooms clean from all manner of dust, by sweeping, washing, and rubbing them. But here clean contrary; for, having first swept them clean, they then strew them all over with sand — yea their very best chambers.

*Henry Teongue*

# 17 June

## 1870 [Clyro, Radnorshire]

Perch went groping about in the brook and brought in a small crayfish which crawled about the table, horns, tail and claws like a fresh-water clean brown lobster. I did not know there were any crayfish in the brook.

*Francis Kilvert*

# 18 June

## 1773 [Selborne, Hampshire]

Some ears of wheat begin to appear. Measles epidemic to a wonderful degree: whole families down at a time. Several children that had been reduced by the whooping-cough dyed of them.

*Gilbert White*

# 19 June

## 1769 [Norfolk]

Old Justice Dawe of Ditchet died last Saturday by drinking.

*James Woodforde*

## 1866 [Oxfordshire]

Smart showers in morning with bright between; this cleared till it was very fine, with flying clouds casting shadows on the Wye hills. Fine sunset. – Tintern to Ross by Monmouth – The afternoon way we much enjoyed, in especial we turned down a grass lane to reach the river at the ferry. It was steep down at first and I remember blue sprays of wych-elm or hazel against the sunlight green further on. Then the fields rose high on each side, one crowned with beautiful trees (there was particularly an ash with you could not tell how many contradictory supple curvings in the boughs), and then orchards, of which this country is full; on the other, with a narrow plot of orchard in which sheep grazed between the rise and the lane, was Goderich castle of red sandstone on the height. Close by the river was a fine oak with long lunging boughs. The country is full of fine trees, especially oaks, and is, like Devonshire, on red soil. We crossed the river whirling down with a swollen stream, and then by lanes to Ross. From the hotel there you see the river enclosing the Oak Meadow and others in its bends. We walked by twilight and moonlight up it, flush, swift, and oily, the moon streaking it with hairs, Addis said, of light. Aspens blackened against the last light seem to throw their scarcer leaves into barbs or arrowheads of mackerel patterns.

*Gerard Manley Hopkins*

## 1871 [Clyro, Radnorshire]

Palmer, the new Cae Mawr gardener, and his wife have moved down from the Vineyards Cottage to the Old Mill. Mrs Palmer could not bear the Vineyards. She said it was so lonely. Miss Bynon, to whom the cottage belongs, took great exception to Mrs Palmer and the fault she found with

the cottage. 'Lonely indeed! What does the lady on the hill want?' asked
Miss Bynon. 'She can see my backdoor.'

*Francis Kilvert*

# 20 June

## 1800 [Grasmere, the Lake District]

On Wednesday evening a poor man called, a hatter – he had long been ill,
but was now recovered and his wife was lying in of her 4th child. The parish
would not help him because he had implements of trade etc. etc. We gave
him 6d.

*Dorothy Wordsworth*

## 1949 [East Anglia]

In further pursuit of drawing-room carpet, call at offices of auctioneer
advertising furniture sale at Fendham House next week, and ask for catalogue.
No catalogues, says clerk. But can have order to view. So as Fendham
get-at-able by slight diversion on journey home, decide to look at carpets
right away. Recall passing through Fendham early in 1939, when was pleasant
little parish in usual style, with full quota of fields and farmhouses, lanes,
woods and pastures. Now all remembered landmarks obliterated by abandoned
aerodrome, and soon haven't least idea where I am. Elderly rat-poisoner at
work on fences a mile back has suggested I follow yellow arrows on tarmac
of perimeter track, but this somehow contrives to bring me back where I
came in. Second attempt, ignoring arrows, brings me within sight of Fendham
church, now marooned in a network of runways. Am still trying to remember
whereabouts of Fendham House in relation to church, and which of three
ways in front of me will take me there, when farm-tractor and trailer bounce
out of adjacent hanger, driver says he's going past gate, and all I need do is
follow him. This eventually results in arrival at destination, where carpets
prove unsuitable.

*Elizabeth M. Harland*

# 21 June

### c.2003 [South of England]

Mistle thrush families are diving into wild cherry trees to get at the ripening fruit. Some of the small cherries have already turned scarlet.

The mistle thrushes will clamber out to the end of frail twigs to reach them, and, like the fat pigeons, they often tumble off as the twigs bend under their weight. As they fly out of the tree, the undersides of the wings flash silver. The young birds are by now as large and sturdy as their parents, though they have a paler head and a more spotty back.

The fruit is also developing on many other trees. On hawthorns, the clusters of berries are now fully formed, and a faint flush of red is showing on some of them. Sloes are forming on the blackthorn bushes but are still quite small and green. On sycamores, the two-winged seeds, like aircraft propellers, are green and large, but they will not spin down until they are brown and dry.

*Derwent May*

# 22 June

### 1775 [Selborne, Hampshire]

A person assures me, that Mr Meymot, an old clergyman at Northchappel in Sussex, kept a cuckow in a cage three or four years; & that he had seen it several times, both winter & summer. It made a little jarring noise, but never cried *cuckow*. It might perhaps be a hen. He did not remember how it subsisted.*

*Gilbert White*

### 1866 [New Forest]

Very fine. Train to Lyndhurst Road and walk into Forest – beeches cut down – warm – pretty country towards Dibden and Southampton. Tents,

*The cry of the female cuckoo is the so-called 'water-bubble' sound.

with folk like gypsies (but they say *no*), peeling rushes for rushlights: you leave a strip of green on the pith for backbone. Beaulieu, the Duke's park, old church and ruins. Village, tide in. Cottage hung with roses, man in front garden tells me he had lived there fifty-three years. I praise the beauty and quiet, but he often thinks he 'ought to a' pushed out into the world – gone to London or some large place.' Boys fishing for bass. The miller's, a piano going inside ('it is the miller's daughter,' no doubt). Rasher and ale at the inn. The young lady at the bar with short curls and towny air finds it 'very dull here'. I walk away at 20 to 9, sunset light over heath and forest, long road. The night-jar whirring.

*William Allingham*

# 23 June

### 1764 [Norfolk]

One Prince a Shoemaker at Bruton came here this Afternoon to measure me for a Pair of Shoes for which I am to pay him when he brings them home 0.5.0. This Prince being a musical Man, I desired him to tune my Spinnett for me, which he did and pretty well, but would have nothing for it. N.B. My chief Intent for sending for him was to tune my Spinnett for I have at present Shoes sufficient.

*James Woodforde*

### 1906 [Olton, Warwickshire]

Cycled through Widney: The Yellow Irises are out in the marsh there now, and at the edge of the stream I found the large blue Water For-get-me-not. While I was stooping to gather some, a beautiful Demoiselle Dragonfly came skimming across the water and lighted on a bunch of rushes. The next moment it was away again. In the meadow I saw several flowers in bloom for the first time – Purple Tufted Vetch, Yellow Vetchling, Water-Cress, Slender Tare, Welted Thistle, and in the lanes Hedge Woundwort and Doves-foot Cranes-bill.

*Edith Holden*

# 24 June

## 1939 [Perth]

Just beyond my window there is a large, full-blown, pink rose at the top of a long stalk. As I was looking out this evening a sparrow glided down through the air and settled on the rose as if it had been a nest. It did not remain for more than a minute, nor did it actually nestle – and I surmise it was hunting for aphides which are not plentiful this season. I was surprised to note how easily the long stem bore the additional weight as if the bird were no heavier than a flower. Indeed after the sparrow had gone the rose seemed in no way to have been ruffled.

*William Soutar*

# 25 June

## 1802 [Grasmere, the Lake District]

Miss Simpson came to colour the rooms. I began with white-washing the ceiling. I worked with them (William was very busy) till dinner time but after dinner I went to bed and fell asleep. When I rose I went just before tea into the garden. I looked up at my Swallow's nest and it was gone. It had fallen down. Poor little creatures they could not themselves be more distressed than I was. I went upstairs to look at the Ruins. They lay in a large heap upon the window ledge; these Swallows had been ten days employed in building this nest, and it seemed to be almost finished. I watched them early in the morning, in the day many and many a time and in the evenings when it was almost dark I had seen them sitting side by side in their unfinished nest both morning and night. When they first came about the window they used to hang against the panes, with their white Bellies and their forked tails looking like fish, but then they fluttered and sang their own little twittering song. As soon as the nest was broad enough, a sort of ledge for them they sate both mornings and evenings, but they did not pass the night there. I watched them one morning . . .

for more than an hour. Every now and then there was a feeling motion in their wings, a sort of tremulousness and they sang a low song to one another.

*Dorothy Wordsworth*

## 26 June

1876 [Slackfields Farm, Derbyshire]
*Hot* Dragging fallow in Langton Close. Horse hoeing.

*Henry Hill*

## 27 June

1773 [Selborne, Hampshire]
Nose-flies, & stouts [either gad-flies or gnats] make the horses very troublesome.

*Gilbert White*

1905 [Barnstaple, North Devon]
On reviewing the past egg-season, I find in all I have discovered 232 nests belonging to forty-four species. I only hope I shall be as successful with the beetle season.

*W.N.P. Barbellion*

## 28 June

1877 [Dorset]
Being Coronation Day there are games and dancing on the green at Sturminster Newton. The stewards with white rosettes. One is very anxious, fearing that while he is attending to the runners the leg of mutton on the pole will go wrong; hence he walks hither and thither with a compressed countenance and eyes far ahead.

The pretty girls, just before a dance, stand in inviting positions on the grass. As the couples in each figure pass near where their immediate friends loiter, each girl-partner gives a laughing glance at such friends, and whirls on.

*Thomas Hardy*

# 29 June

### 1773 [Selborne, Hampshire]

My garden is in high beauty, glowing with a variety of solstitial flowers. A person lately found a young cuckow in a small nest built in a beechen shrub at the upper end of the bostal. By watching in the morning, he soon saw the young bird fed by a pair of hedge-sparrows. The cuckow is but half-fledge; yet the nest will hardly contain him: for his wings hang out, & his tail and his body are much compressed, & streightened. When looked at he opens a very wide, red mouth, & heaves himself up; using contortions with his neck by way of menace, & picking at a person's finger, if he advances towards him.

*Gilbert White*

### 1877 [Dorset]

Have just passed through a painful night and morning. Our servant, whom we liked very much, was given a holiday yesterday to go to Bournemouth with her young man. Came home last night at ten, seeming oppressed. At about half-past twelve, when we were supposed to be asleep, she crept downstairs, went out, and on looking from the back window of our bedroom I saw her come from the outhouse with a man. She appeared to have only her night-gown on and something round her shoulders. Beside her slight white figure in the moonlight his form looked dark and gigantic. She preceded him to the door. Before I had thought what to do E. [Emily, his wife] had run downstairs, and met her, and ordered her to bed. The man disappeared. Found that the bolts of the back-door had been oiled. He had evidently often stayed in the house.

She remained quiet till between four and five, when she got out the dining room window and vanished.

*Thomas Hardy*

1932 [Perth]

Just now as I lifted my eyes to the hillside I saw the trees waving like a wall of fire. If only one could respond to life as the earth to the sun – but the heart is so often a trim little garden with neither the luxuriance nor the conflict of the jungle. It is so easy to retreat within the safe walls of mediocrity.

*William Soutar*

## 30 June

1827 [Cotswolds]

The weather being fine, we took a drive to call on Lady Elcho at Stanway, who has been arrived from London some days, but unfortunately her Ladyship was gone to Cheltenham. On our return in the afternoon we called for half an hour at Mr Bowens' parsonage at Temple Guiting, who shewed us his handsome church, and took us a little circuit in Mr Talbot's grounds which are very pleasantly and tastefully laid out, the ground being undulating, the meadows rich and now all alive with haymakers, the distant plantations covering the horizon, the groves under which we strolled cool and umbrageous, the lawns pleasantly broken with single trees and bordered with thickets, the walks neatly kept, the grotto cool and dark, all bespeaking good taste and opulence. The family is in town: so it is that fashionable people desert their country seats, their rich parks and lovely gardens in the finest season and live there only in the gloomiest months of the year; for when the London season is over, fashion dictates a second edition on an inferior scale at some sea-bathing or watering place or some rambling tour in search of ever-eluding pleasure.

*F.E. Witts*

## 1877 [Dorset]

About one o'clock went to her father's cottage in the village, where we thought she had gone. Found them poorer than I expected (for they are said to be an old county family). Her father was in the field haymaking, and a little girl fetched him from the haymakers. He came across to me amid the windrows of hay, and seemed to read bad news in my face. She had not been home. I remembered that she had dressed up in her best clothes, and she had probably gone to Stalbridge to her lover.

*Thomas Hardy*


## 1995 [Hampshire]

It is around 90° around the house. (I can still only think in terms of Fahrenheit, yards, pints and ounces.) We opened all doors and windows to get a bit of air. Then I had the wheeze of changing into a nightshirt, pretending I was in the tropics, and all was fairly comfortable. The afternoon postman didn't turn a hair.

*Alec Guinness*

# JULY

# 1 July

### 1757 [East Hoathly, Sussex]

Mr Snelling ordered my brother to be entirely debarred from beer, brandy (or any kind of spirits), and meat, and to drink the following for his constant drink, *viz.*, take 1 ounce of cream of tartar, ½ lb of lump sugar, the peel of a lemon; pour a gallon of boiling water on them and let it stand all night, then strain it off and bottle it for use. He also ordered him the cold bath, and blisters behind the ears to be perpetual, notwithstanding he has an issue both in the temple and arm.

*Thomas Turner*

### 1773 [Selborne, Hampshire]

Mr Richardson's garden abounds with fruit, which ripens a fortnight before mine. His kitchen-crops are good, tho' the soil is so light & sandy. Sandy soil much better for garden-crops than chalky.

*Gilbert White*

### 1784 [Powys]

On leaving Welshpool, I was surprised at the goodness, & breadth of the road; and no less at the beauty of the country, diversified by the happiest scenes of wood, cultivation, and population; whereas I was expecting a view of naked wilds: tho that perhaps will soon arrive. The view from the hill over Llanvair, and the stream beyond it, meandring betwixt woods, aided by a glittering setting sun, was truly enlivening; as well as the sound of the church bells, and the buz of the people; but, too soon, I discover'd the little town to be throng'd with market folk, and uproar. T.B. came forth to say, that at the Goat ale-house (to which we had a recommendation) there were no horse-lodgings; and so, he had try'd the Cross-Foxes (the arms of

Sr W.W. Wynn) where, at last, the horses were shelter'd in something like a stable; as for the house, it was fill'd by dancers, and drinkers, celebrating a wedding. I return'd to meet Mr P. and then we retir'd to a seat in the church yard; under an immense yew tree; (of which there are several of astonishing bulk;) whence we often arose to see the dancing, and observe the drunkenness. Heav'ns! What potations of ale, and clangor of unintelligible language! For here the English tongue is little understood. At length, we got tea in our bed room; and had you but seen it, such a broken window! such dirty walls! Few of the very worst English farm-houses cou'd equal it, in badness. The company now began to pair off; one or two of each couple very drunk: Mr P. smoked; & I wrote by the light of two farthing candles.

*John Byng*

# 2 July

1986 [Badminton, Gloucestershire]
Saw three herons together in Vicarage Fields, noble birds, standing as if in earnest conversation. The dogs and I were quite close to them before they loped off, leisurely. No wonder we have lost all our goldfish of late.

*James Lees-Milne*

# 3 July

1946 [Inverness-shire]
When summer was in its first clarity and freshness, I was glad to leave the damp pokiness of my house behind. But now that summer stands still to brood, I am thankful for my cool, stone floor, my bare white walls, my kitchen window, so small that it limits my vision and admits only a slight expanse of overgrown hedge. Overgrown is a mild adjective; the hedge is as tall and thick as a copse. In spring a kindly neighbour offered to trim my hedge. I have a horror of a 'trained' garden. I like unlimited

greenery around me, and my refusal to have the hedge trimmed solved the housing problem for a multitude of thrushes who day-long sing their gratitude.

*Jessie Kesson*

## 4 July

1871 [Clyro, Radnorshire]
Hannah Jones told me about the madwoman of Cwmgwanon. They kept her locked up in a bedroom alone, for she will come down amongst them stark naked. She has broken the window and all the crockery in the room, amuses herself by dancing naked round the room and threatens to wring her daughter-in-law's neck. Then she will set to and roar till they can hear her down the dingle at John Williams house, nearly half a mile.

*Francis Kilvert*

1877 [Dorset]
Country life at Sturminster. Vegetables pass from growing to boiling, fruit from the bushes to pudding, without a moment's halt, and the gooseberries that were ripening on the twigs at noon are in a tart an hour later.

*Thomas Hardy*

## 5 July

1826 [Abbotsford, the Scottish Borders]
Still very hot, but with thundery showers. Wrote till breakfast, then walked and signed the death warrant of a number of old firs at Abbotstown. I hope their deaths will prove useful. Their lives were certainly not ornamental.

*Sir Walter Scott*

## 1943 [Kent]

*Three-fifteen p.m., at the top of Gover Hill, in the avenue that leads down to Oxon Hoath.*

A woman on a chestnut horse has just ridden by, looking romantic against the background of steel-blue shallow hills and bleached cornfields. The sky is thickly clouded, heavy with rain that won't fall. I've eaten chocolate and cherries and read two stupid stories by Somerset Maugham.

I would like to build a tower here, on the top of this hill, with three storeys, a kitchen and living-room on the first, a bedroom and bathroom on the second, and a gazebo and workroom on the third. Perhaps on the top of that, pillars holding up a lintel, but no roof. I would like to lie in the tower quietly for ever.

*Denton Welch*

# 6 July

## 1923 [Lewes, Sussex]

So hot that I furtively undid my stays but not the suspenders.

*Alice Dudeney*

## 1981 [Combe Florey, Somerset]

A weekend of violence at Combe Florey sparked off by the Church fete on Saturday in the ground of Combe Florey House, leaves a bruised and bewildered populace wondering where we have all gone wrong.

Theft and looting – mainly by crazed nonagenarian whites – left two milk bottles broken beyond hope of repair, cakes from the cake stall seriously nibbled, and one book from my own stall of review copies badly foxed.

Needless to say the police were quite unable to contain the violence, which is thought to be non-racial in origin. When I suggested to P.C. Barnes, our village policeman, that he uses CS or even plastic bullets against a particularly quarrelsome group of old dears around the china stall, he revealed that he had not brought them with him.

Various conclusions can be drawn from all this. In the first place, geriatric terrorism must be recognised for what it is – the unacceptable face of the welfare state. This may mean arming the police and reversing the Government's entire economic policy.

Next, the Government must provide play schools for elderly folk where they can work off their aggressive instincts on each other. Massive government spending may be necessary. The overriding question must be whether we, as a nation, can afford a repetition of events at Combe Florey on Bloody Saturday.

*Auberon Waugh*

# 7 July

### 1767 [Ansford, Somerset]

I refused to bury 2 Corpses this afternoon at C. Cary, one that died Yesterday a Woman by name Cooper, and another Woman Peter Longman's Wife the Blacksmith, who died Sunday. The reason of my refusing them, was their not giving me proper notice of interring them. It has occasioned a good deal of talk about me, which I am sorry for, as I only did it, to make them more careful for the future, for the People of C. Cary have been very remiss in respect to that and have gave me a great deal of trouble always.

*James Woodforde*

### 1807 [Over Stowey, Somerset]

We had salmon again for dinner so that for a week past we've had our fill of fish.

*William Holland*

# 8 July

### 1872 [Clyro, Radnorshire]

Reports coming in all day of the mischief done by yesterday's flood. Pigs, sheep, calves swept away from meadow and cot and carried down river with hundreds of tons of hay, timber, hurdles and, it is said, furniture. The roads swept bare to the very rock. Culverts choked and blown up, turnips washed out of the hillsides, down into the orchards and turnpike roads. Four inches of mud at the Rhydspence Inn on the Welsh side of the border, the Sun, Lower Cabalva House flooded again and the carpets out to dry. Pastures covered with grit and gravel and rendered useless and dangerous for cattle till after the next heavy rain.

*Francis Kilvert*

## 1996 [Combe Florey, Somerset]

Sentencing three young men to prison for organising a cockfight in Kelloe, County Durham, the stipendary magistrate, Mr Ian Gillespie, condemned a 'barbaric and illegal practice which is apparently widespread throughout the United Kingdom'.

He is right. These cockfights have been an established feature of country life in Britain for as long as I can remember. Word is passed around and aficionados gather, with great secrecy, in some barn or other. The only sign that anything untoward is happening is usually a huge number of cars parked for no apparent reason in an unlikely spot.

I have never been to a cockfight in England, but I once went to one in Manila, where they are a regular Sunday morning diversion, and found it very boring. A cock, when all is said and done, is no more than a male chicken. As a fighter, it lacks dignity, poise, intelligence or any of the attributes of nobility.

But that is no reason to stop other people diverting themselves in this way. I was interested to learn that although the practice has been illegal since 1835, this was only the fourth prosecution of its kind to go before a British court in the past 50 years.

This may be seen as a tribute to the taciturnity of country folk. In fact, the law is a monument to the way town dwellers think they can control the life of the countryside. The influence is increasingly resented, as villagers on Dartmoor showed last week when they prevented a tourist centre from being built there. Plans included a visitors' centre and cafe and a 70-space car park but, despite these wonderful promises, the local inhabitants announced that they simply do not want to be visited.

*Auberon Waugh*

# 9 July

1785 [Fyfield, Hampshire]
Vast distress of want of water, particularly in ye Hill country, ye farmers at Tangley and Chute obliged to send and buy water at Andover at 1s 6d. per load.

*Henry White*

# 10 July

1923 [Weybridge, Surrey]
At 9.30, the rain having ceased, E.M.F. [E.M. Forster] and I went for a walk by the River Wey. In the sultry twilight the river created a double world in which reflection and reality were indistinguishable. Upside-down was the same as right-way-up. Neither sky nor water moved, and the looming masses and smokey remoteness of riverside trees hung tranced in a stillness under which we flitted like bats, or like our own vague musings as we hovered along the tow-path, staring into the sultry dusk. Shadow melted into shadow: all was painted in subaqueous neutral tones, and the stars were veiled by an imperceptible mistiness. A mile away a line of poplars pointed skyward. 'It's like the life after death,' I suggested, diffidently. My conventional comment failed to satisfy Forster, whose subdued voice, mingling with the unearthly twilight stillness, syllabled a few sayings which have since vanished into the mazes of my forgetfulness.

*Siegfried Sassoon*

# 11 July

1765 [Somerset]
A terrible Accident happend while we were at dinner, which many of us went to see the Body – viz, a poor Boy was dragged and killed by a Horse

about half a Mile from us on the Ilchester Road. The boy was about 14 Years
old – I hope to God the Poor Boy is happy. There was no bone broken
neither was his Skull fractured – but he is dead. We all came home singing,
and I thank God well.

*James Woodforde*

## 1866 [Oxfordshire]

Dull and shallow sunlight. Saw an olive-coloured snake on hedge of
Finchley wood and just before its slough in the road – or at all events a
slough. Oats: hoary blue-green sheaths and stalks, prettily shadow-stroked
spikes of pale green grain. Oaks: the organisation of this tree is difficult.
Speaking generally no doubt the determining planes are concentric, a
system of brief contiguous and continuous tangents, whereas those of
the cedar would roughly be called horizontals and those of the beech
radiating but modified by the droop and by the screw-set towards
jutting points. But beyond this since the normal growth of the boughs
is radiating and the leaves grow some way in there is of course a system
of spoke-wise clubs of green – sleeve-pieces. And since the end shoots
curl and carry young and scanty leaf-stars these clubs are tapered, and
I have seen also the pieces in profile with chiselled outlines, the blocks
thus made detached and lessening towards the end. However the star
knot is the chief thing: it is whorled, worked round, a little and this is
what keeps up the illusion of the tree: the leaves are rounded inwards
and figure out ball-knots. Oaks differ much, and much turns on the
broadness of the leaf, the narrower giving the crisped and starry and
Catherine-wheel forms, the broader the flat-pieced mailed or shard-
covered ones, in which it is possible to see composition in dips, etc.
on wider bases than the single knot or cluster. But I shall study them
further.

*Gerard Manley Hopkins*

# 12 July

## 1916 [Lewes, Sussex]

The tradesmen are terribly rude. I went in to Pryor, the pork butcher, who had 3 pigs' tongues on a blue dish in the window. Pryor, sitting behind the counter reading a newspaper, asks after a pause: 'What's for you?' 'Pigs' tongues, please.' 'You can't have 'em, they're going to be cooked for my tea.'

*Alice Dudeney*

# 13 July

## 1773 [Selborne, Hampshire]

Five great white sea-gulls flew over the village toward the forest.

*Gilbert White*

## 1875 [Chippenham, Wiltshire]

This morning after breakfast I started to walk to Bembridge through Sandown and Yaverland. The morning was blue and lovely with a warm sun and fresh breeze blowing from the sea and the Culver Downs. As I walked from Shanklin to Sandown along the cliff edge I stopped to watch some children bathing from the beach directly below. One beautiful girl stood entirely naked on the sand, and there as she half sat, half reclined sideways, leaning upon her elbow with knees bent and her legs and feet partly drawn back and up, she was a model for a sculptor, there was the supple slender waist, the gentle dawn and tender swell of the bosom and budding breasts, the graceful rounding of the delicately beautiful limbs and above all the soft and exquisite curves of the rosy dimpled bottom and broad white thigh. Her dark hair fell in thick masses on her white shoulders as she threw her head back and looked out to sea. She seemed like a Venus Anadyomene fresh risen from the waves.

*Francis Kilvert*

## 1992 [Saltwood Castle, Kent]

A grey day. A time for planning. We really should operate to a timetable. Things that must have black lines set aside for them (not necessarily every day) are:

(a) House work in Garden House – cleaning kitchen, hanging pictures, plugs on lights etc

(b) Word processor – already 7.30–8.30, provided this working after KK. [his son's labrador] 7.45–8.45?

(c) Filing in summer office – at *least* one hour per day

(d) Cleaning cars}

(e) Scything and forking} possibly alternate

(f) SUNDAY FREE

I must look up old timetables.

*Alan Clark*

# 14 July

## 1906 [Olton, Warwickshire]

Glorious day after a day of heavy rain. On my weekly ride to Knowle, saw the following flowers in bloom since I passed through the lanes a week ago – Field Knautia, Small Scabious, Nipple-wort, Water Dropwart, Corn Sow Thistle, Creeping Plume Thistle and Ivy-leaved Lettuce; as well as several varieties of Hawkweed. Many of the Oak Trees which were so devastated by caterpillars this year are producing quite a new crop of foliage.

*Edith Holden*

# 15 July

## 1758 [East Hoathly, Sussex]

A most prodigious melancholy time; very little to do, for I think that luxury increases so fast in this part of the nation that people have very little or no money to spare to buy what is really necessary. For the too frequent use of spiritous liquors and the exorbitant practice of tea-drinking have in such a manner corrupted the morals of people of almost all ranks that they have rendered industry a stranger to the people in those parts.

*Thomas Turner*

## 1773 [Selborne, Hampshire]
No rain since June 20th at this place; tho' vast showers have fallen around us, & near us.

*Gilbert White*

## 1866 [New Forest]
Breakfast at Crown 9.30. A. T. [Alfred Tennyson], Mrs T., Hallam and Lionel. A.T. and I out at 12. Swan Green forest path, Hailday's Hall, we *swim* through tall bracken. T. pauses midway, turns to me, and says solemnly, 'I believe *this* place is quite full of vipers!' After going a little further, he stopped again and said, 'I am told that a viper-bite may make a woman silly for life, or deprive a man of his virility.'

*William Allingham*

## 1937 [Perth]
*Anecdottle*: There was a farmer in Pullars called – if I remember rightly – Willie Low. When my mother was a child he was an elderly man who had outlived two wives but was courting one of the work-girls. Having made up his mind to propose he took his fancy for a walk up Jeanfield way and suggested that they might wander through the grounds of Wellshill cemetery. He ultimately led the girl to the grave which held his two spouses and, as they stood looking down at the stone, he said: 'How would you like to lie there, Maggie?' and Maggie accepted this unique proposal by answering: 'Fine.'

*William Soutar*

# 16 July

### 1870 [Clyro, Radnorshire]

At tea I sat between Miss and Mrs Oswald and opposite a tongue. May I never sit opposite a tongue again, at least if I have to carve it with a new round-headed small knife as blunt as a fruit knife. I heaved and hacked away at the tongue, cut it up into small bits, and made a complete wreck and ruin of it. The more the knife would not cut and the less tongue there was to give, the more people seemed to want it and asked me to send them some.

*Francis Kilvert*

# 17 July

### 1756 [East Hoathly, Sussex]

In the morn after breakfast we went down to Mr French's to get him to bring me from Lewes ½ oz. cauliflower seed, and when I came there, I found Mr French, his servants. and Tho. Fuller a-catching of rats; so I stayed and assisted them about 3 hours, and we caught near 20. The method of catching them was by pouring water into their burrows, which occasioned them immediately to come out, when either the dogs took them or [we] killed them with our sticks. Just as we had done, Mr John Vine came in. We stayed about ½ an hour and came all away together, Mr Vine and T. Fuller coming round by our house and only for the sake of a dram. Mr Vine, as we came along from Mr French's was making several observances with regard to good economy husbandry. To wit, he said that man who went the road a-timber carrying etc. never hurt his horses if he did not overload them, and he very plainly demonstrated that going with a light load turned out most to the master's advantage in time, and therefore he must of consequence get more money by light loading than heavy.

*Thomas Turner*

# 18 July

### 1867 [Oxfordshire]

Showers and fine; rainbow. – The reason Shakspere calls it 'the blue bow' – to put it down now precisely – is because the blue band edged by and ending in violet, though not the broadest, is the deepest expression of colour in the bow and so becomes the most decisive and emphatic feature there. – At sunset the air rinsed after the rain.

*Gerard Manley Hopkins*

# 19 July

### 1701 [Wotton, Surrey]

A poor [old] Labourer falling off from the Hay Cart, not any considerable height, but pitching on his head, breaking his Collarbone, & doubtlesse disordering his braine, tho neither quite speechlesse, & let blood without effect, died, to my exceeding sorrow & trouble, it being in my Haying.

*John Evelyn*

### 1875 [Chippenham, Wiltshire]

I called on Mrs Martin. She was busy picking pheasants' feathers to make a pillow. Talking of feather beds she said, 'Pheasants' feathers will do very well for a bed, but no pigeons' feathers. People don't like to sleep on pigeons' feathers.' 'Why not?' I asked. 'Well,' said Susan Martin mysteriously, 'folk do say that a person can't die on pigeons' feathers.'

*Francis Kilvert*

### 1876 [Slackfields Farm, Derbyshire]

*Fine* Dragging fallow, turned seeds, mowed orchard.

*Henry Hill*

# 20 July

## 1986 [Essex House, Badminton]

Lunched with the Garnetts [Andrew, an entrepreneur, and Polly Devlin, writer] at Cannwood Farm, their new house near Frome. An old red brick farmhouse much added to. Pretty and higgledy-piggledy, crammed with furniture, ornaments and knick-knacks, children falling over each other, maids with babies, muddle, confusion, jollity; a house such as I could never make. Polly much improved, fine eyes, immensely clever and quick. Took us for a walk in a meadow they own which has been scheduled 'not to be disturbed'. As it has never been 'improved' by farmers or treated with pesticides, it is a tapestry of wild flowers, such as one sees in a Cluny panel and indeed one saw every day in one's youth. Scabious, clover, vetch blue and yellow, cornflowers, marguerites and eighty variety of grass, so Polly says. The field next door, which has been 'improved', utterly dead like a landscape on the moon. To think that A. [Alvilde, his wife] and I have lived to see this change.

*James Lees-Milne*

# 21 July

## 1866 [Oxfordshire]

There is a large-leaved kind of ash which grows in tall close bushes: when the wind blows it the backs of the sprays, which are silvery, look like combs of fish-bones, the leaves where they border their rib-stem appearing, when in repetition all jointed on one rib, to be angularly cut at the inner end. The two bindweeds are in blossom.

*Gerard Manley Hopkins*

## 1870 [Clyro, Radnorshire]

Breakfast 6.45. Mrs H. drove us in the pony carriage to Perranwell Station in time for the 7.35 train to Hayle. The journey lay through a great mining district chiefly tin. The bowels of the earth ripped open, turned inside out in the search for metal ore, the land defiled and cumbered with heaps and wastes of slag and rubbish, and the waters poisoned with tin and copper washings. The Cornish village bare bleak barren and ugly, whitewashed and often un-sheltered by a single tree, grouped or scattered about mountainous wastes.

Above Godvery and all along the North coast there are a great many seals. Once at Godvery the H's saw a fearful battle between a seal and a large conger eel. The seal had got its teeth into the conger and the conger had coiled his folds round the seal's neck and was trying to choke him. The seal kept throwing up his head and trying to toss the conger up out of the water that he might have more power than the eel. It was a fierce and dreadful fight, but at last the seal killed the conger.

The Vicar of St Ives says the smell of fish is sometimes so terrific as to stop the church clock.

We did not know it at the time but while we were enjoying ourselves on the beach a poor miner who had gone out to bathe in his dinner hour was drowning in the very bay near us. The sea fog came rolling up from the Atlantic in a dense purple bank, and the sea changed colour to a deep dark green.

*Francis Kilvert*

### 1993 [Saltwood Castle, Kent]

A dreadful cold wet July, intermittently 'muggy'. I bathed, one length, this morning and cleared a headache (almost a hangover headache caused, I would stress, by that 'Lido Hotel' wine which tasted good, but is clearly full of anti-freeze), but the water is the same colour as the moat, and smells of vegetation.

*Alan Clark*

## 22 July

### 1787

We arrived at Sonning at one o'clock; always in company there; that is the life of the country! A garden full of raspberries and currants, but I dare not eat from a bowel complaint. Saying this is like my predecessor in diary Mr Ashmole; but all diaries, let them be ever so bad, will be read with avidity hereafter.

Nay, I am even vain enough to think this of my Tours, should they exist a hundred years, as descriptive of the manners of our travelling, the rates of our provisions, and of castles, churches and houses that may then be levell'd with the ground.

All diaries are greedily sought for, let them be ever so ill and foolishly written, as coming warm from the heart; for instance, that of the second Ld Clarendon, and those dirty, idle memorials of astrologer William Lilly, and Elias Ashmole, who tells us of every shocking ailment that assailed him and how often he sweated and purged.

Most modern Tours are written (in my mind) too much in the style of pompous history; no dwelling sufficiently upon the prices of provisions, recommendations of inns, statement of roads, etc., so that the following travellers reap little benefit from them.

I have often thought that maps merely for tourists might be made. And have wish'd that some intelligent traveller (for instance, Mr Grose) [Francis Grose, author of *The Antiquities of England and Wales*] would mark on such touring maps all the castles, Roman stations, views, canals, parks, etc., etc., which, accompanied by other common maps, would lead the researching Tourist to every proper point and object; and not subject him (as at present) to ask questions of ignorant innkeepers or to hunt in books for what is not to be found; for till lately we had no inquisitive travellers and but few views of remarkable places.

*John Byng*

# 23 July

### 1904 [Worcestershire]

After dinner Boys and Baines went on the river, & Mother and I went to see Miss Northcroft off, & to buy a boat hook. Then we went to Worcester to feed the swans, we found some, & some cygnets. The cygnets were grey, with almost grey beaks & feet; some of them had feather sheaths still on their young feathers. The swans and ducks fed out of our hands, & one swan bit a hole in my thumb. Some boys were fishing close by, & the fish came for the bread which we gave the swans. We had gooseberries & sponge cake for tea which we had under a horse chestnut tree. We saw a Thrush which was hitting a snailshell against the path, so as to get the snail out, and eat it . . .

*Naomi Mitchison (aged 6)*

# 24 July

### 1780 [Fyfield, Hampshire]

Reaping wheat begun in Fr Berrett's piece N. of ye grove. It was by no means ripe or near it, but was sadly Blighted so that many ears have no corn in them at all, and it is to be feared that this mischief is more general than it is now suspected.

*Henry White*

### 1866 [Oxfordshire]

The wild parsley (if it is that) growing in clumps by the road side is a beautiful sight, the leaf being delicately cut like rue. There is a tree that has a leaf like traveller's joy, curled, and with brick-like veinings. It has clusters of berries which are flattened like some tight-mouthed jars, yellow when unripe, then cherry-coloured, then quickly turning glossy black if gathered. The traveller's joy winds over it and they then are hard to tell apart, unless that it has rougher duller leaves. There was a graceful bit, a stile, with this tree hanging over on the left side, hazel and large-leaved ash on the right, and a spray of the ash stood forward like a bright blind of leaves drawing and condensing the light. Under the bushes on each side was suggestive woolly darkness (and giving on one hand onto the dry stoned bed of a streamlet, where on looking under one saw more light filtering in) and soft round-bladed tufts of grass grew in half-darkness under the stone at the foot of the stile. – No, the berries belong, I now remember, to a rough round-leaved tree (the underside being white). Merely the white-beam, I believe.

*Gerard Manley Hopkins*

# 25 July

1966 [Underhill Farm, Lyme Regis]

Summer here seduces; runs out of hand as well, there are so many things to do in the garden, in the fields; so many invitations not to write, not to think. An invitation I should normally have turned down, to do a double profile on Vanessa Redgrave and a new universal sex-object, a Raquel Welch, came as a sort of temptation to get out into the world again. I don't feel so much that I need the experience of the outer world, but its humiliations. We live here in a detached, self-supporting, self-sufficient world. We see no one, the sun shines, the sea glistens, our birds and insects weave their summer world around us. It is beautiful, like being in a glass sphere whose diameter is the sea horizon, all seventy or eighty miles of it. The sense of enclosure is very small; yet finally one knows it.

The magazine that is commissioning the article is an insult in itself – the egregious *Cosmopolitan*. This morning they wrote saying they wanted the 'ordinary virile man's view' of the two girls. For 'virile' read 'sex-crazed'.

*John Fowles*

1992 [Saltwood Castle, Kent]

We bought the huge Sidney Cooper for £110,000 [a nineteenth-century painting of Saltwood] – which makes things very tight. I will have to sell a little modern art, but what? The 'chair' [by Cézanne] perhaps?

*Alan Clark*

# 26 July

*c.*2000 [Walnut Tree Farm, Suffolk]

How can I be expected to like squirrels when they have left such a debris of half-chewed walnuts beneath the old tree by the barn? Each year they come and raid the tree and vandalise it like the sort of burglars who have to half smash a house, not content with simply stealing things. 'Grow up, act your age. Just take what you need and bugger off.'

*Roger Deakin*

# 27 July

1892 [en route to Birnam, Perthshire]

Scotch papers are refreshingly acrimonious and spiteful provided you agree with them. I sometimes wonder, considering the metaphysical abstruse turn of Scotch intellect, that the articles provided by their political journalists should be brilliant rather than profound. They make *The Times* leaders appear ponderous in comparison. Exceedingly well written and doubtless well informed, or they could not be so versatile in argument, but they concern themselves more with the cut and thrust of arguments of party politics, than with fundamental principles and the evolution of politics. They reserve their powers of metaphysical dissection for philosophy and the Kirk, wherein perhaps they are wise, certainly practical, but it leaves the Scotch open to the accusation of being politicians first and patriots afterwards.

I believe setting aside the great question of religion, the Scotch people as a mass (that is to say Low-landers and Towns-people, as distinguished from the Celtic Highlanders), have never been seriously moved by any political wave since the days of Bruce. Scotch history as written, is a record of intrigue and party politics, creditable or the reverse when the Union was bought and sold.

Conspiracies and rebellions, Darien, Glencoe and the Porteous riots, make lively reading and doubtless all things work together for a result and end, but the only two important factors in Scotch history have been religion and money – (in the sense of commercial growth since the Union). Even in religion they are highly aggressive, in fact ill-natured sceptics might suppose it is the life of the Kirk.

There was an extraordinary miscellaneous scramble in the first-class restaurant-room at Perth. A hard, hairy Scotcher opposite doing it thoroughly in five courses, porridge, salmon-cutlets, chops, ham and eggs and marmalade. Under my chair a black retriever and on my left a large man in knickerbockers, facing a particularly repulsive Scotch mother and young baby feeding on sops. All the company extremely dirty and the attendants inattentive.

*Beatrix Potter*

## 1911 [Cambridgeshire]

Percy and I decided to bicycle. We started about 11.0: went slowly to Barton, and so to Haslingfield: then between Haslingfield and Harston we lay long on the grass, near ricks, listening to owls and the snorting of some beast that drew nigh, to far-off dogs barking, and cocks crowing. The stars were like the points of pendants in the irregular roof of a cave – not an even carpet or set in a concave. We went on about 1.0, and then made a long halt near the G.N.R. bridge on the way to Newton; but no trains passed, so we went on about 1.45 to Shelford; and this was very sweet, so fragrant and shadowed by dark trees, while Algol and Aldebaran and other great shining stars slowly wheeled above us.

We got to the G.E.R. bridge at Shelford – I was anxious to see trains – and half-a-dozen great luggers jangled through with a cloud of steam and coloured lights. There was one that halted, and the guard walked about with a lantern; a melancholy policeman was here, in the shadow. The owls again hooted and screamed and cocks roared hoarsely.

Suddenly we became aware it was the dawn! The sky was whitening, there was a green tinge to east, with rusty stains of cloud, and the stars went out. We went on about 2.30 to Grantchester, where the mill with lighted windows was rumbling, and the water ran oily-smooth into the inky pool among the trees. Then it was day; and by the time we rode into Cambridge, getting in at 3.30, it was the white morning light – while all the places so mysteriously different at night had become the places one knew. We found some bread-and-butter, and smoked till 4.0, when we went out round the garden, the day now brightening up: after which I went to bed, but P. walked till 5.0. The mystery, the coolness, the scent, the quiet of it all were wonderful, and the thought that this strange transformation passes over the world thus night by night seemed very amazing.

*A. C. Benson*

# 28 July

1874 [Chippenham, Wiltshire]

This morning Teddy set up the net and poles in the field opposite the dining room windows and we began to play 'sphairistike' or lawn tennis, a capital game, but rather too hot for a summer's day.

*Francis Kilvert*

# 29 July

1788 [Norfolk]

In the Evening took a ride to Norwich and Briton with me, and there I supped and slept at the Kings Head. In the Evening before Supper I walked into St Stephens and saw the Polish Dwarf Joseph Boruwlaski and his Wife who is a middle-sized Person, he is only three feet three Inches in height, quite well proportioned everyway, very polite, sensible and very sprightly, and gave us a tune upon the Guitar, and one Tune of his own composing. The common price of admittance was one Shilling, but I gave him rather more 0.2.6.

*James Woodforde*

# 30 July

1943 [Jersey]

Margaret and Dorothy here this morning for the last day of this term. I shall be glad to have more time for potato-flour, gardening etc. I like to see the children, but haven't really the time to teach them! Finished drying and weighing flour. Have just over 40 pounds from my 400 pounds of potatoes.

*Nan Le Ruez*

# 31 July

1773 [Selborne, Hampshire]
This morning Will Tanner shot, off the tall meris-tree in the great mead, 17 young blackbirds. The cherries of these trees amuse the birds & save the garden fruit.

*Gilbert White*

# AUGUST

# 1 August

1785 [Fyfield, Hampshire]
Cricket match at Periham between Mr A. Smith and Men of Whitchurch and Andover – won by ye latter.

*Henry White*

1946 [Kent]
. . . Eric [his companion] came in and we quarrelled stupidly over the clipping of the hedge, or some such hollowness. So I hastily made another picnic and took it here at the bottom of the downs, behind Trottiscliffe Church, on the Pilgrim's Way. My heart was very heavy, and the air too is weighing-down and thick. I have walked along the path picking scabious, harebells, cornflowers purple and white and smelling wild thyme – all the flowers purple and mauve except for the two white cornflowers.

There are dummies on low gibbets, set up for the soldiers to rip with their bayonets. There is an engine in a house, all locked, that hums and whirrs everlastingly. High up on the hill was a frilly thin girl and a baby in scarlet.

The buzz of all the insects is like a distant echo of the power-house.

*Denton Welch*

# 2 August

1916 [Oxfordshire]
Reached Southampton about noon. Got on train and came to Oxford about 4 p.m. – No 3 General Service Hospital at Somerville College. Paradise. Strange thing getting landed at Cambridge in August 1915 and Oxford 1916.

Lying in hospital train on his way to London he looks out at the hot August landscape of Hampshire, the flat green and dun-coloured fields – the advertisements of Lung Tonic and Liver Pills – the cows – neat villas and sluggish waterways – all these came on him in an irresistible delight, at the pale gold of the wheat-fields and the faded green of the hazy muffled woods on the low hills. People wave to the Red Cross train – grateful stay-at-homes – even a middle-aged man, cycling along a dusty road in straw hat and blue serge clothes, takes one hand off handlebars to wave feeble and jocular gratitude. And the soul of the officer glows with a fiery passion as he thinks 'All this I've been fighting for; and now I'm safe home again I begin to think it was worth while'. And he wondered how he could avoid being sent out again.

Weather golden and sweet and gracious. The harvest landscape slipping past me as I lay in the train – all pale-golden wheat and silver-green barley and oats. Then Oxford bells chiming 5 o'clock and a piano sounding from across the lawn – someone strumming emotional trash – and the tall chestnuts swaying against the blue, as I lie in a little cream-white room. What an anodyne it all is after Fricourt etc. No need to think of another winter in the trenches, doomed though I am to endure it. Good enough to enjoy the late summer and autumn. And then, who cares?

*Siegfried Sassoon*

## 1943 [Sissinghurst, Kent]

We go to the village fete at Sissinghurst Place. All the village children dress up and there is one little boy who impersonates Montgomery riding in a tank. There are many side-shows. One of them is a dart contest in which people are invited to throw darts at large cartoon figures of Hitler, Tojo and Mussolini. The Mussolini target does no business at all. Hitler and Tojo attract great crowds but people do not want to throw darts at Mussolini as they say he is 'down and out'. Really the English are an amazing race.

*Harold Nicolson*

## c.2000 [Walnut Tree Farm, Suffolk]

It was strange, last night, driving home across Suffolk from the levity of the ukelele orchestra to the just-killed fox on the road at Denham. It was a most beautiful fox, in the pink of condition, its coat thick and a rich, deep red, and, when I gently lifted it up off the road to lay it to rest in dignity behind the hedge, it was surprisingly heavy: perhaps twenty pounds, certainly fifteen. There was no blood and there were no marks on it. Its neck must have been broken as it glanced off a car. Strange that foxes, which are supposed to be so clever, can't learn to avoid the headlights of cars. This fox had come out of Denham woods. It was in such perfect health, yet they say the average life of a fox is no more than three years!

*Roger Deakin*

## 3 August

1800 [Grasmere, the Lake District]
I made pies and stuffed the pike – baked a loaf. Headache after dinner – I lay down. A letter from Wm rouzed me, desiring us to go to Keswick. After writing to Wm we walked as far as Mr Simpson's and ate black cherries. A Heavenly warm evening with scattered clouds upon the hills. There was a vernal greenness upon the grass from the rains of the morning and afternoon. Peas for dinner.

*Dorothy Wordsworth*

## 4 August

1759 [Lancashire]
In the evening I began near Stockton market-place as usual. I had hardly finished the hymn, when I observed the people in great confusion, which was occasioned by a lieutenant of a man-of-war, who had chosen that time to bring his press-gang, and ordered them to take Joseph Jones and William Alwood. Joseph Jones telling him, 'Sir, I belong to Mr Wesley,' after a few words he let him go; as he did likewise William Alwood, after a few hours, understanding he was a licensed preacher. He likewise seized upon a young

man of the town; but the women rescued him by main strength. They also broke the lieutenant's head; and so stoned both him and his men, that they ran away with all speed.

John Wesley

1892 [Sawrey, the Lake District]
I may say that I lost half a day. The hen-quail got out of the window which was unsettling, besides that, I had eaten too many gooseberries the previous day. The cock is certainly tamer without her, a startling little fat bird, but I was disturbed to think of cats. There is a black one in particular belonging to Miss Hutton, which brought in three rabbits on one evening. She is afraid it will end in a rabbit-snare, which is rather rich. It has been seen on its hind legs peeping in at the rabbit hutch, also dogs.

It is not a safe place for Benjamin Bouncer. I walk him about with a leather strap. He is the object of many odd comments from that amusing person McDougall [a gamekeeper], 'Eh, see him, he's basking!' (on his back in the sand), 'Are you aware that rabbit will eat sweeties?, See how busy he is!' He is constantly giving it peppermints which I suspect are pilfered from his sister-in-law Miss Duff.

Beatrix Potter

# 5 August

1946 [Inverness-shire]
On the farm this *is* 'breathing time'. The farm-workers who are not on their brief annual summer holiday – of three days' duration – scythe the thistles round the steading and fill the day with odd jobs. The pace of their life has slowed down. It is as if the men and the earth they work were conserving the last ounce of strength for 'the hairst'.

Jessie Kesson

## 1991 [Melton Constable, Norfolk]

The woodlands around this central Norfolk village are one of the remaining areas where it is possible to see spectacular carpets of wild bluebells. However, there are now two plantations just off the road where the luxuriant spread of hyacinth-coloured flowers will not be back for many years, if ever again. Their absence is the work of an unscrupulous team who systematically stripped the woods of their bluebell bulbs earlier this spring. The bulbs then earn them substantial profits when resold to horticultural dealers. The flower extraction at Melton Constable is not an isolated incident: this year in both Norfolk and Essex protected species of orchid have been stolen from country trust reserves. The team that cleaned out Melton were arrested earlier this month for stealing snowdrop bulbs at another site in Norfolk. Whatever the current legal position, plundering the countryside of its wild flowers must be morally indefensible, making further inroads into an already diminished flora. Just two examples of this are the disappearance of ninety-seven per cent of traditional meadowlands since the 1930s and half of all British woodlands since 1945.

*Mark Cocker*

## 6 August

## 1874 [Chippenham, Wiltshire]

I received this evening a wild strange unhappy note from Susan Strange begging me to come and see her as soon as possible. She was worse and in some trouble of mind about herself. She was also troubled about her daughter Fanny who grieves her sadly by frequently lying and stealing. I told her she must correct the girl in time. 'I do flog her,' she said. 'And the other morning she was a naughty girl and her brother Joseph brought her in to me in her shimmy while I was in bed. I held her hands while Joseph and Charlie whipped her on her naked bottom as hard as ever they were able to flog her.'

*Francis Kilvert*

### 1975 [Belmont, Lyme Regis]

I manage to squeak a young Tawny Owl into believing me a mouse. It sat perched fifteen feet above my head on a dead branch of the old cedar, oblivious of the torchlight, shifting its head from side to side in a desperate attempt to pinpoint this less than satisfactorily authentic sound; a comic little creature.

*John Fowles*

# 7 August

### 1892 [Birnam, Perthshire]

Tried to draw in garden, but was eaten up with midges.

*Beatrix Potter*

# 8 August

### 1811 [Hampshire]

Went with Lord Hinton, who had never fished with a minnow before, and the trout ran so remarkably well that he caught 7 brace of the largest fish we had seen for the season in the space of an hour and half. I killed also one trout, while instructing him how to troll, which was the largest caught this year, weighing 2 lb.

Lord Hinton hooked a trout with a minnow, which was so large as to require nearly twenty minutes to get him to the top of the water; and while we were in the very act of landing him, we had the sad mortification to see him break the tackle and swim away. He was the largest trout I ever saw, and has defeated all the fishermen. I should guess his weight at about 7 lb.

*Colonel Peter Hawker*

### 1892 [Perthshire]

Hopelessly wet, which was the more provoking as Bostock & Wombwell's Menagerie was advertised to be at Dunkeld for one day only. I had no desire to see the performance because of the lion-taming, which I object to, but if there's any show I like, it is a circus. We went down in the wet in the evening and found the thirteen or fourteen vans drawn up in the town square, and covered with a tarpaulin, with several satellite peep shows. In front of one, a vulgar, noisy proprietor was inviting the public to pay tuppence and see the man with a beard six yards long. I had rather not. There was a considerable crowd of dirty natives outside, but having mounted a step ladder on to a pasteboard stage, we found there was no other audience but ourselves.

The animals were splendid, so much healthier and fresher looking than most at the Gardens; Bertram thought the lions, twelve in number, were rather light in the limbs, doubtless by being tame bred, but in my opinion their sleekness made up for it. There was a magnificent lion in a division by himself, and divided by a partition, a lioness and two very little cubs playing like kittens.

At either end of the small van, a polar and a brown bear. They had a very complete variety of beasts, and the only single animal which looked out of condition or unhappy, was one of the pair of performing elephants, who was deplorably ill with a cold. The keeper, a big black-haired fellow seemed much concerned, and invited her 'Nancy, poor old girl', to take part of his supper, but she dropped it and stood with her trunk crumpled up on the bar 'like a sick worm'. The poor thing died three days later at Coupar Angus. They are hopeless if they receive the slightest injury or illness, as they simply mope till they die.

In ridiculous contrast was a little Jack donkey of the very smallest proportions, who was marching about loose under the noses of the lions, stealing hay.

*Beatrix Potter*

# 9 August

1905 [The Lake District]
Travelled up to Carlisle and drove eight miles through Cumberland lanes between banks covered with Harebells, Toadflax, and Hawkweed, crowned

by low hedges waving with the long streamers of Honeysuckle and sweet-scented Bedstraw. In many places the fields were green with Ragweed.

*Edith Holden*

## 10 August

1892 [Perthshire]

He [Donald McLeish, gamekeeper] told another curious story of a fox which he trapped in a snare. When he came in sight of it, it was sitting up with the wire round its neck, but on his going round behind it with the intention of shooting it, it flopped down 'dead'. It actually allowed him to open its eyes and mouth with his fingers, pull it about and carry it home in his game-bag, only dropping the disguise when shut up in an empty room.

It lived six years in a kennel and fed upon porridge. It was so sly, it had a habit of saving a portion of porridge within reach of his chain, then pretending sleep, and pouncing on the hens, which it took into the kennel 'feathers and all'. Lord Fife allowed it to catch as many as it could.

*Beatrix Potter*

## 11 August

1780 [Norfolk]

My great Horse much worse this morning, was walked up to Reeves again and Ben with him, the Dr gave Ben a Draught for him to take – but the poor Horse was so ill on his return, that he could not give it to him, and about 10 o'clock this morning died. I endeavoured to bleed him a little before and sent Will to Gould of Attlebridge to come and see him, but he was dead long before he came. Gould said that he died of a Fever in the Bowels – and that he should have been bled, had a Clyster & some cooling Physic also. Am very sorry for him as he was so goodnatured a Beast. Don't intend to employ Reeves any more as a Farrier. I could not have thought that he would have died so soon. The Death of my poor goodnatured Horse (by name Jack) made me very uneasy all day long. Ben and Will skinned him, we kept one half of him and we gave the other half to Mr Press Custance. Whatever the skin fetches, is to be divided between Will, Ben & Jack.

*James Woodforde*

1870 [Clyro, Radnorshire]
The weather has become intensely hot again. There are such quantities of apricots this year and they all ripen so fast together that there is no knowing what to do with them. A great number have been given away.

*Francis Kilvert*

## 12 August

1774 [Selborne, Hampshire]
Fly-catchers bring out young broods. Mich: daisy blows. Apricots ripen. Some martins, dispossessed off their nests by sparrows, return to them again when their enemies are shot, & breed in them. Several pairs of martins have not yet brought forth their first brood. They meet with interruptions, & leave their nests.

*Gilbert White*

## 13 August

1938 [Antrobus, Cheshire]
We miss the full volume of bird-song at this time of the year (there is a Kentish phrase, 'as dumb as a lark in August'), but not all birds are silent. Yellow-hammers and greenfinches are both singing daily, robins began their autumn song five or six days ago, starlings several times recently have made me think that a thrush is singing, swallows on the wing or on a wire, and the three doves (the turtle, the stock-dove, and the wood-pigeon) all may be heard almost every day. I have even heard a lapwing giving its cheery spring call.

*A.W. Boyd*

# 14 August

## 1911 [Barnstaple, North Devon]

At 4 pm went to the Salmon Pool for a bathe. 87.3 in the shade. The meadow as delicious in the sunshine. It made me want to hop, flirt my tail, sing.

*W.N.P. Barbellion*

# 15 August

## 1865 [Berkshire]

After seeing [Bishopston] church I went along a narrow deep-hedged winding lane, and came to a magnificent walnut tree, the finest by far I ever saw; and opposite a nice-looking small old-fashioned house, at the gate of which were eight children, waiting about with no apparent object: presently I heard a rough, loud man's voice. I thought he was driving them off, but he was counting them: he was in shirt-sleeves, but had a well-dressed companion. They leant over the gate, the rough man called the children, and in his rude way, disguising kindness (ever since the fashioning of this eccentric island-people kindness has been a thing worn under a cloak), he distributed his plums, sending one to the brat in the 'cradle' (perambulating): he would not help me about my road till he had finished the dole. I had half a mind to stop and talk to him – indeed I began about the walnut-tree, and am indebted to him for knowing it is a walnut – but shyness, the plague of this eccentric English nation, broke off our budding acquaintance.

*William Cory*

## 1969 [Belmont, Lyme Regis]

To Wales, to spend a weekend with Tom M [Maschler, his publisher] at his country cottage in the Black Mountains. Tom has a new girlfriend now, called Fay Coventry; a milky, intelligent, quietly self-possessed creature. We hardly saw her, she spent the whole weekend in the kitchen, making jam, cooking, cooking very well, and I think making a web for him to fall into. He zig-zags about her like a daddy-long-legs, half in love with death (marriage to her); and half in love with her (which means using her). I think he is the most *désinvolte* person I have ever met; though there is something cruel in his airy freedom, a contempt for people who don't make an equal amount for themselves. Something cruel and easily hurt also. We went for a walk in the mountains and I can't stand his restlessness, the feel he gives that one must be getting somewhere. So I suggested he went home and left me to idle on in my own haphazard fashion. He was tired, wanted to go home, but I see it offended him, that I could do without him, that I might have some secret, some pleasure perhaps, from which I was excluding him. Like all Jews, he finds it immensely difficult to take any but a cursory interest in nature; yet feels he ought to, because he sees the inconsistency of living in such a wild place and not knowing anything about the life of it; and then again, hasn't the patience, must get on.

*John Fowles*

# 16 August

### 1824 [Somerset]

My boys engaged to attend young Newnham and Langford fishing in the brook; their two companions, with young Peter Hoare, came to breakfast; the whole party went afterwards to fish in the Cam. On my return I found the lads had had good success with their fishing, but young Newnham only caught one, as he thought it cruel to use a worm, and only fished with paste. I really believe he is an excellent young man, although he may in some instances carry his ideas too far.

*John Skinner*

### 1892 [Perthshire]

Went to see Mrs McIntosh in the afternoon, much amused with the old mother, stone deaf and unable to leave her chair, but very affable and merry.

She sat in her arm-chair beside the kitchen fire, and opposite on the other side of the hearth sat two black and tan dachshunds belonging to Miss Grace, very precious and tied to the dresser with a bit of string.

Afterwards went along with the pony nearly to Guay. Met the Tinker caravans with baskets as we came back. What dirty shock-headed little rascals, but as merry as grigs on a fine day.

As to the lowest stratum of tinkers and tramps they are perfect savages, mean spirited and trembling in sight of the county policeman. You see very old ones, and when seasoned, they are tough.

I met a fine looking old woman on the Stanley road the other day whom I remember, not changed in the slightest during the last fifteen years, but the younger members of the gangs are much thinner by comparison, which prevents their increasing to the proportion of a plague, although prolific.

I should think they are very seldom tamed off the tramp. I remember one instance. I wonder what was the result of that little idyll, perhaps as well we do not know. There used to be a rather pretty modest-spoken girl who came round every summer with a company who sold baskets, her granny was blind. One year she did not appear with them, and we were told she had married a young fisherman on the west coast, and settled down.

*Beatrix Potter*

## 17 August

1925 [Lewes, Sussex]
Such a dazzlingly lovely morning felt I must do something, so paid £1 3s for a trouser press for Ernest. It came. I was automatically thanked and he never even unpacked it! Went off first to Bowls and after supper to Chess. In a *fury*, not with him but with my own fool self (for not knowing better), put it in his bedroom.

*Alice Dudeney*

# 18 August

1876 [Slackfields Farm, Derbyshire]
Cutting oats in Lime Close. Fetched one truck of lime from Station. Paid Messrs. Alton, Ales. Expenses, etc.

*Henry Hill*

2004 [Claxton, Norfolk]
Perhaps it's the way in which blackbirds cock their heads or half turn them sideways, as if trying to see things from a different point of view, that creates the impression of them being deeply reflective birds. Throw in their tameness and you cannot help but feel blessed by the trust of these intelligent creatures.

Aside from the two nests tucked into hedges in both the front and back gardens, the thing that's given me most pleasure this year is the berry's-eye view of blackbirds gorging themselves on rowan fruits. We have a hammock slung beneath the tree and as we gazed up so the birds reciprocated while they did a daily tour of the crop, hauling at the gorgeous clusters whenever the fancy took them and then dozing off with just a single berry-like eye keeping sentinel.

Psychologists suggest that small, rotund animals (think of puffins, penguins and owls) mimic the physical attributes of our babies and arouse feelings of tenderness. I suspect that blackbirds, with their plump bellies, share in this uneven distribution of human affection. I discovered curious confirmation of the process as I lay in the hammock because I found myself thinking – as I used to tell my daughters when they were tots – that they looked good enough to eat. Fortunately blackbirds are also good to think about and to hear. The song, that fine, fresh distilled music of the temperate world, is the very essence of the European spring. Sadly the song has lapsed with the end of their breeding, but blackbirds still mark our seasonal round. That fabulous mixture of blackbird black and rowan red forces me to a conclusion at which the rest of nature now hints. Autumn is upon us.

*Mark Cocker*

# 19 August

## 1870 [Clyro, Radnorshire]

Ben Lloyd of the Cwm Bryngwyn reeling up the steep field above Jacob's Ladder carrying a horse collar and butter tub. Just as I came up the drunken man fell sprawling on his back. He got up looking foolish and astonished, and I gave him some good advice which he took in good part at first. I asked if he were married. Oh, yes, and had great-grandchildren. A nice example to set them, I thought. When I said how his wife would be vexed and grieved to see him come rolling home, I found I had touched a tender point. He became savage at once, cursed and swore and threatened violence. Then he began to roar after me, but he could only stagger very slowly so I left him reeling and roaring, cursing parsons and shouting what he would do if he were younger, and that if a man did not get drunk he wasn't a man and of no good to himself or public houses, an argument so exquisite that I left it to answer itself.

*Francis Kilvert*

## 1961 [Machynlleth, Wales]

A few days ago I did the ridge-walk of Pumlumon: that is to say I did one of the finest ridge-walks in all Wales. I started in the north in Montgomeryshire, going by Glaslyn, a shining, circular, plantless, stony-margined lake set high in a purple heather moor. Then down to a long, water-lily lake called Bugeilyn, which means the Shepherd's Lake. But no shepherds live thereabouts now. Only hydro-electricians and their inevitable retinue of Irishmen. Not that there is anything new about Irishmen in the Welsh hills. They were here already in prehistoric times and maybe it was Irish fingers that dropped the little flint arrowheads found in the bog by Bugeilyn; and Irish hands that raised the once great cairns of Pumlumon.

If so I hope they enjoyed Pumlumon as much as I did: the view across Wales; the untrammelled, undulating miles of the high plateau; the mountain silence; the coolness of the uplands after the airless, hot valleys.

It was in a spirit of exhilaration that I came swiftly down the final great slopes of Nant-y-moch. After that who better to give me a lift back to civilisation than one whose joy it is to ring bells? To ring out the bells seemed a fitting end to such a day. So two hours after leaving Pumlumon's summit cairn I was watching a bob major being rung in the great square tower of the church of Llanbadarn near Aberystwyth.

*William Condry*

### 2002 [Claxton, Norfolk]

As I sit in the garden I watch and listen to the swifts swinging over the village in wide arcs before they plane off across the far fields. By early morning they have already been frantically busy for hours, yet their hard scream never loses any of its reckless power. It fires down on the earth like fragments of audible flak and I know that even as the bats emerge towards dusk, these swifts will be still hurtling overhead, still screaming to the heavens.

Suddenly they're back and in a flurry of wing beats make a momentary pass at the houses opposite, before breaking away once more. It looks like a failed attempt at entry to the nest chamber but these creatures are so consummate in their aerial manoeuvre it is hard to believe that anything they deliberately undertake ends in error. Then finally they return and I am rewarded with what I long to see: that half-metre wingspan collapsing down, scraping the gutter edge as it folds away and the bird vanishing into its improbably small hole. The swift's conversion from black meteor to terrestrial flesh-and-bone always has an air of the miraculous, like some magical sword that will enter a scabbard a third the width of its blade.

*Mark Cocker*

## 20 August

### 1892 [Perthshire]

After lunch went to the flower-show which was flat. It was held in what the Scotch call a Marquee. I understand that on the previous night they danced. McDougall said because they were just moribund, a curious reason for dancing.

*Beatrix Potter*

# 21 August

1756 [East Hoathly, Sussex]

*Saturday.* In the morn about 8 o'clock I was sent for down to Mr Porter's to be witness to something, but what I do not know. (But I conjecture it to be articles of agreement between Mr Porter and some other for the sale of a farm of Mr Porter's lying in Essex, and now in the occupation of Tho. Wright). Mr Porter signed one paper, and the gentleman's name that signed the other was, I think, John Benison. He was dressed in a band, and had a gown or cassock on and seemed as if he belonged to some college or hospital. Miss Dinah Binge and myself witnessed both the papers . . . This day the subscription purse of £50 was run for on Lewes Downs when there was only 2 started for the same; *viz.*, Lord Craven's bay mare Princess Mary, and Mr Howe's chestnut horse, which was won by the mare with ease, there being only two heats, though the odds at starting were 21 to 10 on the horse.

*Thomas Turner*

# 22 August

1875 [En route by boat from Oxford to London]

I had an awfully bad night, kept waking up at all hours, thanks to Clarke who snored and ground his teeth like a maniac all the night. This was the first time I had slept in the same room with Clarke, and I was very glad it was the last. We got up at 7, took towels, went across the bridge to the weir and bathed. It was very jolly, the river just there being very wide, and a tremendous rush of water from the weir. We went back to the Hotel and ordered breakfast, and after bullying the waiters and waiting nearly an hour, we got some. It was quite on a par with the supper we had the night before: everything very bad and served in a most uncomfortable style. The coffee was about the substance of mud, the bread was stale and the ham was very salt. The three egg-cups which we used appeared to be the only ones the establishment possessed, as some other fellows that were having their breakfast at another table in the coffee room, had their eggs brought in wine glasses. We asked for a slop basin. The waiter looked as if he thought it quite an unnecessary luxury, and brought us a finger-glass, that, I suppose, being the nearest substitute he could find. After breakfast, whilst the other two packed up and got the boat ready, I walked to the town with my can, and bought half a gallon of milk.

*Howard Williams*

## 23 August

1970 [Belmont, Lyme Regis]
A sparrowhawk in the garden. The only one I have seen this year.

*John Fowles*

## 24 August

1921 [Lewes, Sussex]
After supper Mr Gale came in with acute hump. Thought he was going to cry. Talked about his flat and his furniture. Then, very lugubriously: 'I've got two turkeys in the sitting room.' I – dropping my crochet – *what??*! But he meant carpets.

*Alice Dudeney*

1981 [The Lake District]
When the cars are crawling bumper to bumper through Ambleside and the fells are 'wick wi' fwoak' I sometimes go into the 'back of Skiddaw' country to get away from it all. Here, even in the August holidays, you can be reasonably sure of having untracked hills to yourself and a mountain day free from the irritations of traffic, crowds, noise, litter and all the excesses of mass tourism. You could hardly call it exciting country – the only climbing crags are on Carrock Fell – but the spaciousness of these lonely, heather fells, the vast views stretching from the familar peaks of central Lakeland to the

Scottish hills, the welcome absence of tracks and cairns, and interesting, even dramatic, links with our past together provide an unusual flavour not found elsewhere in the national park. The ruins of the early British hill-fort more than 2,000 feet above sea level on the summit of Carrock Fell, for instance. Why was it built, and how? And the old derelict mines tucked away in remote gills, miles from anywhere; what incredibly hard lives these men must have had in these dark tunnels and shafts so high in the hills! There are nine summits of more than 2,000 feet in this desolate country that John Peel and his little Galloway knew so well and you can collect them all in a far from demanding day – except, perhaps, in bad weather, when you'll need to steer by compass. Knott (2,329 feet) is the highest, High Pike the most northerly summit in the district, and remote Great Sea Fell the most flamboyantly named. Not to be compared with the real Scafell, of course, but I have seen views, in shredding mist, from its rounded summit of a Mediterranean blue Solway and the sunlit Lowland hills that made one feel good just to be alive.

*A. Harry Griffin*

# 25 August

## 1818 [Yorkshire]

Heard of a famous dandy at Harrowgate of the name of Stewart, a relative of Lord Castlereagh, who being asked by the Master of Ceremonies to dance enquired of him if the lady he meant to introduce him to was handsome, and being told she had a good fortune asked if she danced well and being answered in the affirmative said, 'Trot her out.' When he came to her he took out his quizzing glass and having eyed the lady some time through it says to the M.C. 'Trot her back again.'

*Benjamin Newton*

## 1892 [Birnam, Perthshire]

Birnam Games. I did not go. Spent great part of the day standing on two garden benches and a buffet, all three of us, and McDougall looking over the yew hedge. It is an interesting and enviable point of view.

It came to a large proportion of the seven thousand spectators poking away through the small Railway Station, stragglers getting over the white station palings, seven feet high. Mr Kinnaird [the station master] told papa privately he hoped it would be wet, however they were got off safely. It was a gloriously fine day between wet ones.

Watching the people go away there were very few intoxicated, but I was sorry to see three-quarters of those few, wee young boys. The games are singularly more decently conducted than formerly, when drink was sold in the grounds, and great Highlanders were brawling and lying about by the dozen. I remember a long red knife and two savages washing their bloody heads in the river, but no one paid any particular heed. The police body were only there to prevent the *laddies* from dodging through the railings.

*Beatrix Potter*

## 26 August

1921 [Renishaw – home of the Sitwell family, Derbyshire]
The lake is large, ornamental, and too shallow for an effective suicide.

*Siegfried Sassoon*

1934 [Perth]
If you ask me why I deem it worthy to fill up a page such as this day by day – shall I not reply, 'Worth-whileness hasn't very much to do with it'? The most natural reply might be, 'Because I cannot go out and chop a basket of firewood or take the weeds out of the garden path.' Yet that wouldn't be a wholly honest answer. We are all sustained at times by the thought that whatever we may be we are certainly a solitary manifestation of creation; not a single other creature in all the history of the world has been just as our self – nor another will be like us. Why not put on record something of the world as seen by this lonely 'ego': here and there perhaps a sentence may be born whose father is reality.

*William Soutar*

# 27 August

## 1826 [Abbotsford, the Scottish Borders]

Today we journeyed through the hills and amongst the storms; the weather rather bullying. We viewed the Grey Mare's Tail, and I still felt confident in crawling along the ghastly bank by which you approach the fall. I will certainly get some road of application to Mr Hope-Johnstone, to pray him to make the place accessible. We got home before half-past five, having travelled forty miles.[*]

*Sir Walter Scott*

## 1995 [Hampshire]

Jill Balcon, Keith Baxter, Alan Bennett, M [his wife, Merula] and I lunched, in a very casual way, under the tangled strawberry vine and spreading fig tree (with its wooden fruit) in what I refer to as the kitchen arbour. We felt quite jolly in the dappled sunlight and could easily persuade ourselves we were five hundred miles farther south. I went into the kitchen to make coffee and while I was there a fan and her female friend worked their way through the hedge with a gift (God knows what) for me. She didn't spot me. M said I wasn't available and asked her to leave. Luckily the dogs didn't attack, which would have left me open to legal proceedings, I suppose, for occupying my own land and protecting my privacy. The lady has been a nuisance for years, sending me unwanted pyjamas, for instance, at Christmas. I have never met her.

*Alec Guinness*

# 28 August

## 1985 [Badminton, Gloucestershire]

Met Eardley [Knollys, a painter] at Hungerford, The Bear, at eleven this morning. We walked down the canal to Kintbury where we drank ginger

---

[*]The Grey Mare's Tail, situated between Moffat and Selkirk, is the highest waterfall in the Scottish Borders, with a three-part drop of sixty metres. Sir William Hope-Johnstone (1766–1831) was MP for Dumfriesshire from 1804–30. The Grey Mare's Tail is today owned by the National Trust for Scotland.

ale and ate croutons – delicious. Then walked back again. About eight miles in all and I felt very weary. Not so Eardley, who was as spry as ever, and would have walked further. From Hungerford we drove to Littlecote, which is to be resold next week by the bloody tycoon who bought it lock, stock and barrel from the Wills family last month. It is very dreadful that these mushroom millionaires can speculate in this way with England's heritage. But it is not a nice house, an over-restored rich-man-of-the-Twenties house. Best things are the armour and buff jerkins from Cromwellian times that belonged to the Popham family. Interesting Cromwellian chapel, with pulpit but no altar, and original pews, screen and gallery. Great Hall, with shuffle table of inordinate length. Pretty library, with nice black Wedgwood plaster cast busts over the bookcases, which I coveted. Long Gallery, with restored ceiling. No, not a satisfactory or an endearing house.

The tranquillity and isolation of canals. We passed along distant stretches of water between a thick drama of trees, poplar, grey willow, birch. Sometimes a rosy red brick bridge, constructed on a curve, with knapped flint – superb engineering of Regency times. The long tow-path flanked by the brown canal and a hedge of pinkish willow-herb. A world of its own, disturbed by the occasional flight of a moorhen.

*James Lees-Milne*

## c.2003 [South of England]

Lapwings – also known as green plovers or peewits – have finished breeding and are now flocking in the fields and on the muddy shores of estuaries. Even large flocks of them, with their dark green backs, can be hard to make out on ploughed land, but when they fly up the whole sky is full of flashing black and silver. They assemble in the air and move off in rather floppy-looking flight. On the ground they tilt their whole body forward to pick up food, and their long crests sometimes flutter in the wind. Lapwings from the Continent have already begun to cross the North Sea, and will spend the winter wandering round in company with our native birds.

*Derwent May*

# 29 August

### 1879 [Surbiton, Surrey]

Dry, windy morning: slight showers, dry again. Arum – some all red, some with green berries. Moth coloured and humble-bee on thistle-head together, the humble-bee under the broad wing of the moth, happy together.

*Richard Jefferies*

# 30 August

### 1755 [East Hoathly, Sussex]

*Saturday*. This morn my wife and I had words about going to Lewes tomorrow. My reason for not going was on account of my owing Mr Roase some money, and was loath to go till could pay him the balance. Oh! what a happiness must there be in a married state when there is a sincere regard on both sides and each party truly satisfied with each other's merit; but it is impossible for tongue or pen to express the uneasiness that attends the contrary.

*Thomas Turner*

# 31 August

### 1782 [Weymouth, Dorset]

I begin to be heartily tired of this place for it is all sameness and dullness: a gentleman left it some days since, saying he would not stay in any place, where were neither wenching, drinking, or gaming; and neither of the three are practised here . . .

*John Byng*

### 1949 [East Anglia]

Look out of bedroom window at 6.30 am to see a covey of partridges on lawn. Am fascinated by sight of so much potential food so near . . . and yet so far. So is William, who has come upstairs to watch us drink our early tea, and is, as usual, stretched out in his favourite 'British Lion' attitude along one window-sill. A town-bred cat, he is new to live partridges. But instinct tells them what they are. And the expression on his furry face as he watches them, now picking at the grass, now immobile and practically invisible against a flower bed, is highly entertaining. Then one looks skyward, and sees both of us. On previous visits they have imagined themselves unobserved, and have left at their leisure, squeezing between the wood palings one by one. This time there is a warning screech, a whirr of wings, and fourteen feathered bullets hurtle over the palings and take cover in the adjacent hay field. Shall be surprised if they come again, for game birds seem to have developed an uncanny faculty for knowing the date. And although they would be safe enough in our garden, they are not to know that, and from to-morrow think of man as their enemy.

*Elizabeth M. Harland*

# SEPTEMBER

# 1 September

## 1892 [Perthshire]

I shall never forget old Mr Wood coming to Dalguise one hot Monday afternoon in search of 'worms', and producing a present out of his hat of about two dozen buff-tip caterpillars, collected on the road. They ought to have been in a red cotton pocket handkerchief, but they had got loose amongst his venerable grey locks. He is still living and much the same to look at, but what McDougall [a gamekeeper] calls 'a wee bit dumpy', rather past.

*Beatrix Potter*

## 1945 [Kent]

Yesterday we took lunch, ducks' eggs, nut meat, tomatoes, crispbread, cherry jam, honey and coffee in the car and drove to Peckham Old Church on the hill, where we stopped and ate, gazing down over the churchyard to the far view.

As we were eating, the rural district sewage tanks drove up and emptied their loads straight into the woods. We heard the sewage swishing and gurgling and then the smell struck us in the face in sudden gusts. We shut the car window on that side and soon it dispersed; but surely this is a very extraordinary thing to do, to empty sewage straight into a wood.

Afterwards a fair-haired youth, with a darker, very faint beard just sprouting, told us that they sometimes just emptied the sewage into a field, although people had complained, so he supposed they now came and dumped into this lovely wood. He was gentle and docile, and so rather likeable and sad. One felt he was soon going to be ground down.

*Denton Welch*

# 2 September

**1896 [Sawrey, the Lake District]**
Hawkeshead Show. The only prize *we* won was for *common turnips*.

*Beatrix Potter*

**1995 [Hampshire]**
A clap of thunder and then welcome rain for half an hour. Proper rain, not the feeble drizzle we've had a couple of times in the last few days; but I fear it hasn't come in time to save parched trees, which look autumnal and rattle their brittle leaves.

*Alec Guinness*

# 3 September

**1800 [Grasmere, the Lake District]**
A fine coolish morning. I ironed till ½ past three – now very hot. I then went to a funeral at John Dawson's. About 10 men and 4 women. Bread cheese and ale. They talked sensibly and cheerfully about common things. The dead person 56 years of age buried by the parish. The coffin was neatly lettered and painted black and covered with a decent cloth. They set the corpse down at the door and while we stood within the threshold the men with their hats off sang with decent and solemn countenances a verse of a funeral psalm. The corpse was then borne down the hill and they sang till they had got past the Town-end. I was affected to tears in the house, the coffin lying before me. There were no near kindred, no children. When we got out of the dark house the sun was shining and the prospect looked so divinely beautiful as I never saw it. It seemed more sacred than I had ever seen it, and yet more allied to human life. The green fields, neighbours of the churchyard, were as green as possible and with the brightness of the sunshine looked quite gay. I thought she was going to a quiet spot and I could not help weeping very much. When we came to the bridge they began to sing again and stopped 4 times before they entered the churchyard. The

priest met us – he did not look as a man ought to do on such an occasion – I had seen him half-drunk the day before in a pot-house. Before we came with the corpse one of the company observed he wondered what sort of cue 'our Parson would be in'.

*Dorothy Wordsworth*

1871 [Clyro, Radnorshire]
I went to Bettws in light rain and preached extempore on the Good Samaritan from the Gospel for the day. A red cow with a foolish white face came up to the window by the desk and stared in while I was preaching.

*Francis Kilvert*

## 4 September

1872 [Binbrook Hall, nr Louth, Lincolnshire]
My shearling lambs are in a fearfully crippled condition. It is painful to witness the amount of suffering the poor animals have to endure, and all on account of man's sin. No one can look sympathetically over his crambling flocks and herds writhing in the anguish of physical pain, with tongues like pieces of raw flesh and feet a mass of fevered corruption without feeling regret and remorse concerning his sins which have produced such a train of diseases through the ranks of animal life.

*Cornelius Stovin*

1946 [Inverness-shire]
The last bramble-pickers haunt the precincts of the wood; they seem like shadows rather than like people, as they bend over the ditch; their exuberance is gone. They leave the wood – and many unpicked brambles – while it is still early evening. On the road townwards their animation returns; they talk and laugh; they are no longer shadows, they are people, happy, because they are homeward bound; in half an hour they will be back in town, in known territory, away from the strangeness of a vast wood, unfamiliar to them at all times, but overwhelming in the gloaming of a September night.

*Jessie Kesson*

# 5 September

## 1872 [Clyro, Radnorshire]

I was out early before breakfast this morning bathing from the sands. There was a delicious feeling of freedom in stripping in the open air and running down naked to the sea, where the waves were curling white with foam and the red morning sunshine glowed upon the naked limbs of the bathers.

*Francis Kilvert*

# 6 September

## 1872 [Binbrook Hall, nr Louth, Lincolnshire]

Last night in the yard the two waggoners were loudly singing an obscene song. I felt it my duty to hush them.

*Cornelius Stovin*

## 1896 [Sawrey, the Lake District]

In the afternoon we again had that old person Tom Thornley. It is my opinion that he is half-baked, not two minutes would he talk about one thing except ghost stories, whereby he made my mother very uncomfortable.

*Beatrix Potter*

## c.2000 [Walnut Tree Farm, Suffolk]

Yesterday I noticed that on the tin roof of the woodshed, where I had lined plums in rows in the valleys of the corrugated-iron roof to dry in the sun as prunes – an experiment – a spider has noticed the number of visiting fruit flies and other insects, and constructed a funnel-necked web immediately next to the rows of plums. It has got lucky straight away and a dozen victims were struggling in their silky bonds by the late morning.

*Roger Deakin*

# 7 September

1791 [Selborne, Hampshire]
Cut 125 cucumbers. Young martins, several hundreds, congregate on the tower, church and yew-tree. Hence I conclude that most of the second broods are flown. Such an assemblage is very beautiful, & amusing, did it not bring with it an association of ideas tending to make us reflect that winter is approaching; & that these little birds are consulting how they may avoid it.

*Gilbert White*

1985 [Badminton, Gloucestershire]
A lovely, cloudless, golden day. A. [Alvilde, his wife] went out to a luncheon party and I went for a long walk with Folly [the whippet] down the Gloucester–Sharpness canal, two hours from Slimbridge to Frampton. Dragonflies with brown striped bodies, and peacock butterflies. A wind ruffling the water. A few boats passing when the bridges are wound, not up but round. Talked to a middle-aged couple with largish boat moored. They said you could get to Manchester by canal and the River Severn, and then to Leeds by another canal. Felt pleased with myself, happy that I can still walk six miles.

*James Lees-Milne*

# 8 September

1871 [Binbrook Hall, nr Louth, Lincolnshire]
Hands are so scarce that we have made very slow progress with harvest operations. I have still sixty acres of barley down unbound. It is in a very critical condition. The early part of yesterday was very bright and breezy and by noon they had finished binding the wheat. By the time the barley was fairly dry the clouds had gathered and the rain began to fall. I am afraid a second drenching such as continued through the night will spoil the sample. The prospect is a very anxious and dark one. The extreme luxuriance of

the clover may possibly prove fatal to the corn. We need a drying apparatus this morning to save our barley crop from deterioration if not destruction. Perhaps the Almighty may send us one. He has abundance in His stores. He can change the winds and disperse the clouds and dry up the moisture as well as send it. How delightfully welcome the streaks of blue sky which I beheld this morning in looking out from my bedroom window. The barley was no sooner dry than it became saturated a second time. Would it be presumptuous if I urged my case before the Lord?

*Cornelius Stovin*

### 1936 [Perth]

There is a 'worthy' minister at Redgarton, the Rev Dauvit Grahame who is rather too fond of his dram; and some years ago he was called up before his session. When the meeting was about to begin Grahame jumped up and said: 'Gentlemen, a preliminary word, please. I am well aware why you have summoned me here this evening but allow me to ask two questions before we proceed. First, has any man among you assisted me home when I have been the worse of liquor? And second, is there any man among you whom I have *not* assisted home when he was the worse of liquor?' As the answer to both questions proved to be in the negative, the Rev Dauvit turned about – and no doubt left for the inn at Pitcairngreen.

*William Soutar*

# 9 September

### 1871 [Binbrook Hall, nr Louth, Lincolnshire]

Rose this morning about 5 o'clock. I thought I heard the pattering of the rain upon my garden groves. In drawing aside the blind to my utter dismay the water was standing in a pool on the carriage drive, which indicated a heavy fall of rain for several hours. This is the third drenching for my barley. It is a mercy that it had become tolerably dry yesterday, for under the hedgerows it had already begun to sprout. This is a morning of disappointment to us farmers. Yesterday we were vigorously retrieving matters, carrying in the morning and tying in the afternoon and the foreman and I were planning for managing most the binding today. But all our schemes are upset by Divine Providence for some wise end. Perhaps to drive us to prayer to more humble dependence upon His Almighty power and wisdom and love. He makes us behold His severity as well as goodness. How dark and gloomy the prospect! How thick and hazy the air! How leaden the skies! Yesterday I was pulling ketlocks out of the turnips, also neadles, redrobbin and scarlet poppies. It is a proverb that weeds grow apace. Experience brings home the truth. There is not a weed now growing in my turnip fields but will come to maturity and yield its thousandfold increase many months before the turnip itself. It forms part of the curse still lingering in the ground. What a tenacious hold they still have upon our soil. If we cease our vigilance they soon become predominant. A skilful and persevering hand is required to maintain empire over this department of natural laws and forces.

*Cornelius Stovin*

# 10 September

## 1892 [Perthshire]

There have been two gentlemen from Belfast at the hotel, who tried to take in little Mr Peter Grant at the Lending Library, in some ingeniously complicated way which I could not follow. Something about the three volumes of a novel, and taking one back and getting another whole set, until he claimed eight books instead of two. He actually wanted to argue the point with me, said the aggrieved Peter, a clear proof that the inhabitants of Ulster are Scotchmen. I do not know if he was a representative man of any mark, but he assured Mr Grant with relish that Belfast would fight.

Mr Grant himself – 'Peter' – my grandfather says to me 'Peter' etc. is an intelligent little man, but if anything, too fluent. His remarks are worth hearing, but he button-holes, and has an embarrassing short sighted habit of peering close up to you with a puckered, spectacled face. He is a retired soldier, and has strong views on compulsory army retirement, vice-superannuated prime ministers. Mamma detests him.

*Beatrix Potter*

# 11 September

1892 [Perthshire]
Went to [Dunkeld] Cathedral. They keep up one old custom, I mean locking the door during service. One may hear the rasping of the key during the final prayer. I wonder what happens if anyone faints, not that I imagine a native capable of such an indiscretion.

*Beatrix Potter*

# 12 September

1958 [Keswick, the Lake District]
These misty, gentle mornings are the epitome of early autumn. Blue smoke arises vertically from the farms, the mountains are half-hidden in cloud, and sounds carry far across the valley in the still air. The hedges in the lane which leads down to the lake-marsh are tangled with honeysuckle, pale flowers and scarlet berries both together, with the heavy heads of ripening haws, green crab-apples and elder leaves which show the first hint of autumn purple. The stooks of the corn in the fields lean damply and rather drunkenly together, and six magpies are gathered in a little knot on the stubble until first one, then two, and then all rise fluttering in the air. They strike at one another with wings and feet outthrust, more like gamecocks than magpies; their severe black and white loses its severity here against the golden stubble and is gay and lively. Their clattering voices mix with the other morning sounds: a clucking hen, a heron on its way to the lake, and the sound of running water. There is a very old ash tree near the river; its upper branches are mouldering away, riddled by goat-moths and

woodpeckers, and its trunk is just a hollow shell. Out of its roots a runnel of decayed earth and owl pellets spreads into the grass; not one owl but many, indeed generations of owls must be responsible for so many pellets. They are made up of fur, little bones and skulls of mice, shrews, and voles, and some of the skulls still have the orange teeth characteristic of these small rodents. Everything – trees, grass, and hedges – is hung with dew-soaked cobwebs.

*Enid J. Wilson*

# 13 September

### 1756 [East Hoathly, Sussex]

At home all the morning. About 11.30 I went to Mayfield in order to see a cricket match, *viz.*, Lindfield against Mayfield. When I came to Mayfield, there were four of Lindfield out, but Lindfield got 52 runs the first innings and Mayfield 48, which made Lindfield 4 ahead. Lindfield got 31 the second innings, which made them 35 ahead of Mayfield, who went in and got them with only one wicket up. I came home about 6.50. I paid for the standing of my horse 2d., which was all I spent, for I neither ate nor drunk while I was gone, nor nothing before I went but dry bread and cocoa, tea and some coffee mixed . . . My opinion concerning the game was that Lindfield kept the field best and batted best in general, but could not bowl. And what is remarkable, they was all tradesmen, and but one above 25 years of age, and I think eleven of very civil men.

*Thomas Turner*

### 1816 [Yorkshire]

Rode through a most beautiful country to Otley. The roads in many places for a mile or two scarcely passable, the first four miles from Rochdale excessively bad, two miles in the middle between Halifax and Bradford very bad, a mile down to the bridge over the Aire between Bradford and Otley, these parts are the worst, but it is a matter of great surprize that the whole of the road should be in such indifferent repair and some execrably bad through the whole of this manufacturing district, that the whole and sole cause where the road is not pitched is the not letting the water off or breaking the stones and that the whole distance from Congleton to Otley there were not 20 persons employed in either of these occupations, notwithstanding they tell you half the people are out of employ and every three miles at furthest there is a shilling turnpike for chaise and pair. The environs of Rochdale, Ripponden, Halifax, Bradford, the bridge over the Aire and Otley are beautiful in the extreme and were it not for the reflection that the greatness of Great Britain depended I may say principally on the defacing of the hand of nature in these parts by the hand of man, which produces not only riches in every way from exportation and taxation at home and raises in time of war an innumerable population which is seen over the whole district for the armies, one could not help regretting that scenes so romantic and lovely should be impaired and destroyed by the black steam engines, but the yarn, the cloth, the cotton, the morals of the people destroyed by being crowded together and the hammers of the water engines perpetually affrighting quiet and comfort from vallies in which at first view one would imagine were placed by nature in the most remote and sequestered situations for the peculiar residence of innocence and peace. The seats or rather the villas of the manufacturers like the citizens in the neighbourhood of London have neatness to recommend them but scarcely any character through the whole district that distinguishes one very much from another.

*Benjamin Newton*

## 1987 [Badminton, Gloucestershire]

Went to the tedious annual meeting of the local branch of the CPRE [Campaign to Protect Rural England] in the hall at the House. I sat at the back so I might escape, which I did after ninety minutes. A nice young man from the National Parks Commission gave a talk, but I could hardly hear him. Deaf and blind, what is the use of my attending such occasions? He wore a signet ring on his middle finger, usually a sign of bedintness among men. Looking at the audience, I noticed as usual that they were all of the middle-class; none from the lower, and needless to say not one of the Somerset family. One may deride the middle classes, but it is they who really care about country things. Having looked through Simon Blow's book on hunting, I think I hate the upper classes. Their arrogance, their unquestioning superiority is, or until recently was, insufferable.

*James Lees-Milne*

# 14 September

### 1791 [Selborne, Hampshire]

Hop-picking goes on without the least interruption. Stone-curlews cry late in the evenings. The congregating flocks of *hirundines* on the church & tower are very beautiful, & amusing! When they fly-off together from the Roof, on any alarm, they quite swarm in the air. But they soon settle in heaps, & preening their feathers, & lifting up their wings to admit the sun, seem highly to enjoy the warm situation. Thus they spend the heat of the day, preparing for their emigration, &, as it were, consulting when & where they are to go. The flight about the church seems to consist chiefly of house-martins, about 400 in number: but there are other places of rendezvous about the village frequented at the same time. The swallows seem to delight more in holding their assemblies on trees.

*Gilbert White*

### 1947 [Crouch, Kent]

As I was driving home by the Pilgrim's Way above Wrotham Water I came upon a mass of scarlet and red in the corner of a field, that I first mistook for a bright new farm implement. Then as I drew nearer I saw that the mass was soft and not shiny. I then half-explained it to myself as a bundle or folded tent belonging to some very brilliant gypsy. Only when I was almost upon it did I realise that the heap was a man and a woman lying in each other's arms on the stiff dried-up grass. They seemed perfectly still, locked and twisted together intricately – the black legs and arms of the man over the vivid scarlet sausage of the girl's dress. I wondered if they would always remember this Sunday, or whether it would be lost in a vast heap of other clinging, clutching holidays. Below them the cars rushed by on the arterial road; a man got out of a high old-fashioned Morris, clutched up a handful of yellow flowers and thrust them through the top of the almost shut window to fall on the head of an unheeding child.

*Denton Welch*

# 15 September

1907 [Inverness-shire]
I donned a kilt for the Highland Ball at Glenfemess. It was anxious work at first, as it is a garment with no notion of privacy, and delights in giving all present tantalising glimpses of things unseen. However, with careful manipulation and a pair of drawers, I got through the evening tolerably. It was quite comfortable to dance in, but should be a godsend to mosquitoes.

*Sir Alan 'Tommy' Lascelles*

# 16 September

1791 [Norfolk]
A Hare being seen near my House by Ben I went out with my Dogs, found her, had a very fine Course and killed her. Dinner to day Jugged Hare, very good.

*James Woodforde*

# 17 September

1907 [Inverness-shire]
A peaceful weekend, in which little of interest happened . . . Even if it weren't Harewood, it would always be a most comfortable house to stay in. There are four essentials to comfort – shaving-water that will stay hot for

an hour, boot-jacks in every bedroom, grapes for breakfast, and *Ruff's Guide [to the Turf]* in the rear [lavatory].

Harewood has them all except, oddly, the last.

*Sir Alan 'Tommy' Lascelles*

### 1944 [Kent]

What shall I write about? Shall I write about the bright morning with the sharp bird notes and the delicious spongy cooings of the pigeons on the roof of this house? Shall I write about the noises of the aeroplanes, the last flower on the wisteria that I can see mauve and pitiable out of my window? Shall I write about the war ending? Or my breakfast of porridge, toast and marmalade and coffee? Or just about autumn. Waking up cold in the morning coming back cold through the low blanket of mist by the waterfall last night – from the pub on Shipbourne Common, where Eric bought me a thimbleful of cherry brandy for three shillings, and we heard the loud-mouthed woman holding forth on cubbing before breakfast.

In this house now – in the big part which Eric and I are sleeping in because Mrs Sloman is away, I have an eighteenth century wooden mantel in my room, taken from an old house. Then there is a china green basin and brass locks with drop handles to the doors. The furniture 'limed oak', ugly, and a chinchilla Persian cat is sleeping and grunting and dribbling on my bed. Outside the window a tractor is humming. Eric is having a cold bath, so that the water pipes sing.

*Denton Welch*

## 18 September

### 1995 [Combe Florey, Somerset]

A young man walking outside York recently found a dead badger by the roadside and decided its head might look nice on his living-room wall. So he cut off the head, took it home . . . and put it in his fridge.

What nobody had told him was that since some drivelling new law passed by the present Government, it is illegal to take a dead badger home with you, or possess part of one. As a result, James Pipes, 21, was sent to prison for three months.

The brief news report does not tell us how York police discovered that Pipes was keeping part of a dead badger in his fridge. Perhaps they possess ultrasound detection equipment in their helicopters, able to pinpoint pieces of dead badger to within inches. Or perhaps it was part of a routine inspection of fridges they have up north, to ensure they are not eating each other.

But we must congratulate York police on bringing this young criminal to book. If it had not been for James Pipes, the dead badger might still be lying intact by the roadside, adding its fragrance to the Yorkshire air. Can we really think three months in prison is enough?

*Auberon Waugh*

## 19 September

1988 [Belmont, Lyme Regis]
Peter Benson was born in 1956; he is thirty-two years old. He comes to help in the garden every Wednesday. Last week he said he must charge £4 an hour, so I pay him 15–16 for his usual stint here. He brought two short stories he had published in recent collections today. I like him, both as a writer and a human being. His quickness and obliqueness. They are a different breed from us, I mean my generation. Knopf sent me Harold Brodkey's stories the other day. I feel slightly they are speaking a different language; the unsettling thing is that it is the same.

*John Fowles*

## 20 September

1720 [Oxfordshire]
Yesterday was a great Foot-race at Woodstock, for 1400 libs., between a running Footman of the D. of Wharton's and a running footman of Mr

Diston's of Woodstock, round the 4 Mile course. Mr Diston's Man, being about 25 years of Age (& the Duke's about 45), got it with ease, out-distancing the Duke's near half a Mile. They both ran naked, there being not the least scrap of any thing to cover them, not so much as Shoes or Pumps, wich was look'd upon deservedly as ye Height of Impudence, & the greatest Affront to the Ladies, of wich there was a very great Number.

*Thomas Hearne*

## 21 September

1991 [Yorkshire]

Of all the hilltop villages in this part of the country, none sits more solidly upon on its ridge than Bolsterstone. Up here the Pennine air seems always fresh because we are almost 1,000 feet above sea level. The other day we took the ridge-top path that runs eastwards from the village. There wasn't a breath of breeze under a cloudless sky. No sound came to us as we went along through wiry grass burnished by a rainless month and late harebells were still shining bravely. Cows were grazing the high pasture over the wall to our left as we sat to look back. The squat tower of the dark-stoned church crouched among its graveyard trees, but we could see nothing of the medieval castle that once dominated the settlement. Below our belvedere, to the south, More Hall and Broomhead reservoirs, like the harebells, reflected a Mediterranean sky. At the head of Ewden Dale, beyond the reservoirs, the purple profile of the Broomhead Moors dominated the horizon and, now and then, we heard the 'pop, pop' of a shooting party on what, in Edwardian times, was England's record-breaking grouse moor. However, our immediate ridge-top world was quiet. Over the wall a resting cow had her eyes closed and ears back as she chewed her cud. An ear flicked off a visiting fly. We were all at peace up here.

*Roger A. Redfern*

# 22 September

1906 [Perthshire]

Walked to the Lake of Menteith and back across the hills. Unlike most of the Scotch lochs the shores are flat and marshy and surrounded by large beds of reeds, which are a great resort of Water-fowl of all kinds. The Lake is noted for the large number of Pike it contains. The walls of the little inn-parlour on the edge of the Lake are hung round with fine, stuffed specimens in cases, that have been captured in its waters.

Rowed across to Inchmanhone Priory on one of the two islands. Here were huge old Spanish Chestnut trees, supposed to have been planted by the monks, and the largest Nut trees I have ever seen; also the Box tree, said to have been planted by Queen Mary.

*Edith Holden*

# 23 September

1979 [Sanna, Ardnamurchan]

I saw a wren today as I walked the shoreline. Or rather I did not quite see it but glimpsed it, creeping among the rocks. What a skulking slithering side-on creature this bird is! I was strongly tempted to make the old sign of avoidance. The wren is the true bird of ill-omen and not your obvious childish raven. One can readily understand why they held wren hunts in the experienced Middle Ages, why whole villages abandoned themselves to sticks and cries and madness. You may find a wren in your tame garden but that is only because it was there first. Wrens have undomestic souls.

*Alasdair Maclean*

# 24 September

*c.*2003 [South of England]

More mice are coming into houses at night. Many of them are house mice, which live in gardens and under hedges as well as indoors, especially in the summer. In a house, they will visit many places in the course of a night, finding routes above ceilings and behind wainscoting.

Besides small scraps of food that have been dropped on the floor, they eat plaster and glue. They have good night vision and keen ears. In the morning, their small black droppings show where they have been. Long-tailed field mice, or wood mice, also venture into houses in the winter. They are larger and browner than house mice, with more conspicuous ears and a dangling tail. However, they are less likely to make their home in a house.

*Derwent May*

# 25 September

1698 [Wotton, Surrey]

A report of many suddainly dying by being abroad somewhere in Barkshire in a stinking fogg.

*John Evelyn*

1877 [Dorset]

Went to Shroton Fair. In a twopenny show saw a woman beheaded. In another a man whose hair grew on one side of his face.

*Thomas Hardy*

1892 [Perthshire]

Employed all day drawing a ram's head, borrowed from Mr Hendry the *Flesher.*

*Beatrix Potter*

# 26 September

### 1818 [Yorkshire]

Had a thorn taken out of the middle of that part of the body which Derham calls a large cushion of flesh by my wife last night.

*Benjamin Newton*

# 27 September

### 1876 [Slackfields Farm, Derbyshire]

*Dull* Carting manure into Birches. 9 loads. Delivered two colt foals at Mr Bailey's Chaddesden.

*Henry Hill*

### 1758 [East Hoathly, Sussex]

In the morn my brother and self set out for Eastbourne where we arrived about 7.30. We breakfasted at Mr Sam Beckett's, where we also dined on a shoulder of lamb roasted with onion sauce and potatoes (my family at home dining on a sheep's head, lights etc. boiled; Master Watford, being at work for us, dined with them.) We came home about 10.20, but not sober, and I may say by the providence of God my life preserved. For being very drunk, my horse took the wrong way and run into a traverse with me and beat me off, but, thanks be to God, received no damage. Oh, what a poor creature I am after so many weak endeavours to prevent getting in liquor, that I must still remain so silly!

*Thomas Turner*

# 28 September

## 1781 [Fyfield, Hampshire]

Tobacco leaves gathered and cut green by R. Smith, then dried and proved to be excellent, with a fine flavour like ye Havannah Segars. Smoked at ye Parish meeting at Easter and much appreciated.

*Henry White*

## 1870, Michaelmas Eve [Clyro, Radnorshire]

I went out for a walk with Mr G. Venables over the Doldowlod suspension bridge across the Wye and up the Llandrindod road.

We fell into conversation about Wordsworth and the following are some of Mr George Venables' recollections of him.

'I was staying at Ambleside with some people who knew Wordsworth and was introduced to him there. Then I went over to tea at his house, Rydal Mount. Wordsworth's sister Dorothy was in the room, an old woman at the time. She was depressed and took no part in the conversation and no notice of what was passing. Her brother told me he attributed the failure of her health to the long walks she used to take with him, e.g. from Llyswen to Llanthony.

'He said he met "Peter Bell" on the road between Builth and Rhayader.

'One evening riding near Rydal I saw Wordsworth sauntering towards me wearing a shade over his eyes, which were weak, and crooning out aloud some lines of poems which he was composing. I stopped to avoid splashing him and apologised for having intruded upon him. He said, "I'm glad I met you for I want to consult you about some lines I am composing in which I want to make the shadow of Etna fall across Syracuse, the mountain being 40 miles from the city. Would this be possible?" I replied that there was nothing in the distance to prevent the shadow of the mountain falling across the city. The only difficulty was that Etna is exactly North of Syracuse. "Surely," said Wordsworth, "it is a little N.E. or N.W." And as he was evidently determined to make the shadow fall the way he wanted it I did not contradict him. Wordsworth was a very remarkable looking man. He looked like an old shepherd, with rough rugged weather beaten face, but his features were fine and high cut. He was a grand man. He had a perfectly independent mind and cared for no one else's opinion. I called upon him afterwards at the Stow, Whitney. He was very kind to me there. He used to say that the Wye above Hay was the finest piece of scenery in South Britain, i.e. everything south of himself.'

Francis Kilvert

### 1970 [Belmont, Lyme Regis]

Back to Lyme. Now it's Eliz [his wife], arguing and weeping through the whole journey. I despise her, ignore her, etc., etc. I feel my head will burst open. At home we argue into the small hours. Now she wants to sell Belmont. We are to have little houses dotted over the landscape, staying a few months in each: I ought to be able to write anywhere. I listen to her, and think of the garden. The strawberry-tree is in flower. I try to explain I can write here because there is peace here; that I need a known environment, one I feel no drive to get to know and explore, in order to stay cooped up with a book. I can't go into the unknown from the unknown.

John Fowles

## 29 September

### 1803 [Over Stowey, Somerset]

Dined on a Michaelmas Goose, Mrs Southcomb did not join us, an apple fell on her head in the orchard which discomposed her much.

William Holland

### 1949 [East Anglia]

Took part in Brains Trust at Spixworth last night, when one of the questions asked was 'Are modern children pampered too much?' The dictionary defines 'pamper' as 'to feed luxuriously . . . to gratify (tastes, etc.) to excess'. And the natural tendency of most parents is to lavish gifts upon their children, to over-indulge, pet, and protect them, forgetting that in doing so they are stifling their children's initiative, sapping their rightful independence and teaching them, not to take care of themselves, but to be helpless in a world that is merciless to the weak. Rejoicing as I do in the greater freedom accorded to to-day's children, their emancipation from the bad old days when they might be seen but not heard, and when too often arguments were closed with the strap or the slipper, I yet wonder sometimes if the pendulum hasn't swung too far in the other direction. And if too many grown-ups, as well as children, are not beginning to sit down, expecting somebody else to get on with the job, instead of taking off their own coats, and setting to work.

*Elizabeth M. Harland*

## 30 September

1778 [Norfolk]

Rheumatic Pain very bad all night and still continues so – I took some Flower of Brimstone in some strong Beer about 11 this morning, before that took some Gin and after Gin some Brandy. My Pain continued all Day about me.

*James Woodforde*

1966 [Underhill Farm, Lyme Regis]

Along the beach to Stanton St Gabriel. A peach-gray day, very dying yet mellow. We picked about for fossils. To me, much more enjoyable than any day in Spain. I simply don't want to travel any more.

*John Fowles*

# OCTOBER

# 1 October

**1826 [Abbotsford, the Scottish Borders]**

Wrote my task, then walked from one till half-past four. Dogs took a hare. They always catch one on a Sunday – a Puritan would say the devil was in them.

*Sir Walter Scott*

**1849 [East Anglia]**

To-night finished re-heeling and soling the family socks.

*Elizabeth M. Harland*

# 2 October

**1800 [Grasmere, the Lake District]**

A very rainy morning. We walked after dinner to observe the torrents. I followed Wm to Rydale, he afterwards went to Butterlip How. I came home to receive the Lloyds. They walked with us to see Churnmilk force and the Black quarter. The black quarter looked marshy, and the general prospect was cold, but the Force was very grand. The Lychens are now coming out afresh, I carried home a collection in the afternoon. We had a pleasant conversation about the manners of the rich – avarice, inordinate desires, and the effeminacy unnaturalness and unworthy objects of education. After the Lloyds were gone we walked – a showery evening. The moonlight lay upon the hills like snow.

*Dorothy Wordsworth*

1892 [Perthshire]
Wet, very *weet*.

*Beatrix Potter*

## 3 October

1870 [Clyro, Radnorshire]
How odd, all the news and letters we get from Paris now coming by balloons and carrier pigeons.

*Francis Kilvert*

1995 [Hampshire]
Last night the baby deer which has been enchanting us and our neighbours was killed. Gunshots, far too close, were heard shortly after dark but we think it was killed by a fox. Its mangled body was found this morning a hundred yards from the house. Perhaps it was wounded by shot and finished off by a fox. The dogs sense everything. They were apprehensive last night and again this morning. They, I am sure, are guiltless. They have never chased deer; looking on them as goats and therefore sacred to my wife.

*Alec Guinness*

## 4 October

1781 [Fyfield, Hampshire]
Sent Mr Powlett's Reflecting Telescope home by Sop [a servant] and a Truckle Cheese.

*Henry White*

## 5 October

1836 [Stafford]
Went with Reggy [her husband] to the school and paid a visit to Sally Read to enquire about poor John Maey who, exhibiting insanity, (it being in the

family) has been taken to Forston Asylum. One would almost think this were Satan's device to retard the progress of the Gospel in this parish, as the poor fellow had through grace been led to the knowledge of the saviour and the value of his soul previously, and had in consequence given up his evil ways of drinking and smuggling, and had warned his former companions. Called at Farmer Flower's and walked by the riverside.

*Emily Smith*

1870 [Clyro, Radnorshire]
A dark foggy afternoon. At the Bronith near the Cottage a yellow poplar spire stood out against the dark woods above. At the Bronith spring a woman crippled with rheumatism and crying with the pain, had filled her tin pail and was trying to crawl home with it. So I carried the pail to her house.

*Francis Kilvert*

## 6 October

1757 [East Hoathly, Sussex]
This day how are my most sanguine hopes of happiness frustrated! I mean in the happiness between myself and wife, which hath now some time been continued between us, but, Oh, this day become the contra[ry]! The unhappiness which has, almost ever since we were married, been between us has raised such numberless animosities and disturbances – and amongst our friends – that I think it hath almost brought me to ruin. What the causes of it is I cannot judge. I cannot judge so ill of my wife as to think she is only to blame, and I think I have tried all experiments to make our lives happy, but they all have hitherto failed of their end. I can see nothing that so much contributes to our unhappiness as an opposition that proceeds from a contrariness or at least spitefulness of temper, but an opposition that seems indicated by our very make and constitution.

*Thomas Turner*

## 1826 [Abbotsford, the Scottish Borders]

Went to see Colonel Thornhill's hawks fly. Some part of the amusement is very beautiful, particularly the first flight of the hawks, when they sweep so beautifully around the company, jingling their bells from time to time, and throwing themselves into the most elegant positions as they gaze about for their prey. But I do not wonder that the impatience of modern times has renounced this expensive and precarious mode of sporting. The hawks are liable to various misfortunes, and are besides addicted to fly away; one of ours was fairly lost for the day, and one or two went off without permission, but returned. We killed a crow and frightened a snipe. There are, however, ladies and gentlemen enough to make a gallant show on top of Whitlaw Kipps. The falconer made a fine figure – a handsome and active young fellow with the falcon on his wrist. The Colonel was most courteous and named a hawk after me, which was a compliment. The hawks are not named until they have merited that distinction.

*Sir Walter Scott*

## 1892 [Perthshire]

What an aggravating old person Mr Lowe the post master is! You go down in a hurry with two or three small affairs, say a postal order and three stamps. He says in a forbidding manner 'let us do one thing first: *haveyougotapenny*'? He works out the change on his fingers, and after all has to carry on the halfpence to the next transaction, which you work out for him as he has collapsed into a state of imbecility. 'I *think* that's right' says he, regarding you sideways with evident suspicion.

He is a fat, hunched old fellow, with little piggy eyes, a thick voice and wears a smoking-cap with a yellow tassel, and he has immense hands with which he slowly fumbles about for the stamps, which he keeps amongst the stationery in empty writing-paper boxes. He puts on wrong postage 'shall we say tuppence? (!)' and will sauce anybody who is unprovided with small change; he wants reporting.

*Beatrix Potter*

# 7 October

## 1874 [Chippenham, Wiltshire]

For some time I have been trying to find the right word for the shimmering glancing twinkling movement of the poplar leaves in the sun and wind. This afternoon I saw the word written in the poplar leaves. It was 'dazzle'. The dazzle of the poplars.

*Francis Kilvert*

# 8 October

## 1861 [Inverness-shire]

At a quarter to nine, we reached the inn of Dalwhinnie – 29 miles from where we had left our ponies – which stands by itself, away from any village. Here again, there were a few people assembled, and I thought they knew us; but it seems they did not, and it was only when we arrived that one of the maids recognised me. She had seen me at Aberdeen and Edinburgh. We went upstairs: the inn was much larger than at Fettercairn, but not nearly so nice and cheerful; there was a drawing-room and a dining-room; and we had a good-sized bed-room. Albert had a dressing-room of equal size. Mary Andrews [a wardrobe-maid] who was very useful and efficient and Lady Churchill's maid had a room together, every one being in the house; but unfortunately there was hardly anything to eat, and two miserable starved Highland chickens, without any potatoes! No pudding, and no fun; no little maid (the two there not wishing to come in), nor our two people – who were wet and drying their things – to wait on us! It was not a nice supper.

*Queen Victoria*

## 1937 [Antrobus, Cheshire]

Quite a number of stoats have been in evidence lately, and one was surprised into an action of which I had hardly thought it capable. It was crossing a little green lane and ran almost under my horse's feet, but with a good turn of speed it just got clear and proceeded to fly the ditch; it didn't appear to jump across but simply sailed through the air at the level at which it was running, and when it reached the farther bank it disappeared in a twinkling.

*A. W. Boyd*

# 9 October

1761 [Norfolk]
I was very bad all last night and all this day, having got a bad boil upon my Posteriors.

*James Woodforde*

# 10 October

1876 [Slackfields Farm, Derbyshire]
*Fine* Fetched 1 ton of coals from Salterwood. Carted 5 loads of manure into Hep Green.

*Henry Hill*

1989 [Northamptonshire]
It was a warm, sunny day for a cruise downstream on the River Nene from Oundle to Ashton Lock. Two pairs of great crested grebes were swimming in the yacht basin and we were told that both pairs had bred successfully there earlier in the year. The waterfowl on the river were mostly predictable and included numerous mallard, occasional coot and moorhens, a few black-headed gulls and two pairs of mute swans with cygnets at widely separated points. A gaggle of fifty to sixty Canada geese was interesting for, in previous cruises at this time of year, we had seen only odd pairs. No cruise seems quite complete without a kingfisher, so we were delighted to see one fly rapidly upstream below a line of riverside willows. Big aeshna dragonflies zoomed low above the water but we saw no swallows or martins. Over a patch of seeding thistles, a charm of goldfinches was dancing. We moored

beside a wooded island and had a picnic on the grass while a swan sat sunbathing on the cement surround of the lock, then we walked to the lovely village of Ashton. Abundant on a grey stone wall was pellitory, that curious aberrant stingless nettle with red stems and tiny green flowers. A mass of ivy covered much of the wall's top and two red admiral butterflies were feasting on the flowers. We bought drinks at the Chequered Skipper Inn and enjoyed them at a table on the village green. The inn displays a fascinating signboard, on one side, the upper side of the butterfly and, on the other, the underside, picked out in nails driven into the wood close together, their heads painted to make two excellent portraits of the butterfly. The chequered skipper is a scarce butterfly in Britain, being confined to a few restricted areas, one of which is the neighbouring Rockingham Forest.

*L. P. Samuels*

# 11 October

1852 [Balmoral, Inverness-shire]

After luncheon, Albert decided to walk through the wood for the last time, to have a last chance, and allowed Vicky and me to go with him. At half-past three o'clock we started, got out at Grant's, and walked up part of *Carrop*, intending to go along the upper path, when a stag was heard to roar, and we all turned into the wood. We crept along, and got into the middle path. Albert soon left us to go lower, and we sat down to wait for him; presently we heard a shot – then complete silence – and, after another pause of some little time, three more shots. This was again succeeded by complete silence. We sent someone to look, who shortly after returned, saying the stag had been twice hit and they were after him. Macdonald next went, and in about five minutes we heard 'Solomon' give tongue, and knew he had the stag at bay. We listened a little while, and then began moving down hoping to arrive in time; but the barking had ceased, and Albert had already killed the stag; and on the road he lay, a little way beyond *Invergelder* – the beauty that we had admired yesterday evening.

*Queen Victoria*

# 12 October

### 1892 [Perthshire]

I have an unconquerable aversion to listening to accounts in the first person of supposed supernatural visitations.

*Beatrix Potter*

### 1992 [Saltwood Castle, Kent]

Poor 'E' [his Rottweiler] is now in terminal decline. I had to carry her off to bed and down the second flight front stairs today. I could have never have done that in the great days of the 'room fighting'. For the first time she is herself really low, and hangs her head as in the last minutes in the bullring. Thank God for the long break in Scotland, where we have a lovely picture of her, beautiful in the heather.

*Alan Clark*

# 13 October

### 1836 [Staffordshire]

Begun weekly accounts. I paid John's, Mary's, Cozens' bills amounting to £10/15/-. We dined early and Reggy walked in to Fordington where a sermon was preached for the Irish Society [set up to convert the Irish to Protestantism] by Mr Collisson. I gave Reggy my subscription of 5/- for the Irish Society and 5/- to that department for the special purpose of educating negroes in the West Indies. Fire at Broadmayne. Drew a good deal.

*Emily Smith*

# 14 October

### 1906 [Olton, Warwickshire]

Bright and cold after a week of damp, rainy weather. Walked to Catherine de Barnes to get some Dogwood berries, which I knew were plentiful in the hedges about there. The Hips made a great display along the route, especially on a wild piece of common ground we crossed, covered with gorse and briars. I noticed great numbers of Finches here feeding on the berries. Some of the Gorse bushes were in flower, these with the bushes of Scarlet Rose-berries, and trailing Blackberry briars, covered with red and yellow leaves made fine patches of colour in the bright sunshine. I saw some Hare-bells and Sow-Thistle in flower, and some Crab apples on a tree, which I vainly tried to reach.

*Edith Holden*

# 15 October

1800 [Over Stowey, Somerset]

After dinner my wife and William went out to gather mushrooms and I was left in the Parlour in a kind of dozing way, when I was roused by a rumbling noise. I started up and ran to the door and found it was Mrs Southcomb, my wife's sister, and Grace her maid. Poor woman she had a fit as soon as she was out of the carriage. She always has a fit when in the least hurried for which reason she came this day from Honiton in the Parish of South Molton without getting out of the Chaise, between forty and fifty miles and only changed horses, once, at Tiverton. They were in readiness as soon as she got there for had she got out of the chaise it would have brought on a fit. She has had these fits ever since the death of her husband eight or nine years ago. An extraordinary woman tho' so nervous and quivering on all occasions yet so determined that nothing can move her from her Resolutions. So very much attached to her Husband that she cultivates the Memory of him on every thing she does. She must live and die in the same house that he did, loves or hates every person that he did. In short the memory of her husband seems to be the primum mobile of her life. After her fit she cheered up and grew chatty and agreeable. The driver and horses sleep here tonight by Mrs Southcomb's request as a reward for his merit and attention and great care in bringing her safe.

*William Holland*

# 16 October

## 1784 [Selborne, Hampshire]

Mr [Jean Pierre François] Blanchard passed by us in full sight at about a quarter before three pm in an air-balloon!!! He mounted at Chelsea about noon; but came down at Sunbury to permit Mr Sheldon to get out; his weight overloading the balloon. At a little before four pm Mr Bl landed at the town of Romsey in the county of Hants.

*Gilbert White*

## 1878 [Surbiton, Surrey]

Wasp and very large blue-fly struggling, wrestling on leaf. In a few seconds the wasp got the mastery, brought his tail round, and stung once or thrice; then bit off the fly's proboscis, then the legs, then bit behind the head, then snipped off the wings, then fell off leaf, but flew with burden to the next, rolled the fly around, and literally devoured its intestines. Dropped off the leaf in its eager haste, got on third leaf, and continued till nothing was left but a small part of the body – the head had been snipped off before. This was one of those large black flies – a little blue underneath – not like meat flies, but bigger and squarer, that go to the ivy. Ivy in bloom close by, where, doubtless, the robber found his prey and seized it.

*Richard Jefferies*

## 1892 [Perthshire]

Up the road some flakes of snow, much crackling of withered leaves, no deer. Gathering moss on the way down did hear a noise which on a lawful day I should have attributed to the Gas Works, but being the Sabbath concluded it must be the *Red King* or a *Rabbit snoring*.

*Beatrix Potter*

# 17 October

## 1968 [Lyme Regis]

These walks, on which I see nothing unusual, confirm in me my love of this countryside very strongly. I do not want to live anywhere else in the world. I never want to live for more than a few days at a time in London again.

*John Fowles*

# 18 October

## 1870 [Clyro, Radnorshire]

Old James Jones was breaking stones below Pentwyn. He told me how he had once cured his deafness for a time by pouring hot eel oil into his ear, and again by sticking into his ear an 'ellern' (elder) twig, and wearing it there day and night. The effect of the eel oil at first was, he said, to make his head and brains feel full of crawling creatures.

*Francis Kilvert*

## 1892 [Perthshire]

I remember hearing old Dr Irving tell, when I was a child, that he had introduced safety pins to the civilised world. He saw a gypsy wife with her plaid fastened with an odd twist of wire, and thinking it ingenious, took it as a pattern to the Museum in Dunkeld. I remember his lamenting that he had not taken out a patent. – The same mistake that uncle Booth made with the yellow train-grease, both articles are in universal demand now.

The demand for the latter sprang into being with railways; but I should have thought unthinking, that safety pins dated from primeval times before the invention of dressmaking, when people of both sexes wore shawls and sheets. I believe, on reflection, the Romans are represented to have fastened their Togas with a kind of double brooch, in appearance rather like a chain sleeve-link. Brooches and buckles are Celtic and Greek. I suppose it was the application of the principle to wire which was a new departure. How old is wire? The spirit of enquiry leads up a lane which hath no ending.

*Beatrix Potter*

# 19 October

1949 [East Anglia]

A telephone call to ironmonger seven miles and two stations down the line, suggesting he should rail us the articles I now have no time to collect elicits the information that this simple transaction no longer possible. Nowadays a railway lorry must collect the goods, take them to a depot fifteen miles in the opposite direction, whence they will in due course be railed to us . . . a twenty-mile journey with a change of train en route. While goods formerly consigned to a station two miles away, and picked up on arrival by the consignee must now go on to a station eight miles away, from which they're delivered once a week. The trouble with the official mind is that it likes everything to look well on paper, and to take a large view. It makes no allowance for special cases, and life, particularly in the country, is full of these. Since man has only survived the ages because of his adaptability, cannot help feeling that the country that allows itself to become too rule-ridden risks the fate of the dinosaur and other prehistoric creatures. And wonder how I should ever get through my day if I adopted these methods.

*Elizabeth M. Harland*

# 20 October

1800 [Grasmere, the Lake District]

William was disturbed in the night by the rain coming into his room, for it was a very rainy night.

*Dorothy Wordsworth*

1935 [New Forest]

On the window-sill is a pot of forest pickings that is the epitome of its autumn colouring; and a sombre colouring at that. Some crisp brown fern, a branch of hawthorn leaves of that burnished purple-red that is so exquisite a setting for the smouldering crimson of the haws – but this year there are no haws, – just a touch of vivid green and gamboge yellow on the botched bramble leaves, a tuft or two of ling, and half a dozen scarlet hips; and with them the cool blue-green of a tiny sapling fir, one of those countless self-sown seedlings that cry to be pulled up at every turn. They choke the hollows and blur the outlines; we keenly appreciate the serious efforts of the forest's present administration to deal with this menace to its beauty.

*Janet Case*

# 21 October

1874 [Chippenham, Wiltshire]

John Hatherell said he remembered playing football with the men on Sunday evenings when he was a big boy and the Revd Samuel Ashe, the Rector, trying to stop the Sunday football playing. He would get hold of ball and whip his knife into the bladder, but there was another bladder blown the next minute. 'Well,' said the Rector in despair, 'it must go on.'

*Francis Kilvert*

*c*.2000 [Walnut Tree Farm, Suffolk]

The October winds, the equinoctial gales, have arrived and turned the trees into waves of sound, the wind gushing and sighing through them all night. It is through trees that we appreciate and judge the strength of the wind.

To make all this noise, the leaves must still be on the trees, although the wind is busy blowing them off, bashing the branches together to shake them free. It is as if the wind were sent specially to do the job.

In a big wind you wonder whether a tree with many trunks, such as a hazel, or any coppice tree, is designed to withstand wind by dispensing the stress through multiple, slender, streamlined shoots.

*Roger Deakin*

# 22 October

### 1899 [Surrey]

I had not realised until quite lately how life in England is permeated by suspicion, like the Frensham's Vicar's, of social intercourse between girls and young men. Our own vicar protested solemnly a few weeks ago, against the opening of evening classes in the schools, for girls: his reason being that in gathering the girls together, we very practically advertised to the village youths at what time of night they may be found.

I think the vicar's suspicion is tacitly endorsed by society in general. When one considers, it is a somewhat rare thing to see men and maidens together, 'courting': and the sight is viewed with a grudging tolerance at best. House-mistresses, of course, object to 'followers': and the maids know it. But there is a wide-spread feeling that for a man and girl to be seen together is not quite right. Hence the interviews are furtive: they take place in bye-lanes, or are postponed till dark. A girl who should neglect such precautions would certainly be regarded as wanton, and would suffer for it.

*George Sturt*

# 23 October

### 1892 [Perthshire]

A perfect hurricane and driving showers of snow. Immediately after breakfast got over the wall to survey the domain of the McInroy's [Mr McInroy of Lude, a neighbour], who yesterday departed back to Lude.

A nasty dirty place, no wonder the young man was always in the road. The five young ladies and the 'dearling clinker' and screeching voices may well have been audibly irritable if they were accustomed to a fine place and nineteen miles of deer forest.

It is the melancholy fact that the distinguished Mrs McInroy came from Stockport, and Mr McInroy, in spite of his kilt, is but a mushroom laird (his father bought it from the Robertsons forty years ago, which is but a grain in the hour-glass in a land where every other chieftain is descended from Fergus McFungus, though, for the matter of that, the kilt is rather a sign of an Englishman, or at all events town.)

*Beatrix Potter*

# 24 October

1985 [Badminton, Gloucestershire]
After sunset this evening I look at the moon with and without my spectacles. With them, the moon is three-quarters full, and clear. Without spectacles, there are four moons interlocking. Covering my right eye and seeing only with my left, the moon is ovoid and divided into sections, as though it were a heart with veins; much larger than life; nothing else visible in the gloaming. In the distance I could hear the stags roaring during the rut, a sound more melancholy than expectant of pleasure, more *post* than *ante coitum*.

*James Lees-Milne*

# 25 October

1799 [Over Stowey, Somerset]
This is my Wedding Day when we are to have something better than ordinary for dinner. We were married eighteen years to this day.

*William Holland*

1870 [Clyro, Radnorshire]
At Maesllwch Castle last week four guns killed seven hundred rabbits in one afternoon.

*Francis Kilvert*

1986 [Belmont, Lyme Regis]
Foul murder. When I came down this morning there was a small sea of feathers on the terrace, beside the Coade gatepost. I took William [his grandson] out to look at it. A steel-blue and russet bird flew, flashed away

from the ivy behind the gatepost: a male sparrowhawk. Below, the remains of the collared turtle-dove that had been its breakfast. A pair of the doves have been with us for some time, and one was growing quite tame, compared with its usual nervous self. Nature red in tooth and claw, and the sparrowhawks grow rarer every year or the number of times I see them; but this upset me.

*John Fowles*

## 26 October

1768 [Norfolk]

I had a poor little Cat, that had one of her ribs broke & that laid across her Belly and we could not tell what it was, and she was in great pain. I therefore with a small Penknife this morning opened one Side of her and took it out, and performed the operation very well and afterwards sewed it up and put Friars Balsam to it and she was much better after, the incision was half an inch. It grieved me much to see the poor creature in such pain before, and therefore made me undertake the above, which I hope will preserve the Life of the poor Creature.

*James Woodforde*

## 27 October

1949 [East Anglia]

Am always fascinated by seed-catalogues. And am certain that the average housewife could be much more adventurous when planning the next crops for her kitchen garden. My list for next Spring's planting includes currant tomatoes, apple cucumbers, Chinese cabbage (to be eaten both raw and cooked), celeriac, the old-fashioned Jersey bean, sweet peppers, Northumberland pot leek, South African marrows (the fruits, the size of a cricket ball, are cooked whole), and, for next winter's decoration, a packet of ornamental gourds.

*Elizabeth M. Harland*

# 28 October

### 1799 [Over Stowey, Somerset]

A great bustle – Wm Frost and Mr Amen carrying apples to the cart for cyder. They are taken down to Hewett's to be made through his hair cloths which is not the fashion of this county. Mr Amen thinks it is impossible for the cyder to be good as it is not made after the fashion of the county. I tell him he is a blockhead and that he knows nothing of the matter. 'Why Sir, I have made hundreds of hogsheads of cyder in my time.' 'Silence you Ass.'

*William Holland*

### 1870 [Clyro, Radnorshire]

Hot coppers, too much wine last night and an ill temper this morning. Reading *Puck* by 'Ouida', a book Morrell lent me. The authoress seems to have a rabid hatred of women and parsons.

*Francis Kilvert*

# 29 October

### 1946 [Inverness-shire]

The farm labourers' brief respite, after the ardours of leadin' the hairst, is over; the 'tattie hairst' is near. The end of this month catches the lilt of an old song in the voices of the bairns forming the tattie squads:

> Fa saw the tattie-lifters,
>
> Fa saw them gaun awa'?
>
> Fa saw the tattie-lifters
>
> Mairchin' doon bi Ballahaugh?
>
> Some hive sheen an' some hiv stockin's,
>
> Some hive nane awa.
>
> So fa saw the tattie-lifters
>
> Mairchin' doon bi Ballahaugh?

That song was maybe appropriate twenty years ago. The young tattie-lifters who sing it now sing it wi' their tongues in their cheeks. They've a' got baith 'sheen and stockin's' and they earn as much in one day as the bairns who first sang the song earned in a week.

*Jessie Kesson*

# 30 October

## 1812 [The Lake District]

My reason for stopping at Penrith was to see Ullswater, one of the finest of the lakes, and the only one I could reach without going nearly forty miles out of my way. I hired a gig, and got a weaver's boy for a pilot; and, in six miles, reached the village of Pooley, at the foot of the lake. Nothing can be more romantically beautiful than the richly wooded hills that form the side scenery, and the majestic heights which compose the background of this landscape; in a word, the view creates a sort of sensation which we feel on hearing Mozart's music, seeing Shakespeare's tragedies, hearing John Braham sing, or seeing ourselves surrounded by a good evening flight of wild fowl.

*Colonel Peter Hawker*

## 1966 [Underhill Farm, Lyme Regis]

Eliz [his wife] has been away for ten days now. I live like a hermit, my closest companion the little blue tit that roosts under the canopy every night. The weather is very fine, cool but clear; the moon huge each night. It can't be good for me; I wear old clothes, don't wash, eat bits of food at wrong hours, let the kitchen proliferate into piles of mess and dirty dishes, drift around the fields and let them become parts of me, like the wild life. Yet this last is a beautiful experience, in itself and because not many generations more will ever know it. Science and over-population must swamp nature; of course there will be reserves and naturalists still, but by 2066 no one will be able to have this strange symbiosis with nature. I live like [Richard] Jefferies, like John Clare. I can't celebrate it in words – not lack of words so much as the knowledge that cannot surpass their words. I mean I become an element of nature myself. The other day two boys came, with guns, and asked me if they could shoot pigeons. I said no in a gentle series of explanations about why nature existed and how lovely I knew, from my own past, it was to have a gun in one's hands, but . . . that great but. I was weak. I thought myself mean to stop their fun, and nearly said yes. But they were like two wild creatures too; and I outwitted them. If I'd said how dare you, get off my land, they'd have poached out of sheer and justified spite.

*John Fowles*

# 31 October

### 1892 [Perthshire]
Standing on the Bridge, Dunkeld looked very deserted, nothing but stray dogs. Mr McKenzie, the Minister, came up the middle of the road, swaying his arms about and peering through his spectacles. I don't think he recognised me till I had shaken hands. His viciousness did not appear, he has a particularly kind, fatherly manner, and is an indefatigable parish minister. He gets into ill-favour by taking sides with rather unchristian vehemence in the thousand-and-one squabbles of his large parish, and by the unpardonable sin of being unable to pay his debts.

*Beatrix Potter*

### 1950 [East Anglia]
Spend most of the day digging up hundreds of the best chrysanthemum plants, secateuring stems to within six inches of stools, and removing them to glasshouse (a friendly market gardener's) and cold frame (our own) for next season's cuttings. Evening spent with family as Mother is celebrating her birthday, though not in the traditional manner. According to the ancient Celts, this was the last day of the year, and they lit enormous bonfires at night. When cold, the ashes of each were scattered in a circle, when everyone who had helped to make the fire then put a stone inside, and if next day any stone was found displaced or damaged, it was believed that its owner

would die within the year. Later superstitions centre chiefly on one's future husband or wife. I have peeled apples and thrown the single coil of skin over my left shoulder in my time, though I can't in the least remember what initial resulted. (And am sure it wasn't Adam's!) But have never eaten a salt herring before going to bed, when one's future partner should appear with a cup of water in one's dreams. Nor have I roamed blindfold in a cabbage field, and pulled up a stalk, when a clean one presages a poverty-stricken husband, earth on the roots a rich one, a hard stalk a strong man, soft a weak-willed, a short stem a short man, a long stalk a tall, and so on. And I'm not going to try it now, either, says Adam, as we pass a field on our way home, and I suggest a little scientific investigation.

*Elizabeth M. Harland*

# NOVEMBER

# 1 November

## 1877 [Oxfordshire]

My cousin, Sarah Swift Dew, who lives with us went by the first train for a situation to Devonshire – Winscott, near Torrington. At noon today tolls ceased to be payable at both the Lower Heyford Turnpike Gates, and Bicester King's End gate (Bicester & Enstone Turnpike Trusts), & at Kirtlington Gate; & at Souldern Gate. The Heyford gates were removed today. The Commissioners of the Bicester & Enstone turnpike road have agreed to sell the Heyford Bridge Toll House & garden & the site of the Heyford Town Gate House & garden both in the parish of Lower Heyford, to Corpus Christi College, Oxford, for the sum of £60. Turnpike roads undoubtedly have done good service in times past, but their day seems to be over. The pulling down of these Turnpike Gates, or rather however the extinction of these Turnpike Trusts, will save me tenpence every Monday. I copied the Inscription on the Board at Souldern Gate which was as follows: 'Souldern Gate. Tolls Payable at this Gate. For every Horse, Mare, Gelding, Mule, Ass, Ox, Bullock, & other Beast of Draught drawing in Carriage, not exceeding 5 Pence. For every Horse, Mare, Gelding, Mule, or Ass, not drawing, a sum not exceeding 1d. For every drove of Oxen, Cows, or neat [bovine] Cattle, a sum not exceeding 12 Pence per Score, and so on in proportion for any greater or less number 12 Pence. For every Drove of Calves, Pigs, Sheep, or Lambs, a sum not exceeding 6 Pence per Score, and so on in proportion for any greater or less number 6d. Double Toll on Sundays.'

*George James Dew*

# 2 November

### 1698 [Yorkshire]

This day I was with one Mr Fiddis, a minister at Holderness, who told me that, about six years ago, going to bed at a friend's house, some had out of roguery fixed a long band to the bedclose where he lay. About half an houer after he was got to bed they begun to pull, which, drawing the bedclose off by degrees put him into a sudden fright, and, looking up, he did really think and believe that he saw two or three spirits stirring and moveing about the bed, and says but that he discovered the string, and the partys confessing the fraud, he durst almost have sworn that he really saw strange things, which shews the effects of suddain frights.

*Abraham De La Pryme*

### 1794 [Norfolk]

My Maid Molly has declared herself with Child, more than half gone. Molly is with Child by one Sam Cudble, a Carpenter of the Parish of Coulton, and he says that he will marry her – The Man bears a fair Character – However, in her Situation, it is necessary for me to part with her as soon as possible. To Morrow therefore I intend at present to dismiss her. She is a very poor, weak Girl, but I believe honest.

*James Woodforde*

# 3 November

### 1789 [Selborne, Hampshire]

Planted 150 cabbages to stand the winter: dunged the ground. Grapes all very bad. Two swallows were seen this morning at Newton vicarage house, hovering & settling on the roofs, & out-buildings. None have been observed at Selborne since October 11. It is very remarkable, that after the hirundines have disappeared for some weeks, a few are occasionally seen again sometimes, in the first week in November, & that only for one day. Do they withdraw & slumber in some hiding-place during the interval? for we cannot suppose they had migrated to warmer climes, & so returned again for one day. Is it not more probable that they are awakened from sleep, & like the bats are come forth to collect a little food?

*Gilbert White*

## 4 November

1802 [Grasmere, the Lake District]

I scalded my foot with coffee after having been in bed in the afternoon – I was near fainting, and then bad in my bowels. Mary waited upon me till 2 o'clock, then we went to bed and with applications of ginger I was lulled to sleep about 4.

*Dorothy Wordsworth*

1944 [Jersey]

A man aged 42 has killed his wife, aged 30, and hanged himself afterwards because she went with Germans. It is said that there will be many more such tragic happenings. Residences, supposed to be pro-German, have been tarred. And a man was found placing a large quantity of dynamite to blow up a certain shop because the owner has always sold at black market prices and now only sells to the Germans. Horrid man – I went to the shop once and found him much too familiar.

*Nan Le Ruez*

## 5 November

1942 [Antrobus, Cheshire]

Out in the middle of the mere to-day a Bewick's swan was swimming. It kept aloof from a family of mute swans and paid no heed when the four cygnets flew up and down the mere. A little later two more swans came circling high over the water, calling 'how-how' in gentle, high-pitched tones. They were two more Bewick's swans, and as they dropped lower the original bird answered their call and joined them in the air. Then all three gradually came lower and lower, dropping their feet and spreading the webs to act as brakes at the end of each circle. When at last they planed down to the mere, they put their bills in their scapulars and went to sleep. Probably it is not long since they left the Arctic, for they are seldom seen here so early in winter.

*A. W. Boyd*

## 6 November

### 1881 [Surbiton, Surrey]

Thrushes singing, the first for a very long time, in copse, garden. Larks singing and soaring. Chaffinch, Greenfinch call. Sunny after clouds, warm blue sunshine. Two buttercups. Redwings, kuck, kuck.

*Richard Jefferies*

## 7 November

### 1773 [Norfolk]

I had a very restless Night last night being very feverish. Was very heavy all day Yesterday, I took some Brimston & Treakle & Cream of Tartar last night going to bed. I did not go to either Church to day being but indifferent. I eat no Meat all day to day & am the better for it.

*James Woodforde*

### 1997 [Bardsey Island, Wales]

*S. then cyclonic 3-4*

Calm and dry. Col. back on the island – Ernest scooted him and the post across when the wind dropped yesterday afternoon. After shopping in Pwllheli (bare trees and Nanhoron reminded me this is a year I've seen none of their leaf-change and fall) I got back to winter digging and clearing. I stuck a few clippings of the Euonymus in a vase on the kitchen windowsill to enjoy the reddish seedpods against glossy green leaves. I lit a bonfire of hedge trimmings and garden rubbish before the pile could be colonised by creatures – the hedgehogs ought to be safely tucked up, but shrews stay active – in the coldest weather, they can apparently slow their metabolism right down by *shrinking* their internal organs – and wrens are always on the lookout for winter shelter. Last year, when I reached down to drag out the old bluetit box from where it had fallen behind the windbreak, there was an eruption of six or seven of them, a whole family stuffed inside.

*Christine Evans*

## 8 November

### 1874 [North Wales]

Walking with Wm. Splaine we saw a vast multitude of starlings making an unspeakable jangle. They would settle in a row of trees; then, one tree after another, rising at a signal they looked like a cloud of specks of black snuff or powder struck up from a brush or broom or shaken from a wig; then they would sweep round in whirlwinds – you could see the nearer and farther bow of the rings by the size and blackness; many would be in one phase at once, all narrow black flakes hurling round, then in another; then they would fall upon a field and so on. Splaine wanted a gun: then 'there it would rain meat', he said. I thought they must be full of enthusiasm and delight hearing their cries and stirring and cheering one another.

*Gerard Manley Hopkins*

### 1967 [Underhill Farm, Lyme Regis]

The road to the farm is metalled. Sad to see the old flint track go, but it was becoming impossible to negotiate in second gear.

*John Fowles*

### 1979 [Sanna, Ardnamurchan]

Today is a Fast Day in the Parish. That does not mean a day devoted to fasting, as an outsider might innocently imagine. A Fast Day is a sort of buckshee Sunday, a day with all the rules and regulations pertaining to Sunday save that it lacks a church service. To thoroughgoing believers, deprived of the chance to congregate for a good gossip or a great sucking of peppermints or a counting of heads and a labelling of them or a flaunting of new bonnets, the Sunday atmosphere without the churchgoing must be like the work without the wages.

*Alasdair Maclean*

# 9 November

### 1956 [The Lake District]

Sometimes you come across in a quiet fold of the northern hills a person whose aspect, indeed, whose whole attitude to things about him, is a living proof of some proud, forgotten ancestry. In one such place there is an elderly woman whose head with its high cheekbones, tall forehead, and noble carriage would not look out of place on an old coin and whose tongue is as keen as her mind. She was talking about 't'rough ground near Cunningarth', where she lived as a child and where now a number of archaeologists are laying bare the three occupations, one above the other, of the fort, Olenacum, at 'Old Carlisle'. To me, an inexpert helper, the finding of the broken pots and the everyday things of these occupations is an exciting task. It seems a pleasant place, too, this green plateau between Skiddaw and Solway where the skylarks sing in the blue November air as happily as they probably did over the smoking ruins of the first town or the walls of its successors. But to the woman in the hills it is otherwise; she is still repelled and fascinated by something she is part of and does not understand. 'Maybe it was t'travellers (gypsies) who camped down by t'beck an' maybe not; I feared to by t'place at dusk when I was sent on errands – there was more there than you'd ever see.' Go there at night and you might agree with her. The sleeping countryside has a power all its own.

*Enid J. Wilson*

# 10 November

1799 [Over Stowey, Somerset]
None of the Pooles at Church, poor Nathaniel is not buried. Went to Aisholt in the afternoon, found Ricks calm and composed but wonderfully bloated. I counted ten of my own Parishioners there. The farmers complained that they could not sow wheat.

*William Holland*

1944 [Jersey]
Mrs S. Le B. and Beryl came and brought us four small cooking-bowls, one small tin of black boot-polish, some pepper and lentils, all of which they had in their 'secret hoard' in the shop. What lovely presents!

Thieves have come again, for Dad has discovered that a good and large waterbutt has disappeared. We were remarking today that we all feel better in health and much less tired than some months ago, and we put it down to the sugar-beet syrup, which we've been making again lately, and eating it on our bread and drinking it with milk. I'm sure that is what has given us fresh energy. But what a job it is to make.

*Nan Le Ruez*

# 11 November

1799 [Somerset]
Rain last night too and the morning not very promising, tis surely dreadful weather. Briffet is here to kill the sow. A horrible looking fellow, his very countenance is sufficient to kill anything, a large hulky fellow, a face absolutely furrowed with the small pox (a very uncommon thing in these days of innoculations) two ferret eyes and a little turned up nose with a mouth as wide as a barn door and lips as thick and projecting they look like two rollers of raw beef bolstered up to guard against, as it were, the approach to his ragged rotten teeth. However, he is a good pig killer.

*William Holland*

## 1878 [St Harmon, Radnorshire]

School. Flood falling. So far the second greatest flood of this century. Before breakfast I went down to the bridge to see how the Jenkins family were. Soon after I passed last night the river came down with a sudden rush and wave and filled the road full of water and they had to escape to the trap, carrying their children on their backs, wading through water knee deep, and leaving 3 feet of water in the house, the house also being surrounded by water and the water running in at front and back. Mr Stokes kindly rode down from the Old Court to see if they were safe, the water was then up to his horse's girths. Many people were flooded out of their houses at Letton and Staunton and spent the night on the Bredwardine Bridge watching the flood. A number of cattle and colts were seen to pass under the bridge in the moonlight and it was feared they would be drowned. Some women saw a bullock swept down under the bridge at noon to-day. Mr W. Clarke told me that the Whitney iron railway bridge was carried away last night by the flood and 2 miles of line seriously damaged. No trains can run for 3 months, during which time the gap will be filled by coaches.

*Francis Kilvert*

## 1918 [Lewes, Sussex]

*Armistice signed.* I was typing in the middle bedroom when Ernest called up from the yard: 'Alice, it is over.' He wouldn't come out again but I tied on Nelson's [the dog] red, white and blue bow and off we went into the High Street. Everything and everyone delirious. All the dogs out, all with bows and all twisting round your legs in the crowd. A lot of soldiers outside the Town Hall collared Mackay Clarke, the Rector of All Saints, bundled him up on to an impromptu platform, roared at him to make a speech. So there he was, with his ginger moustache and his sweating carrot red face, waving his arms about, moving his lips, and nobody heard one blessed word for the shouting and laughing and roaring. And lots of people were crying and one old woman outside Stone's shop said: 'But think of them poor boys what 'ull never come back.'

*Alice Dudeney*

# 12 November

*c.*2000 [Walnut Tree Farm, Suffolk]

I have a hedgehog in residence behind the Aga. It's a young one, no bigger than my outstretched hand, and I found it in a stupor, exposed by my track in broad daylight. Young hedgehogs are vulnerable to this kind of inexplicable malaise at this time of year; lacking enough body mass to withstand sudden cold, they seem to run low on blood sugar and grow torpid. This leaves them dangerously exposed to attack by winter-hungry crows, or magpies, or hawks. In any case, once they have grown this cold, they often simply lose the ability to get up and look for food and water, and decline further into death.

I brought this animal inside and placed it beside the Aga, where it curled up and slept for hours before stirring and eating some cat food. It then drank vigorously for six minutes, emptying a large dish of water, then slept again, creeping inside a cardboard box of dry leaves of ash and mulberry. The cats take little interest in it, as they're quite used to sharing their feeding bowl with wild hedgehogs. The little thing has gradually gained strength over the last twenty-four hours and has explored the kitchen, eaten more food and retired into the box again, where it noisily goes about its occupational therapy with the leaves.

There's something medieval about a hedgehog: the scavenging peasant of the undergrowth, the hedge bottom. What we love about them is their vulnerability, which they share with human babies: the way they curl up in that foetal ball, shielding the soft furry underbelly.

I'm trying to work out what that sound is, exactly, inside the box. Is it chomping, the squeaking of one mandible against another? The animal is an indefatigable trencherman or woman.

*Roger Deakin*

# 13 November

### 1871 [Clyro, Radnorshire]

'What a fine day it is. Let us go out and kill something.' The old reproach against the English. The Squire has just gone by with a shooting party.

*Francis Kilvert*

### 1946 [Inverness-shire]

The old order has changed. Short years ago November was one of the two months marked apart in the farm workers' year. It held joyous Martinmas. Then did the farm servant receive his six months' 'fee'. His pockets jangled; his wife wore a new floral 'peenie'; his loons war 'rigged' wi' new beets. And happy in the knowledge that any outstanding accounts wi' the 'soutar' or the grocer were honourably closed, he himself asked little more than a jaunt to the nearest town, a meeting, a crack, and a pint with those of his kind; the relaxing, exquisite knowledge of a whole day's respite from labour. And yet, contrarily enough, the bar of the 'Gordon Arms' hummed wi' a braid Scots conversation that embraced naething ootside the limits o' 'the Mairns', 'the maister', *and* 'the work' – subtle busman's holiday!

Now the farm servants' status has been modernised. He's the proud possessor of a 'forty-eight hour week'. All gains bring their losses. Martinmas and all its local colour and joyousness has disappeared from the farm servants' calendar.

*Jessie Kesson*

# 14 November

### 1838 [Falmouth, Cornwall]

Tried a horse & found it wanting.

*Barclay Fox*

1928 [Lewes, Sussex]
Another thrilling day. The electric men came to put electric light in the drawing room.

*Alice Dudeney*

## 15 November

1774 [Norfolk]
I caught a remarkable large Spider in my Wash Place this morning & put him in a small Glass Decanter & fed him with some Bread, & intend keeping him.

*James Woodforde*

## 16 November

1826 [South Cave, Yorkshire]
This is Cave Sittings Day very fine and Sunshining. A Town's Meeting last night at Tindale's where there was the most quarrelling I ever knew at a meeting of this kind but not at all on the Town's affairs. Wm. Cousens & Matt. Pickering begun the fray Pickering having two Guineas a year less licence to pay than Cousens on account of his house not being rated so high, they called each other every thing but respected friends – Then Ths. Levitt and old Loncaster began, so fierce that one would have thought that it would have soon been over but it was kept up with spirit a long time. Ths. Levitt told Loncaster he was the town's fool, and the town was not very wise or else they would not have appointed a real fool Constable. There were several people drunk, but I enjoyed nay saw it quite composed as I take care never to drink so much as to lose the little sense I possess. I came away about half past ten. Several staid until four or five O'clock the next morning.

*Robert Sharp*

# 17 November

1976 [Combe Florey, Somerset]
Philistines in Leeds have beaten up two artists who were planning to shoot at budgerigars with an air pistol in an attempt to extend the frontiers of art. This is the sort of thing which makes my blood boil.

Of course it is a delusion that the public can ever be educated in an appreciation of the arts. But what on earth is the Arts Council's purpose if not to protect artists from the need to ingratiate themselves with the vulgar throng?

In Somerset, we have no such difficulties. With the help of generous grants from Somerset County Council, the Ewart-Biggs Memorial Fund etc., our budgerigar shoots are strictly private affairs. Luckily, as chief landowner in the village, I not only have *droit de seigneur* or *jus primae noctis* over the village maidens (a right seldom exercised now that their average age is 93) but have also retained full shooting rights.

This means I can order any old age pensioner I choose to bring out her budgerigars for me and my friends to shoot at. If the old dears are upset by this, I comfort them by saying: '*Ars longa, vita brevis.*' If they go on complaining, I point out how lucky they are it is only their budgerigars I have chosen to shoot.

*Auberon Waugh*

# 18 November

1987 [Belmont, Lyme Regis]
Too much happens to me, I never have the time to record it. Increasingly I doubt if it is worth recording. In a way it is partly the insidious shadow of death, like the cramming of too much into the last days of a holiday. And partly my contempt for what I have long hated about the snapshot, the amateur's photograph – that secret desire to have it recorded that one was somewhere, some place, some time: *bref*, that one was.

*John Fowles*

# 19 November

### 1942 [Antrobus, Cheshire]

A goldeneye duck was swimming on the small 'flash' by the roadside, attended by six black-headed gulls, which were waiting to pounce on anything it caught during a dive. It swam nervously about, turning quickly to one side or the other, but the gulls took it for a game of follow-my-leader and would not be shaken off. At last the goldeneye lost patience, and with wide open bill darted at the nearest gull and at the same moment made a sudden shallow splash dive; it had to do this twice, and the second time I think it actually struck the gull, which flew off with a loud squawk. They all then left it alone to dive and feed in peace.

*A.W. Boyd*

# 20 November

### 1782 [Norfolk]

Mr Custance told me this morning that he had a few Days ago about 80 Turkies, geese, Ducks, and Fowls stolen from [him] in one night – many of them that were fatting. This is the time of the year that many idle Fellows from Norwich go about the Country stealing Poultry to send them to London to make a Penny of them. I never had any stolen yet, but daily expect it. Burrows of Morton had but a few Days ago also taken from him Poultry to the Amount of 3 or 4 Pds value.

*James Woodforde*

### 1865 [Beeley, Chatsworth Estate]

A fine day one of our Gees missing, I expect someone hath stolen it.

*William Hodkin*

### 1979 [Sanna, Ardnamurchan]

I never hear of a suicide without feeling a great rush of awe and pity. Nothing except the stars at night could be more amazing or more unfathomable.

Three such acts have taken place in this area, to my knowledge, and though all were before my time and all no more to me originally than some childishly-heard anecdote, I have invested each one since with something of my own death. All return to me at intervals with their unsolved and insoluble mystery.

All three were men and all three chose to drown. That is a Hebridean form of self-destruction, a kind of acknowledgement or a resumption of origins. The children in Ardnamurchan chant as they play, 'Water to water, for good or ill, if the sea doesn't get you, the river will.'

Of the first of these I know nothing, save that he committed himself to the care of a deep pool in Allt Sanna, where it runs by the crofts. That was a cold death, colder than most, for that stream comes down from the Glendrian Hills and makes one's bones ache on the hottest day in midsummer. The particular pool he selected, too, is always sombre, taking its appearance from something within itself rather than from its surroundings, as lesser pools do.

Yet the purity of the act, it seems to me, had been corrupted. There were occupied houses a hundred yards away and the neighbourhood is a pleasant one. On the far side of the stream at that point a sloping field, once cultivated – cultivated then, I guess – tilts up to the west, as stubbornly green as the pool is black. Sunlight sticks to that field like glue. I could never have killed myself in such a place. I should have glanced up and my eyes would have betrayed my will.

Of the other two local suicides one was a poor madman who lived in Sanna when my grandmother was a girl. And when I say 'madman' I do not mean your licensed fool or your village natural; in the Highlands we take our madness more seriously than that. This was a strange, disturbed fellow who strode about the township stark naked but kept his thoughts veiled and so offended no one in those strict but unpriggish days. He submerged himself in the sea one morning, off a certain rocky ledge that at high water drops down sheer for ten or twelve feet below the surface. He was found when the tide went out, spreadeagled on the rock face like a climber, clinging for dear death to the seaweed.

That was a post-Reformation ending. No Highlander of old could have held on so determinedly. Lightness of spirit would have buoyed him up if lightness of body had not.

The third suicide was the one I like best, the one that best combined the time, the place and the loved one. This man was a gamekeeper who drowned himself by wading into a mountain tarn miles from anywhere, below Meall nan Conn in Glendrian. The setting he chose was a wilderness of grey stone and coarse grass, untainted by bird or beast. Before he went into the water he stuffed his game bag and his pockets with pebbles, with consonance that is to say. On the shore of the tarn – oh supreme artist! – he left a loaded rifle.

*Alasdair Maclean*

## 21 November

1799 [Somerset]
Met the two Miss Rolins from Stowgursey. They were dressed very smart yet trudging along in the dirty road with a servant maid attending. I never think young ladies appear to advantage along a dirty highroad and I would advise all ladies when obliged to pass thro' dirt not to draw their petticoats too high behind for I can assure them that they discover in so doing more than is to their advantage. The female leg never looks so well behind as before.

*William Holland*

## 22 November

1976 [Combe Florey, Somerset]
To the Village Hall of Highclere in Hampshire, where Archbishop Marcel Lefebvre confirms my two older children in the Old Religion. It is a sad sight indeed to see the once mighty Catholic Church reduced in England to an ageing foreign prelate and a dozen or so assorted clergymen in a draughty village hall.

The English have no tradition for fighting religious wars, unlike the French. At the time of the Reformation practically the entire hierarchy defected without a whimper. So now, they have all followed 'Pope' Paul VI and his drivelling advisers into the heresies of indifferentism and modernism, denying the Papal authority of SS Pius V and X, on whose holy memory any claim to an existing authority must rely.

In church on Sunday – another draughty village hall – the preacher reminded us that the Church is bound to win through in the end, unlikely as this may now seem: one of the signs of the end of the world will be when the Jews are finally converted to the Christian religion.

When I have the good fortune to meet a Jew I often worry about the extent of my obligation to try and convert him to Christianity. Perhaps in the ecumenical spirit of the times, one can leave them in error a little longer.

*Auberon Waugh*

## 23 November

1876 [Slackfields Farm, Derbyshire]
*Cold* Pulling and carting turnips.

*Henry Hill*

1957 [Machynlleth, Wales]
With the sighting this autumn of a party of five grey squirrels and numerous records of others seen or killed here and around Dolgellau, the final establishment of the species in this part of Wales may be said to have begun and the period of infiltration to have ended. This infiltration has been instructive. It is now some years since individual grey squirrels, shadowy and elusive pioneers, began to be reported here. But their advance has never appeared steady. Several times they have seemed to die out but always they have eventually been replaced.

So three-quarters of a century after its introduction into England the American species conquers Wales to the coast. Compared with its rapid advance across the Midlands and into the border counties its progress since then has been slow. This was natural enough, impeded as it was by a barrier of difficult, treeless country. But it was here that the grey squirrels showed their adaptability by trekking out of the woodlands up into mountain country and down into west Wales. One of them was trapped when crossing a high Montgomeryshire moorland some years ago. However much one may regret the advance of the grey squirrel it is difficult not to marvel at its success.

*William Condry*

## 24 November

1801 [Grasmere, the Lake District]

A rainy morning. We all were well except that my head ached a little and I took my Breakfast in bed. I read a little Chaucer, prepared the goose for dinner, and then we all walked out. I was obliged to return for my fur tippet and Spenser it was so cold. We had intended going to Easedale but we shaped our course to Mr Gell's cottage. It was very windy and we heard the wind everywhere about us as we went along the Lane but the walls sheltered us. As we were going along we stopped at once, at the distance perhaps of 50 yards from our favorite Birch tree. It was yielding to the gusty wind with all its tender twigs, the sun shone upon it and it glanced in the wind like a flying sunshiny shower. It was a tree in shape with stem and branches but it was like a Spirit of water. The sun went in and it resumed its purplish appearance the twigs still yielding to the wind but not so visibly to us. The other Birch trees that were near it looked bright and cheerful, but it was a creature by its own self among them . . . A shower came on us when we were at Benson's. We went through the wood – it became fair – there was a rainbow which spanned the lake from the Island house to the foot of Bainriggs. The village looked populace and beautiful. Catkins are coming out palm trees budding – the alder with its plum coloured buds. We came home over the stepping stones. The Lake was foamy with white waves. I saw a solitary butter flower in the woods.

*Dorothy Wordsworth*

# 25 November

1775 [Selborne, Hampshire]

Many phalaenae appear. Strange that these nocturnal lepidoptera should be so alert, at a season when no day papilios appear, but have long been laid-up for the winter. Trees will not subsist in the sharp currents of air: thus after I had opened a vista in the hedge at the E. corner of Baker's hill, no tree that I could plant would grow in the corner: & since I have opened a view from the bottom of the same field into the mead, the ash that grew in the hedge, & now stands naked on the bastion, is dying by inches, & losing all its boughs. Phalaenae appear about hedges in the night time the winter thro'.

*Gilbert White*

# 26 November

1924 [Lewes, Sussex]

At lunch no Ernest [her husband]. I waited till half past one, worried myself into a fit of acute indigestion, kept looking out the window for an ambulance: actually (how mad it seems!) went to the outside lavatory to see if he had hanged himself. Then remembered that he'd said he was going to Brighton.

*Alice Dudeney*

# 27 November

1759 [East Hoathly, Sussex]

Paid James Marchant 2s. for making 8 pair of fearnought spatter dashes [gaiters].

*Thomas Turner*

1945 [Kent]

We went to the preview of Miss Awcock's sale at the Stewardess's cottage in the Cedar Walk of Oxon Hoath. Under the great saga pancake trees squat the little brick house, behind wrought iron grilles. Opposite is the walk with the round pudding bay-trees to the huge kitchen gardens with their grand gates.

Miss Awcock is over seventy. She and her father before her must have been agents for Oxon Hoath for nearly a hundred years.

Now she is being turned out because the new owner, Cannon, says she is completely hopeless and inefficient and Sir William Geary left nothing in his Will about the cottage being hers for life. She is going to live in one room in Tonbridge and a subscription has been got up for her. It reached £375 I think.

The things in her cottage are charming, because quite untouched, unvarnished and unmessed about. Some are almost black with the rich grain showing through the polished dirt. A charming little Sheraton sideboard with Tambour cupboard was like this. Then there is a little castor, dented-in, 1716, which Eric [his companion] is going to bid for, for me. And a good country Chippendale chair that has lost its top splat and pieces off its legs. The seat also has been incorrectly rushed over, but it is nice and worthy, with crisp carving.

The rooms were pretty with old mantels, eighteenth-century, put into the old building, and fragments of panelling in the passages. Everything cared for over many years with no change. Very un-spectacular, but with that untampered air that is very rare.

There is no bathroom, electric light or water laid on. Not even a tap, I think, in the kitchen.

The step at the bottom of the boxed-in stairs was semi-circular. The room one entered into had a brown, thickly painted Adam mantel, and under it the only pretentious, ungenuine thing in the house, a strong, bricky open grate, painful with the pretty mantel.

We left in a hurry because we saw Phil and Peggy Mundane Arswhole appearing at the door; luckily they went straight upstairs, so we wriggled out at once.

*Denton Welch*


# 28 November

1949 [East Anglia]
Much drama and incredible amount of noise over week-end, thanks to Helen Pig, who begins to limp one day, and run at the nose the next. Am sure that

she has cut her foot on the broken glass that keeps turning up whilst the yard is dug out, but any efforts on our part to look at the injured member result in complete non-success. The new symptom appearing, we hastily consult text-books, when we are horrified to learn that the two together may mean foot-and-mouth. We cannot believe that Helen has it. But since this fell disease must start somewhere, and at present we are as imaginative about them as a mother with her first baby, Adam rings up the vet. The vet arrives, takes a precautionary glance at Hepsibah and Hazel, then opens the door of Helen's stye. An unbelievable uproar immediately commences. Am sure the entire neighbourhood must imagine a brutal murder about to be committed, William Cat mews in sympathy from the ridge of the stye roof, the builders cease work and as one man gather round to offer advice, whilst Helen's screams redouble. All this is caused simply by an attempt to pen the invalid in one corner of the stye, and put a halter on. Once this is accomplished, her shrieks give place to a heartrending whimper, her temperature is taken (she hasn't one), and her feet are examined. (One has a small cut.) Presently vet departs, leaving us some medicine to be put in her food, night and morning, till bottle done, and says keep her where she is for the next five days, letting him know at the end of that time if she hasn't recovered. This morning Helen presents a perfect picture of piggy placidity, her limp almost gone.

*Elizabeth M. Harland*

## 29 November

1841 [Falmouth, Cornwall]
The deluge of 1841. The rain poured down in streams instead of drops, the low lands are inundated, walls & hedges are washed away. The water in some of the houses at Penryn is 4 or 5 feet deep & the inhabitants with their pigs are taking refuge in the top storey according to my father's report, who went to Carclew this morning. The road about Stewart's bone mill is converted into a rapid river 3 or 4 feet deep in some places. The like has not been known in this country within the memory of man. It is a happy thing for the old ladies that they can read of the covenant made with our

forefathers that the world should never be drowned again, for certainly this looks somewhat suspicious.

*Barclay Fox*

### 1851 [Surrey]

All painted after breakfast – [Holman] Hunt at grass; myself, having nearly finished the wall, went on to complete stalk and lower leaves of Canterbury-bell in the corner. Young, who was with Hunt, said he heard stag-hounds out; went to discover, and came running in in a state of frenzied excitement for us to see the hunt. Saw about fifty riders after the hounds, but missed seeing the stag, it having got some distance ahead. Moralised afterwards, thinking it a savage and uncivilised sport.

*John Everett Millais*

### 1954 [Sissinghurst, Kent]

H. [Harold, her husband] said that Nigel [their son] had sounded him on whether I would ever consider giving Sissinghurst to the National Trust. I said, Never, never, never! *Au grand jamais, jamais.* Not that hard little metal plate at my door! Nigel can do what he likes when I am dead, but so long as I live, no National Trust or any other foreign body shall have my darling. It is bad enough to have lost Knole but they shan't take Sissinghurst from me. That at least is my own.*

*Vita Sackville-West*

## 30 November

### 1923 [Lewes, Sussex]

After lunch Mrs Hart turned up. Fur coat – Australian black rabbit – which only cost £7 7s! Felt increasingly that a fur coat I must and will have.

*Alice Dudeney*

---

*Vita Sackville-West died in 1962. In 1967, ownership of Sissinghurst was transferred to the National Trust.

# DECEMBER

# 1 December

### 1773 [Norfolk]

Soon after Dinner we all went to Cary and saw some very remarkable Feats of Horsemanship, performed by a Man just come to Town and he performed exceeding well – gave him o.1.o. He rode full galop upon three Horses, laid down on them & got up on his feet on them with Ease with two Horses also standing upon two Quart Pots, between two Horses, stood on his head one Horse on a full gallop, hanging with his Head downwards & his hands touching the ground full Galop & taking up 4 Handkerchiefs. Another Man rode full Galop standing upon his Feet in the Saddle & a Boy on the Man's Head. Great Numbers of People present near a Thousand. It began at 3 and lasted till five o'clock.

*James Woodforde*

### 1878 [Oxfordshire]

A new reading-room at Chesterton, built solely at Lord Jersey's expense, was opened on Oct. 28, 1878, at evening. I went into it on the afternoon of that day, & met Lady Jersey & the Vicar of Chesterton just going into it as I was coming out. Whether it will be as attractive as the 'Red Cow' public house at the other end of the village remains to be seen. The Farm labourers of rural England spend for the most part all their spare money at the alehouse, & live upon the poor rates in old age.

*George James Dew*

### 1968 [Lyme Regis]

At last to Belmont.

I wander round the empty rooms, trying to make up my mind what needs doing first. The three main problems: the floor over the cellar in the east room is rotting; so is the south-west room, the damp beading up almost to the ceiling; and the central heating. Then a host of minor ones – windows to be knocked in, walled up, the wiring to be seen to, the stables to be saved (they're like one huge sponge at the moment), the garden, the fencing – I draw up endless lists. And enjoy it, the peace and quiet after London, the feel of the house, almost a gratitude that something is going to happen after its ten empty years. It has a kind of female feel, this Belmont, I don't know why; a bit of an old whore, with its splendid facade, and all the mess that lies behind the facade rooms.

And as for the garden, it is a whole world – a jungle of bramble, but still with relics of its former grandeur, still some old shrubs surviving. The magnolia tree is in full bud; the japonica is coming into flower, some sort of delicate little white ornamental onion also. I hacked my way through to the linhay near the bottom, a nice little building two stories high. We'll make a summerhouse out of that. Discovered another huge pittosporum, a palm-tree, an auracaria, apples. It is a garden full of levels and terraces and lost corners, and seems more like ten acres than its actual one and a bit. I don't see its state or ruin really. There are so many enjoyable things to do and discover. Like a huge toy.

*John Fowles*

# 2 December

## 1933 [Antrobus, Cheshire]

These popular little beetles the ladybirds are now hibernating in sheltered places – in crannies, under loose bark, or in any other suitable sanctuary. I have found them sometimes in large numbers in the nesting-boxes occupied during the summer by tree sparrows, and often they will invade a house and can be found in corners and behind shutters if an undue passion for cleanliness doesn't drive them away. A few years ago scores took possession of a room in my house, and I have just been reminded of this by a two-spotted ladybird which flew on to a paper I was reading – aroused, no doubt, by the heat of the room.

I have been called to task for calling them beetles (which, of course, they are), and have found people who liked to see them and were perfectly willing to pick them up, and yet were horrified to think that anyone could even touch a beetle! I think that much of this antipathy is due to the common error of calling the objectionable cockroach a 'black-beetle', which, as somebody has quite truly pointed out, is neither black nor a beetle.

Ladybirds are most likely valuable allies of the farmer and gardener, for they are great devourers of the various species of aphis which do so much harm in our orchards and gardens, and I have seen a record of their eating of the eggs of the destructive Colorado beetle, about which there was so much ado last summer when it was found on potato plants near the docks at Tilbury.

*A.W. Boyd*

## 3 December

### 1767 [Norfolk]

My Man Luke Barnard acquainted me this morning that he did not like his Wages, and unless I would raise them, he must leave me, which he is to do at Lady Day next, and his Year being up Yesterday, I am to give him at the Rate of five Pounds a Year till Lady Day without any new Cloaths &c. I am not very sorry, He is a willing Fellow, but indolent & too fond of Cyder.

*James Woodforde*

### 1788 [Fyfield, Hampshire]

Hamper from London containing ye Natural History of Selborne presented by ye author [his brother Gilbert]. A very elegant 4to, with splendid engravings and curious investigations.

*Henry White*

# 4 December

**1908 [Barnstaple, North Devon]**
Went to the Veterinary Surgeon and begged of him the skull of a horse.
Carried the trophy home under my arm – bare to the public view. 'Why,
Lor', 'tis an ole 'orse's jib,' M— said when I got back.

*W.N.P. Barbellion*

# 5 December

**1965 [Underhill Farm, Lyme Regis]**
The purity of the sun here: white, silver, gold. I have never been more
conscious of it. And how the sea changes in texture, colour, transparency
– especially the first. If the waves run from the west they catch in the
evening a kind of imperceptible brownish glaze on the westward slopes;
the eastward are a glaucous grey-green. Very much the soft light in the
aquatints.

Boredom with books, talk about ideas and books, trends and cultures, the
intellectual life of our day; it is like a flood, a natural disaster. So many voices.
Finally they blend in a universal scream.

Rats: they come round the back door at night and when we come out,
blinded by the light, they cannon off the walls and take all the wrong
exits. I could have killed one the other night. But even a rat has a right
to live.

*John Fowles*

# 6 December

**1852 [Stafford]**
Rather a trying morning at lessons and with one or two letters to write.
We drank tea at 7 and half past 7 drove into Dorchester to hear Charles
Bingham lecture at the Town Hall on Switzerland. It was a nice lecture,

but rather too vast as to subject and too sketchy, but much of interest in matter and manner. Came home at quarter past 10. Had a fire in my bedroom all day.

*Emily Smith*

# 7 December

1780 [Fyfield, Hampshire]
Bottled off the pipe of Port wine. Dr Sheppard and Mr Griffith had 1 qr. of it. Mr Ekins had 1 qr., it ran 56 dozen exactly, and 4 bottles and 1 of thick. All done in excellent order and without accident till 30 doz were danced over and 2½ broken by a drunken beast from Andover.

*Henry White*

1973 [Belmont, Lyme Regis]
A fine badger on the lawn, when I went out to piss after one of our late whist sessions. He sniffed and sniffed in the torchlight, then lumbered quickly off.

*John Fowles*

# 8 December

1817 [Over Stowey, Somerset]
A sad accident happened this day at Stowey. Verrier's grandson a little boy that lived with his grandfather in carrying a knife to cut leather from Clitson the Shoemaker to his father, a Currier in Stowey, in running through the street with it in the dark stumbled over some loose stones and fell on the blade of the knife which ran into his neck and killed him on the spot. This has affected the grandfather very much, an industrious mason at Stowey of some note.

*William Holland*

# 9 December

## 1801 [Grasmere, the Lake District]

After dinner it was agreed we should walk . . . William did not go with us but Mary and I walked into Easedale and backwards and forwards in that large field under George Rawnson's white cottage. We had intended gathering mosses and for that purpose we turned into the green Lane behind the Tailor's but it was too dark to see the mosses. The river came galloping past the church as fast as it could come and when got into Easedale we saw Churn Milk force like a broad stream of snow. At the little foot-Bridge we stopped to look at the company of rivers which came hurrying down the vale this way and that; it was a valley of streams and Islands, with that great waterfall at the head and lesser falls in different parts of the mountains coming down to these Rivers. We could hear the sound of those lesser falls but we could not *see* them. We walked backwards and forwards till all distant objects except the white shape of the waterfall, and the lines of those mountains were gone. We had the Crescent Moon when we went out, and at our return there were a few stars that shone dimly, but it was a grey cloudy night.

*Dorothy Wordsworth*

## 1873 [Chippenham, Wiltshire]

Mrs Coates told me of her son Reuben's noble conduct to his dying sweetheart Sarah Hains. He would not be ashamed of her nor cease walking with her though her dropsical size drew all eyes and many suspicions upon him.

*Francis Kilvert*

# 10 December

## 1988 [Belmont, Lyme Regis]

An exceptionally fine day. I worked for an hour down the bottom, in the very mild sunshine, near the woodcock orchids, showing green in the leaf-litter. As always nowadays I am swamped with the number of things I would like to do in the garden. It drowns me, overwhelms me, my behindness.

*John Fowles*

1997 [Bardsey Island, Wales]
Shopping and a visit to the Archifdy in Caernarfon (researching the building of Bardsey lighthouse and its effect on the island community). The moon was clear on my left as I drove home down the long peninsula, and Jupiter and Venus bright and beckoning ahead.

As a symbol of 'good will' and sociability, robins are misplaced on Christmas cards – there was a tremendous fight outside the kitchen window this morning. Reminded me of Gwyneth Lewis's lines

> *Nid tincial tiwn ond bygwyth trais*
> *mae cân gylfinir a dryw'r helyg*

(Not pretty tunes but threats of violence/are the songs of curlew and willow warbler).

*Christine Evans*

# 11 December

1950 [Sissinghurst, Kent]
At 11.45 a.m. Jim Lees-Milne picks me up with Jack Rathbone [Secretary of the National Trust] and we go down to Hertfordshire to see Bernard Shaw's house which he left to the Trust. We first go into the garden. A sloping lawn and rough grass intersected with a few rose-beds. A bank, with a statue of St Joan. A hut in which he worked. Everything as he left it. Postcards, envelopes, a calendar marking the day of his death [2 November, 1950], curiously enough a Bible and prayer book and Crockford's Directory, a pair of mittens. The grass path and the bed around the statue of St Joan are strewn with his ashes and those of Mrs Shaw [who died in 1943]. The Trustees and the doctor got both urns and put them on the dining-room

table. They then emptied the one into the other and stirred them with a kitchen spoon. They then went out into the garden and emptied spoonfuls of the mixture on to the flower-beds and paths. All this some fifteen days ago, but the remains are still there. Just like the stuff Viti [Sackville-West, his wife] puts down for slugs.

*Harold Nicolson*

1971 [Belmont, Lyme Regis]
Bridport. I buy a Neolithic axe, Cornish greenstone, in an antique shop. £4.50.

*John Fowles*

## 12 December

1799 [Over Stowey, Somerset]
The man in the Poorhouse raving. Mr Reeks of Aisholt died last night in the Horrors – A Worthless little man and a disgrace to his profession. He killed himself by drinking. Was brought up to trade but did not succeed well in anything being idle and dissolute. Then he entered some Hall in Oxford, was there a few weeks but never wore a Gown all that time. Entered into Holy Orders, married a Miss Brice and had the Living at Aisholt with her even before the Father's death. Then gave himself up entirely to drinking and brought himself to the Grave in the very prime of life. He did not want intellect but was very satirical, vulgar and even abusive in his language especially when he had got a little liquor.

*William Holland*

## 13 December

1852 [Staffordshire]
Awful Day to us! After prayers dear Edward came over suddenly from Dorchester to say an express had come from Mrs Dolphin in Town by

Lydia's butler to say our deluded sister Lydia had run off to Scotland with that most vile of men Dr Lees. Yesterday at 4 this vile step was taken. God support my precious husband and his brothers under this bitter, bitter trial and direct them what to do and awaken the unfortunate creature to repentance.

*Emily Smith*

## 1995 [Combe Florey, Somerset]

Many Britons will experience violent and contradictory emotions on learning that some part of the great art collection at Castle Howard has been sold partly in order to buy off a younger son. There can be no doubt that these magnificent country houses and the society they supported were Britain's greatest contribution to human civilisation after Shakespeare.

In the new democratic age it is sometimes pretended that we are a nation of footballers, but it is no good pretending we are much good at football. Even today, far more people visit a stately home every year than ever attend a football match. They are the quiet majority, recognising that the country house was our greatest collective achievement.

But it is no good denying that the system was founded and sustained by an elementary injustice – the cruel and unnatural system of primogeniture, whereby the eldest son grabs all the family loot and turns his brothers and sisters out to make their own ways in the world.

This may have resulted in beautiful houses, well-managed estates and contented peasants, but it also created half the social problems that afflict us: an angry exiled urban intelligentsia prone to foolish Left-wing opinions, hatred of the rich, class snobbery and all the rest of it. No other country in the world sees a person's death as sufficient reason to confiscate most of his estate; no other country has ever proposed 98 per cent as the top rate of income tax where the income is derived from savings.

If the English country house culture must be destroyed, what, I wonder, will take its place? The football culture will never appeal to more than a noisy minority, but there must be something to emerge from an intelligent and ingenious race reduced, by foolish education policies, to making Plasticene worms. I think I see the beginnings of it in the Wallace & Gromit animated models. Their brilliant creator, Nick Park, is a Prince of a new Plasticene age. Wallace and Gromit are the inheritors of everything our former pride had planned.

*Auberon Waugh*

# 14 December

## 1784 [Fyfield, Hampshire]

Frost rather harder, but not so severe to feel. Waggons move about in abundance, though ye roads are no better. Coaches stay at Andover every night and make 2 journey days instead of one to London.

*Henry White*

## 1864 [Beeley, Chatsworth Estate]

Wrote a letter to J.G. Cottingham, Sir, having recd. a letter from you yesterday respecting a grass field as you call it that I am ploughing up adjoining Belley Plantation. Will you kindly inform me on what grounds you object a lowering and Game Damages for the same. This field is doing me no good as it is, another year or two it would be no better than the wild common, it is now growing over with heath and gorse. If I must not plough it, what must I do with it, I think it hath cost me money enoughf allready without having the expens of tilling it again in a few more years: that field alone hath cost me more than 100£ tilling and fencing. I have done enough in that field for it to be my own, Therefore if there is no Game damages I shall not expect to receive any but if there is any damages done I certainly shall expect you to pay for all the damage there is done.

Mr Norman had one dozen pigeons, William ploughing in the far piece Father with him most of the day, I fetched one ton of linseed cake from Rowsley Station, Aaron helped me unload it, he was thrashing most of the day, my back is very lame. Mr H. Lees and Mr Thompson had each 1/2 ton of cake, Mr Thompson paid me for his.

*William Hodkin*

# 15 December

1756 [East Hoathly, Sussex]

In the forenoon went down to John Watford's and agreed to take of him one fat hog of about 10 or 12 stone, to be ready in the month of February, at 2s.2d. per stone, and to weigh no feet and ears if I kill him at home ...

*Thomas Turner*

# 16 December

1872 [Chippenham, Wiltshire]

Dame Matthews used to live at the Home Farm at Langley Burrell. She was a member of the family, but she must have lived a long time ago, as Mrs Banks remarked, because she called cows 'kine'. The Dame used to sit in the chimney corner and near her chair there was a little window through which she could see all down the dairy. One evening she saw one of the farm men steal a pound of butter out of the dairy and put it into his hat, at the same moment clapping his hat upon his head.

'John,' called the Dame. 'John, come here. I want to speak to you.' John came, carefully keeping his hat on his head. The Dame ordered some ale to be heated for him and bade him sit down in front of the roaring fire. John thanked his mistress and said he would have the ale another time, as he wanted to go home at once.

'No, John. Sit you down by the fire and drink some hot ale. 'Tis a cold night and I want to speak to you about the kine.'

The miserable John, daring neither to take his hat off nor go without his mistress's leave, sat before the scorching fire drinking his hot ale till the butter in his hat began to run down all over his face. 'Now, John,' she said, 'you may go. I won't charge you anything for the butter.'

*Francis Kilvert*

# 17 December

### 1672 [Northamptonshire]

Richard Porter caught a marten in a trap. Mr Ward spent the night at Dr Hollowhead's and when he was taking off his leggings a strange dog came up behind and bit his shin, and they feared the dog was mad, because next day in the fields it bit a man two or three times, and since then they have heard nothing about it. Thomas Pole bought a lantern, to be hung by the kitchen door. Father returned the guns to my brothers.

*Thomas Isham*

# 18 December

### c.2000 [Walnut Tree Farm, Suffolk]

A tortoiseshell taxies up the windowpane, flexing its wings as if seeking the optimum angle for flight. The little insomniac should be fast asleep, immersed in hibernation, its metabolism slowed to the point of torpor. Instead, its colours are vivid with life, antennae raised straight, and the fur on its back luxuriant. Now it suns itself beneath my anglepoise. Amazing to see such beauty of summer in winter.

*Roger Deakin*

### 2004 [Claxton, Norfolk]

It was one of those classic winter days when the cloud never lifted and the daylight never really blossomed overhead. It was also that moment on a December's afternoon when even this murky greyness started to ebb away. In fact it was so dull I had a job to pick out the deer that I could hear crashing through the undergrowth and whose going was punctuated by a series of harsh, throaty calls.

Chinese water deer have previously been restricted to wetlands like the Broads, although recently I've noticed them breaking out of this ecological restriction. Throughout the year I've seen several of their small, sandy corpses at the roadside even on the outskirts of Norwich. If they finally adapt to ordinary farmland it is difficult to see what could limit their spread. Nor would I like to second-guess what the impact might be of any consequent rise in population.

In the Yare valley, however, they are now an integral element of the scene. This deer bucked and jinked along the dyke then finally realised that the only real source of panic was the pounding trochee of its own heart: It slowed, stopped, then turned and we watched one another as the Yare valley steadily dissolved around us.

Pools of mist were gathering in the hollows and long, soft shoals of white wound round the alder carr until only the tops stood proud as disembodied islands of vegetation. The dusk landscape re-asserted its powers of mystery and swallowed down the deer. I was left to walk home alone along the raised bank, which stretched through the mist-tide like some weird dream causeway that led back to the shores of the living.

*Mark Cocker*

## 19 December

1986 [Lyme Regis]
We came back from London, picking up the car at Axminster; but something odd even before we got out there. The front room curtains were drawn closed. I go to unlock the front door; no good, the inside latch is up. I went around the house. No sign of a break-in, no ladder. At last, doing it more carefully, I see the bedroom door on to the balcony: it is open; and that, finally, is how I get in myself.

We were burgled in September, when in the USA; and now again, and much more thoroughly. They had seemingly been through everything, every room (my study door was forced open), every drawer. I called the police, and we spent the next two hours with them. The Benjamin Martin Gregorian [an eighteenth-century telescope] is gone; all my trade tokens; all Eliz's remaining jewellery; the little French silk-suspension clock we had for years; all current stamps; a box of cutlery; Eliz's camera; my pocket calculator; a chocolate ice-cream from the flat refrigerator, its paper left on the floor.

My first reaction is at its seeming senselessness, amateurishness at how much was *not* stolen: no pottery, no books, no paintings, nothing of what an antique-aware burglar must have gone for. Eliz is in despair, it seems most at the idea that some stranger having been through everything. We both share a contempt of worldly possessions in the usual sense. The police must think us an odd couple – the one (me) so unconcerned, the other (Eliz) renouncing all ownership and putting all the blame on Lyme and our living here.

*John Fowles*

# 20 December

1800 [Over Stowey, Somerset]
Family up and we are at Breakfast in Margaret's room that Betty may make a full display of her inundations down stairs.

*William Holland*

1946 [Inverness-shire]
This is a time when I find it difficult to look at the countryside impersonally. I see it as it were, with 'Christmas eyes'. I can now pass the great fir wood unseeingly but the glow and glint of the most obscure holy tree catches my eye. I sniff the air expectantly. The sentimentalist in me keeps hoping for a white Christmas. And even when my expectations are not fulfilled, when my eyes keep beholding a black, ploughed world, I can still console myself that night will come – night which is never really dark even without the aid of moonlight, for December nights, one and all, have a silver glint and a promise of white frost in their smell.

*Jessie Kesson*

# 21 December

1778 [Selborne, Hampshire]
Vast flocks of fieldfares. Are these prognostic of hard weather?

*Gilbert White*

1944 [Jersey]

We had to take two fowls to the Parish Hall for the Germans to eat at Christmas. It is awful, when so many Jersey folk will be without a Christmas dinner. But it is best to let them have what they want otherwise they will take it by force, and may punish us too.

*Nan Le Ruez*

# 22 December

1801 [Grasmere, the Lake District]

Still thaw. I washed my head. William and I went to Rydale for letters. The road was covered with dirty snow, rough and rather slippery. We had a melancholy letter from C., for he had been very ill, though he was better when he wrote. We walked home almost without speaking . . . We stopped a long time in going to watch a little bird with a salmon coloured breast – a white cross or T upon its wings, and a brownish back with faint stripes [undoubtedly a cock chaffinch]. It was pecking the scattered Dung upon the road. It began to peck at the distance of 4 yards from us and advanced nearer and nearer till it came within the length of Wm's stick without any apparent fear of us . . . I found Mary at home in her riding-habit all her clothes being put up. We were very sad about Coleridge. Wm walked further. When he came home he cleared a path to the necessary – called me out to see it but before we got there a whole housetop full of snow had fallen from the roof upon the path and it echoed in the ground beneath like a dull beating upon it . . . We stopped to look at the Stone seat at the top of the Hill. There was a white cushion upon it, round at the edge like a cushion, and the rock behind looked soft as velvet, of a vivid green and so tempting! The snow too looked as soft as down cushion. A young Foxglove, like a star, in the Centre. There were a few green lichens about it and a few withered Brackens of fern here and there and upon the ground near. All else was thick snow – no footmark to it, not the foot of a sheep.

*Dorothy Wordsworth*

1876 [Slackfields Farm, Derbyshire]
*Fine* Ploughing in Great Marsondy. Hedge topping. Paid for boots and shoes 13s 9d. Mr Copestake, for 2 bags fourths £1. 15. 0d; Mr Georges for drapery 17s 0d; Groceries and expenses 5s 6d.

*Henry Hill*

## 23 December

1830 [Abbotsford, the Scottish Borders]
To add for this day to the evil thereof, I am obliged to hold a Black-fishing court at Selkirkshire. This is always an unpopular matter in one of our countries, as the salmon never do get up to the heads of the water in wholesome season, and are there in numbers in spawning-time. So that for several years during the late period, the gentry, finding no advantage from preserving the spawning fish, neglected the matter altogether in a kind of dudgeon and the peasantry laid them waste at their will. As the property is very valuable, the proprietors down the country agreed to afford some additional passage for fish when the river is open, providing they will protect the spawning fish during close-time. A new Act has been passed, with heavy penalties and summary powers of recovery. Some persons are cited under it to-day; and a peculiar licence of poaching having distinguished the district of late years, we shall be likely to have some disturbance. They have been holding a meeting for reform in Selkirk, and it will be difficult to teach them that this consists in anything else save the privilege of obeying such laws as please them. I shall do my duty, however. Do what is right, come what will.

Six black-fishers were tried, four were condemned. All went very quietly till the conclusion, when one of the criminals attempted to break out. I stopped him for the time with my own hand. But after removing him from the Court-house to the jail he broke from the officers, who are poor feeble old men, the very caricature of peace officers.

*Sir Walter Scott*

1843 [Falmouth, Cornwall]

Mud very general. A bright frosty Christmas is a poetical creation. It is very long since we have realised it in these parts. I gave dinners of beef & potatoes to some 40 or 50 in my parish to dress on Christmas day.

*Barclay Fox*

## 24 December

1903 [Barnstaple, North Devon]

Went out with L to try to see the squirrels again. We could not find one and were just wondering if we should draw blank when L noticed one clinging to the bark of a tree with a nut in its mouth. We gave it a good chase, but it escaped into the thickest part of the fir tree, still carrying the nut, and we gave up firing at it. Later on, L got foolishly mischievous – owing, I suppose, to our lack of sport – and unhinged a gate which he carried two yards into a copse, and threw it on the ground. Just then, he saw the Squirrel again and jumped over the hedge into the copse, chasing it from tree to tree with his catty [catapult]. Having lost it, he climbed a fir tree into a Squirrel's drey at the top and sat there on the tree top, and I, below, was just going to lift the gate back when I looked up and saw a farmer watching me, menacing and silent. I promptly dropped the gate and fled. L, from his Squirrel's drey, not knowing what had happened, called out to me about the nest – that there was nothing in it. The man looked up and asked him who he was and who I was. L would not say and would not come down. The farmer said he would come up. L answered that if he did he would 'gob' on him. Eventually L climbed down and asked the farmer for a glass of cider. The latter gave him his boot and L ran away.

*W.N.P. Barbellion*

1967 [Underhill Farm, Lyme Regis]

First violets in flower.

*John Fowles*

# 25 December

## 1755 [East Hoathly, Sussex]

Being Christmas Day my wife and I both at church in the morning, the text Hebrews 9.26: 'But now once in the end of the world hath he appeared to put away sin by the sacrifice of himself.' My wife and I stayed the communion; gave, each of us, 6d. At home all day. On reading Derham's notes on Boyle's lectures I find he says that Mr Boyle demonstrates that so slender a wire may be drawn from gold that from one ounce of gold a wire may be drawn 777,600 feet in length or 155 miles and a half. In the even Tho. Davy here and supped with us and stayed till 11 o'clock but drunk nothing, only 1 pint of mild beer. We read Smart's poems on immensity, omniscience and power.

*Thomas Turner*

## 1782 [Norfolk]

This being Christmas Day I went to Church this Morn' and then read Prayers and administred the Holy Sacrament. Mr and Mrs Custance both at Church and both received the Sacrament from my Hands. The following poor old Men dined at my House to day, as usual, Js Smith, Clerk, Richd Bates, Richd Buck; Thos Cary; Thos Dicker; Thos Cushing; Thos Carr — to each besides gave 1/0 — in all 0.7.0. I gave them for Dinner a Surloin of Beef rosted and plenty of plumb-Pudding. We had mince Pies for the first Time to-day.

*James Woodforde*

## 1801 [Somerset]

The Singers at the window tuned forth a most dismal ditty, half drunk too and with the most wretched voices.

*William Holland*

## 1870 [Clyro, Radnorshire]

As I lay awake praying in the early morning I thought I heard a sound of distant bells. It was an intense frost. I sat down in my bath upon a sheet of thick ice which broke in the middle into large pieces whilst sharp points and jagged edges stuck all around the sides of the tub like chevaux de frise, not particularly comforting to the naked thighs and loins, for the keen ice cut like broken glass. The ice water stung and scorched like fire. I had to collect the floating pieces of ice and pile them on a chair before I could use the sponge and then I had to thaw the sponge in my hands for it was a mass of ice.

*Francis Kilvert*

## 1973 [Belmont, Lyme Regis]

Christmas Day, on our own. We had a walk along to the cress-bed beyond Pinhay Bay, and picked the first cresses. Totally deserted, a very lovely blue and sunlit day. The sun set as we came back to the Cobb, sinking huge into a mist-bank over Torbay; a resplendent deep pink and reluctant orb. We had the cress with our goose.

*John Fowles*

## 1997 [Bardsey Island, Wales]

*S.E. severe gale 9.*

A dreadful night, but the wind has eased down a little. It seems strange after all that violent noise to look out on the same landscape. We have not heard yet how much damage there may be, or where, but we seem to have come through. The old caravan's wrecked, but that was due for clearing anyway. As soon as it was light, Ernest went down to check the boat.

We had our traditional walk after lunch. The tide was high up the beach; we stood for a time watching the wild white spray furiously smashing, pure energy as it meets the rock; drawing in its breath as if with rage as it falls back.

We are lucky to have the Rayburn to cook the turkey – it will probably be days before the power is back on, such a big area is affected. We have a fire to sit by, plenty of candles and no holes in our roof.

*Christine Evans*

*c.*2003 [South of England]

A robin was recently reported going into a garage, getting locked in, and setting off the burglar alarm. It is not surprising that robins are seen as Christmas birds, because when the days are short they associate with human beings in the hope of getting food more quickly.

This is partly because food is so often put out for them, but also because they connect animal activity in general with food supply. They will be on the lookout when moles are turning up molehills, when there may be something they will want in the fresh earth. So a robin sitting on a garden fork, watching a human working in the garden, really sees this provider of worms as no more than a kind of large mole.

*Derwent May*

# 26 December

1842 [Falmouth, Cornwall]

To Penjerrick to dine with my people as usual on roast beef & plum pudding. Got home in time to join the Christmas revels taking place at our house. We had 28 at tea of 6 years old & upwards, from little Minny up to Sterling. The evening went off most brilliantly, & the fund of enjoyment so easily given to so many little hearts, was not the least enjoyable part of it. From the venerable effigies of Father Christmas with scarlet coat & cocked hat, stuck all over with presents for the guests, by his side the old year, a most dismal & haggard old beldame in a night cap & spectacles, then 1843, a promising baby fast asleep in a cradle. Then we had a 'galvanic shock', which was played on Juliet Sterling & myself, blinding us & dressing up our hands & arms into the exact imitation of the baby's by the aid of a little paint & flannel, to the no small consternation & surprise of the patient on removing the bandage. Then with the aid of a good mask, nightcap, knee-breeches, pillow, & coat & waistcoat of my father's I was enabled to make a very passable elderly Friend & bestow some wholesome advice on the children & on Sterling who was vastly entertained. We then had lots of tableaux vivants which were very good, then supper, then fireworks, then everything else, & we separated in high good humour with ourselves & our company.

*Barclay Fox*

## 1911 [Barnstaple, North Devon]

With the dog for a walk around Windy Ash. It was a beautiful windy morning – a low sun giving out a pale light but no warmth – a luminant, not a fire – the hedgerows bare and well trimmed, an Elm lopped close showing white stumps which glistened liquidly in the sun, a Curlew whistling overhead, a deep cut lane washed hard and clean by the winter rains, a gunshot from a distant cover, a creeping Wren, silent and tame, in a bramble bush, and over the five-barred gate the granite roller with vacant shafts. I leaned on the gate and saw the great whisps of cloud in the sky like comets' tails. Everything cold, crystalline.

*W.N.P. Barbellion*

## 1928 [New Forest]

A hateful thing is done here, done every Boxing Day, but I never happened to hear of it until this year. On Boxing Day the boys of the village go out in company to the woods to hunt the squirrel. Their game is to stone them to death. Squirrels are wary and shy and the hunters none too skilful, but they do take toll of them. I do not know the origin of this ugly sport. A forester who has known of it the last five-and-twenty years knew of a tradition that the squirrels eat the tops of the yews, and that this practice is a yearly punitive expedition, but I expect it has a more primitive source than that. Is there not some tradition that connects the red squirrel with Judas Iscariot? – something older still. The primitive 'hunting of the wren', which [Sir James] Frazier includes [in *The Golden Bough*] among primitive agricultural or even pre-agricultural rites, used also to be practised here, but happily now has been discontinued. It was not confined in this place to any one day in the year. When will the squirrel hunt die out? While deer and fox and hare are hunted the village boys may say with reason 'Why not the squirrel too?'

*Janet Case*

# 27 December

### 1769 [Selborne, Hampshire]
Here & there a lamb.

*Gilbert White*

### 1784 [Fyfield, Hampshire]
The rigour of ye frost much abated this morn, tho it froze very smartly, seems mild and pleasant compared to the violent severity of yesterday. Snow lies deep as everywhere. Horse tracks in general obliterated excepting where waggons have passed.

*Henry White*

### 1973 [Machynlleth, Wales]
This winter in Wales we have lost the battle of Cow Green and thousands of oystercatchers have been shot by permission of the Secretary of State for Wales and the Minster of Agriculture. Why? Because the birds are allegedly reducing the number of cockles in an area where cockling is a local industry. But if the cockles have declined, what proof is there that the oystercatchers are responsible? It could be pollution of the water by the local tinplate factories. More likely it is because the cockles are being over-fished by man, just as whales are. There is another point. Even if oystercatchers are reducing the cockle population, will this shooting produce any reduction of oystercatchers in Burry Inlet? Will not their place be taken immediately by oystercatchers from less favourable feeding grounds? Who better than the Ministry of Agriculture to know that the shooting of woodpigeons is a futile exercise? And what about rabbits? In pre-myxomatosis Pembrokeshire millions of rabbits were trapped every year. But this only encouraged the rest to breed more enthusiastically to keep the numbers up. Surely it should have been proved conclusively that oystercatchers were responsible for a reduction in cockles before these horrible and probably futile killings were allowed. Whatever happened to British justice?

*William Condry*

## 28 December

1801 [Grasmere, the Lake District]

William, Mary and I set off on foot to Keswick. We carried some cold mutton in our pockets, and dined at John Stanley's where they were making Christmas pies. The sun shone but it was coldish. We parted from Wm upon the Rays. He joined us opposite Sara's rock. He was busy in composition and sate down upon the Wall. We did not see him again until we arrived at John Stanley's. There we roasted apples in the oven. After we had left John Stanley's Wm discovered that he had lost his gloves. He turned back but they were gone. We were tired and had bad head aches. We rested often. Once Wm left his Spenser and Mary turned back for it and found it upon the Bank where we had last rested. We reached Greta Hall at about ½ past 5 o'clock. The Children and Mrs C. well. After Tea message came from Wilkinson who had passed us on the road inviting Wm to sup at the Oak. He went. Met a young man (a predestined Marquis) called Johnston. He spoke to him familiarly of the LB [*Lyrical Ballads*]. He had seen a copy presented by the Queen to Mrs Harcourt. Said he saw them everywhere and wondered they did not sell. We all went weary to bed. My Bowels very bad.

*Dorothy Wordsworth*

1865 [Beeley, Chatsworth Estate]

Mrs and I got home again by the 9 am train, Wm. began ploughing in the south field, I went with him and helped him to start. Killed Buckley a pig helped G Bond and M Downs a little, the church singers came at night, a fine day.

*William Hodkin*

## 29 December

1755 [East Hoathly, Sussex]

Dr Snelling went away after breakfast. I paid him half a crown for cutting my seton and likewise am to pay John Jones for his horse's hay, oats, etc.

18d. which together make 4s. Oh, could it have been imagined that he could have took anything of me, considering that I paid him £39 for curing my wife, great part of which I paid him before he had it due, and all of it within 5 months after he had performed the cure. I always do and ever did use him after the best manner I was capable of when he was at our house. He was that man that never gave my servants anything, no, not even the meanest trifle that could be. Notwithstanding they always waited on him like as if they were his own servants. Oh, thou blackest of fiends, ingratitude, what an odious colour and appearance dost thou make! Oh may the most ever-to-be-adored Supreme Excellency that sees and views all our most private and secret actions and even knows our most secret thoughts before we bring them into action guide me with His grace that I may never be guilty of that hateful crime, nor even so much as to indulge an ungrateful thought . . .

*Thomas Turner*

## 1917 [Lewes, Sussex]

At midday a great whack and the sycamore fell! I was heart-rent – cried and cried – made a sort of top muslin blind to the little landing window to hide the cruel patch of branchless sky, then arranged a jug of holly on the window ledge to spray across the lower panes and give the illusion of branches.

*Alice Dudeney*

## 1938 [Perth]

It is the premonitory shadows which force the moment into intensified brightness; and, since the coming year may hold in its womb a crisis more decisive than that which is but overpassed, we look out upon the ending year with the consciousness that when again another year is at an end we may remember this moment as the ending of a time. Stillness is now in the air, and grass smoothly brightened by the wintry sun. The bare rods of the apple trees glitter as if varnished, the wings of the pecking crows shine darkly like roughened metal. Lesser birds curve over the hedge and alight with no sound – it is the quiet which assumes the breathlessness of apprehension.

In it we listen for children's voices, the whistle of a boy, the sound of a hammer or of a bell – these to be memories of a moment still lifted above the triumph of machines.

*William Soutar*

## 30 December

### 1916 [Tiverton Smithy, Cheshire]

A fine, warm sort of day, breezy with clouds about. Found [a fox] at Huxley and ran nicely for about a mile, then turned left-handed and hunted him very slowly back to Clotton cover and lost him. Took a goodish fall over some post-and-rails with a big ditch on the far side. All grass, but a lot of wire. Very little to jump – typical Cheshire fences. Drew Stapleton and Waverton blank. Found at Crow's Nest at 2.30, but he was twice headed on the road and ran a short circle out by the railway and back past cover, and after that they never had a line. A very disappointing hunt; scene very moderate all day.

*Siegfried Sassoon*

### 1926 [New Forest]

Country life is a rare begetter of mixed feelings. You feel you would like everyone to have his fill of it, but when the motor parties leave their broken meats and half-smoked cigarettes behind you are not sure. You jib at the prospect of the tarred road instead of the rough sandy one that divides you from the wild. It will bring more charabancs and cars, more people to enjoy, but somehow you can never suffer gladly the sophistication of a solitude. Not everybody wants one yet. You find them camping close by someone's garden gate. But should we not do well to husband some few solitudes against the time they do? I wonder. Is that casuistry? When a green corner is put up for sale for building plots you mourn the loveliness disturbed. But you cannot blink the fact that there is a crying need for houses. Here as elsewhere is a cottage famine. But delectable sites are not as a rule designed for workmen's cottages.

It makes your heart ache to see the finest oak in the countryside cut down to let light in upon the crops. But they tell you it is good for farming.

*Janet Case*

# 31 December

### 1786 [Norfolk]
This being the last Day of the Year, we sat up this Night till after 12 o'clock – then drank Health and happy New Year to all our Somersett Friends &c. and then went for Bedfordshire alias to bed.

*James Woodforde*

### 1874 [Chippenham, Wiltshire]
Edwin Law told me of an infallible receipt for warming cold and wet feet on a journey. Pour half a glass of brandy in each boot.

*Francis Kilvert*

### 1881 [Surbiton, Surrey]
2000 peewits in same field. Thrushes singing morning yesterday. Buttercup, avens, white nettle flower. Peewits feed among sheep until dusk then lost in shadowy mist, utter but one cry now in the depth of winter or summer, 'peewit'.

*Richard Jefferies*

### 1973 [Belmont, Lyme Regis]
An exceptionally mild winter, even for here; we've had no frosts yet; even a Portugese cistus in flower; on Christmas Eve I picked two splendid narcissi. The passion-flowers on my balcony have been fruited heavily this year; still orange rugby footballs by the dozen. The birds seem reluctant to eat them, alas. A negative sign of the mildness must be the absence of marsh tits (only one seen so far) and of tawny owls.

*John Fowles*

1997 [Bardsey Island, Wales]

'Nine-tenths of our life is well forgotten in the living,' wrote William Carlos Williams. I suppose every year changes each of us, subtly, though we don't recognise how or why. I've had so much more time to discover things, birds, especially; I never really saw a wheatear before — their slanting flight, the way their stripes of silver and chocolate brown catch the light. I didn't consider it necessary to know the names of everything — that names are only the labels we put on things - but knowledge of the detail is a kind of honouring the pattern.

The fulmars are back; after four months' silent wandering over thousands of miles in the Atlantic, long dark night and their pituitary glands have prompted them back to the noisy cliff-ledge nest-sites, although they will not breed until May. And the lights are on in Wil Gwyddel's lambing shed at Gwagnoe. The cycle goes on.

*Christine Evans*

# Biographies

ALLINGHAM, WILLIAM (1824–89) Born in Ireland, he worked first as a customs officer before settling in England in 1863. He was well-connected in the literary world and counted among his friends Coventry Patmore, Thomas Carlyle and Tennyson. He is best known for his poetry, most notably 'The Faeries' ('Up the airy mountain') and his diary which appeared in 1907.

BARBELLION, W.N.P. (Bruce Frederick Cummings) (1889–1919) By profession a naturalist on the staff of the Natural History Museum in London, he suffered acute ill-health from childhood, and from early manhood knew he was doomed to an incurable and progressive paralysis. Despite this his diaries, first published in 1919 shortly before his death, with the title *The Journal of a Disappointed Man*, are remarkable for their forensic observation and vivid style.

BENNETT, ALAN (1934– ) Born in Yorkshire and educated at Oxford, he is a dramatist and actor. He first appeared on stage at the Edinburgh Festival Fringe in 1960 in *Beyond the Fringe*. He has written for theatre and television, including *Forty Years On*, *Habeas Corpus*, *Kafka's Dick*, *An Englishman Abroad*, *The Madness of King George* and *The History Boys*. *Writing Home* (1994) includes essays and reflections as well as excerpts from his journal. In *Untold Stories* (2005) he wrote candidly and movingly of the mental illness that afflicted his mother and other family members.

BENNETT, (ENOCH) ARNOLD (1867–1931) The son of a Staffordshire solicitor, he was destined to follow in his father's footsteps but determined to become a writer and moved to London. A phenomenally successful novelist and playwright and influential reviewer with a prodigious output, his best-known books were set in the Potteries of his home region. His journal covers the years from 1896 to 1929.

BENSON, A(RTHUR) C(HRISTOPHER) (1862–1925) Son of E.W. Benson, Archbishop of Canterbury, he was master of Magdalene College, Cambridge. A prolific author, he wrote many volumes of biography, family reminiscences, criticism and verses, including 'Land of Hope and Glory'. His diary, comprising some five million words, starts in 1897 and ends in 1925. Extracts were first published in 1926.

BIRCHALL, DEARMAN (1828–97) Born in Leeds and educated at private schools in York and Croydon, he went into the cloth trade in Leeds. He started his own business in 1853, but was only a sleeping partner after he moved to Gloucestershire in 1869. His firm won prizes for cloth at various International Exhibitions. His first wife died two years after their marriage in 1861 and he remarried in 1873. He was then living at Bowden Hall, Gloucester, where he housed his collection of china, fabrics and paintings.

BOYD, A.W. (1885–1959) Beginning in 1933, he wrote a weekly Country Diary in the *Manchester Guardian*, which formed the basis of his book, *The Country Diary of a Cheshire Man*. He lived in the parish of Antrobus, near Northwich. 'Cheshire', he noted, 'is essentially a farming county. Its dairy herds and Cheshire cheese need no eulogy, and speak for the quality of its grass-land' – much of which at the time he was writing (the Second World War), was under the plough.

BROWN, GEORGE MACKAY (1921–96) Born in Stromness, Orkney, which he rarely left, Mackay Brown was a novelist, short story writer, poet and news-paper columnist. His subject was what was on his doorstep, the rich lore of the islands. His books were many, including the novels *Greenvoe*, *Magnus* and *Beside the Ocean of Time*, which in 1994 was shortlisted for the Booker Prize. His *Collected Poems* appeared in 1995. Sir Peter Maxwell Davies set to music many of his poems and other works. His weekly column for *The Orcadian*, 'Under Brinkie's Brae', named after the hill under which Stromness nestles, describes whatever took his fancy, be it the introduction of a new radio station or an outing to a neighbouring island.

BYNG, JOHN (1743–1813) For the whole of his later life the 5th Viscount Torrington was known as Colonel John Byng. It was under this name that he compiled the day-to-day accounts of his summer holidays, spent in a succession of riding tours, which were eventually published as *Rides Round Britain*.

CASE, JANET (nds) Obliged to give up her work and life in London, she settled finally in 1922 in the New Forest, which she explored endlessly and which she loved, especially its birds. In 1925, she was invited by the *Manchester Guardian* to become one of its regular country diarists, signing herself J.E.C.

Her final contribution appeared in June 1937, when she was in a nursing home, from where she observed a 'glorious' beech tree and two big white butterflies.

CLARK, ALAN (1928–99) Son of Kenneth Clark, author of *Civilization*. He was Conservative MP for Plymouth (Sutton), 1974–92, Minister of Trade, 1986–92, and Minister of State, Ministry of Defence, 1989–92. His books include *The Donkeys: A History of the BEF in 1915; The Fall of Crete; Barbarossa: The Russo-German Conflict, 1941–45* and *Aces High: The War in the Air over the Western Front.* His diaries cover the period 1972–99, when he was privy to the internal workings of the Thatcher government. He had a well-deserved reputation as a ladies' man.

COCKER, MARK (1959–) Author and naturalist, formerly employed by the Royal Society for the Protection of Birds, English Nature and Birdlife International. He lives in the Norfolk countryside. His books deal with modern responses to the wild, whether found in landscape, human societies or in other species. He has written for the *Guardian*'s 'Country Diary' column since 1988.

CONDRY, WILLIAM (1918–88) On 9 October 1957, Condry wrote his first 'Country Diary' for the *Manchester Guardian*, which was signed with his initials, 'W.M.C.' It was not until 1966 that he and his fellow diarists had their names acknowledged in full. In fact, he had kept a diary since 1927. He was the doyen of Welsh naturalists and the author of several books, including *Natural History of Wales, Wildlife, My Life, Pathway to the Wild* and *A Welsh Country Diary*, as well as a book about Thoreau.

CORY, WILLIAM (1823–92) Educated at Eton, where he was assistant master for twenty-six years, he was the author of the 'Eton Boat Song'. An accomplished classical scholar, he wrote verses in Latin and Greek. His best known poem is perhaps 'Heraclitus'.

DE LA PRYME, ABRAHAM (1671–1704) At St John's College, Cambridge, he met Sir Isaac Newton, which sparked his interest in the occult. As a curate in Hull, he compiled local histories. He was given the living of Thorne and in 1701 was elected a fellow of the Royal Society. His diary includes public events, anecdotes and notes on archaeology and topography.

DEAKIN, ROGER (1943–2006) Writer, documentary maker, environmentalist, for the last six years of his life he kept a record in forty-five lined exercise books of his daily life, work, thoughts and memories which was distilled into *Notes from Walnut Tree Farm*, published posthumously. He was a founder director of the arts/environmental charity Common Ground in 1982. For the last forty years of his life he lived in an Elizabethan moated farmhouse on the edge of Mellis Common, near Diss, Suffolk. He was the author of the acclaimed *Waterlog*, in which he described his experiences of 'wild swimming'. This was followed by *Wildwood: A Journey through Trees*, a celebration of the transforming magic of trees.

DEW, JAMES GEORGE (1846–1928) A relieving officer in Oxfordshire, he kept a diary which is a closely observed record of nineteenth- and early twentieth-century life.

DUDENEY, ALICE (1866–1945) Once deemed 'a rival to Thomas Hardy', she was an English writer of short stories and novels. She kept a diary from 1910 until her death, with only a short gap for the years 1914–15. Publication, however, was withheld for forty years, in deference to local sensibilities.

EVANS, CHRISTINE (1943–) Brought up by her Welsh grandmother until she was eighteen months old, Evans, a poet, imagines her first words might have been Welsh. When she was eight her father gave her a copy of *Early Morning Island* by R.M. Lockley, whose descriptions of the Pembrokeshire islands cast a spell on her that has never gone away, though she was born in West Yorkshire. She is the author of several collections of poems, including *Looking Inland*, *Falling Back (The Shepherd's Widow)* and *Cometary Phases*.

EVELYN, JOHN (1620–1706) The second son of a wealthy Surrey landowner, he was always a man of substance, though not independently well off until 1699 when he inherited the family estate at Wotton. He went to Balliol College, Oxford, then read law before travelling extensively on the Continent. Throughout his long life he was an eye-witness to many epochal happenings, including the Restoration of Charles II, the Second Dutch War, the Plague and the Great Fire of London. His epitaph described this era as 'an age of extraordinary events, and revelations'. In 1664 he published *Sylva, or a Discourse on Forest Trees*, which was highly influential and made him a celebrity. Of his eight children, only one survived him. His immense *Diary* extends from 1620 in the reign of James I to 1706 in the reign of Queen Anne, a time of enormous transformation.

FEA, PATRICK (*c.*1710–96) An Orkney laird, he kept a diary over a period of thirty years from 1766. Details of his early life are meagre, though it seems likely he was born in Orkney, at Airy, his father's farm in Stronsay. In 1723 he became a Freeman of Kirkwall. After Culloden, having been identified as one of a group of 'hotheaded young men' who supported the Jacobite cause, he hid from Hanoverian troops in caves in Orkney. The farm where he lived, worked and wrote his diary, which gives a detailed if terse account of his daily life, lies at the head of a long shallow bay at the south end of Sanday, Orkney's third-largest island.

FOWLES, JOHN (1926–2005) English novelist, best known for *The Magus* and *The French Lieutenant's Woman*. His journals were published in two volumes, the second one posthumously. As well as describing in unflinching and, at times, uncomfortable detail the life of a writer, they are also remarkable for Fowles's interest and empathy with nature, which he much preferred to the hoop-la of the literary world.

FOX, BARCLAY (1817–55) Born in Falmouth, Cornwall. His father was a notable scientist and the family were Quakers. His diary, which he kept from the age of fourteen until shortly before he died, is notable not only for its chronicling of provincial life in the mid-nineteenth century but for its portraits of three eminent Victorians: John Sterling, John Stuart Mill and Thomas Carlyle.

FOX, CAROLINE (1819–1871) Born in Cornwall the same day as Queen Victoria, the younger daughter of Robert Were Fox, scientist and inventor, she led a very active social life despite living so far from fashionable society. Of a delicate disposition, she had a Quaker upbringing. Her diaries, written from the age of seventeen, are crowded with a remarkable gallery of characters, including Tennyson, Wordsworth, Carlyle, John Stuart Mill and many others.

GATES, PHIL (nds) A prolific author and academic, he graduated from Oxford University in 1973. Subsequent research has focussed on plant breeding methods and desert trees. He has written extensively for newspapers and magazines and has produced numerous books, many for young people. He has been the *Guardian*'s country diarist for County Durham since 1988 and the *Northern Echo*'s country diarist since 1984.

GRIFFIN, A(RTHUR) HARRY (1911–2004) Though he started his climbing career in the 1930s, he could still be seen on the Lakeland hills well into his eighties. Among climbers he was legendary as a repository of oral history. He wrote more than a dozen best-selling books and was a long-time contributor to the *Guardian's* 'Country Diary' column. He was born in Merseyside but his family moved to Barrow-in-Furness on the southern edge of the Lakeland Fells when he was still a child. A notable climber, he was an even more notable chronicler, having started out as a cub reporter on a local newspaper. Often bracketed with Wainwright of walking guide fame, he was critical of the deleterious effect his books had on the fells because of the number of visitors they encouraged.

GUINNESS, SIR ALEC (1914–2000) One of the outstanding actors of his generation, he was born in London. He made his first professional appearance in 1933, and went on to become a member of the Old Vic. During the war he served in the Royal Navy. He starred in numerous films, including *Kind Hearts and Coronets*, *The Bridge on the River Kwai* and *Star Wars*. His theatre work includes *The Cocktail Party*, *A Voyage Round My Father* and *Habeas Corpus*. He was George Smiley in a television adaptation of the spy novels by John le Carré. Knighted in 1959, his diary of 'a retiring actor' covers 1995–6.

HARDY, THOMAS (1840–1928) English poet, novelist and short story writer, famed for such books as *Jude the Obscure*, *Tess of the D'Urbervilles* and *Far from the Madding Crowd*. He was born in the Dorset hamlet of Higher Brockhampton. School was three miles away, which distance he walked twice daily for a number of years. Not surprisingly, walking figures significantly in his fiction, as indeed do the countryside, its creatures and its characters. Later he moved to Dorchester, his home at Max Gate becoming a place of pilgrimage.

HARLAND, ELIZABETH MARY (nds) She is perhaps best known for her book *No Halt at Sunset: The Diary of a Country Housewife*, the majority of whose entries first appeared the *Eastern Daily Press* and which was first published in 1951. She wrote a number of other books, including *Two Ears of Corn*, *Farmer's Girl* and *Well Fare the Plough*.

HAWKER, COLONEL PETER (1786–1853) Starting in the army as a cornet in 1801, he was a captain of the 14th Light Dragoons during the Peninsular War. He was badly wounded at Talavera, and retired from the army in 1813. He became lieutenant-colonel of the North Hampshire militia. He patented an improvement to the pianoforte and devised alterations for firearms, which were demonstrated at the 1851 Exhibition. He was a keen sportsman and author of the much-acclaimed *Instructions to Young Sportsmen*.

HEARNE, THOMAS (1678–1735) His parents' poor circumstances sent Hearne first into day labour, but his exceptional academic skills were recognised and he was sent to school and subsequently to St Edmund Hall, Oxford. He became an assistant keeper at the Bodleian Library and remained there, refusing offers of other posts, until 23 January 1716, when he was shut out for refusing to take the oath to the Hanoverian dynasty. He spent the rest of his life in St Edmund Hall, continuing his work as an antiquary. His diary, kept from 1705 until his death, was frequently dangerously outspoken and finally filled 145 volumes.

HILL, HENRY (1833–99) He took over the tenancy of Slackfields Farm, a 200-acre farm to the east of Horsley village in Derbyshire, in 1871. He was the second son of John and Mary Hill of Higham. His father was a miller. His diaries give a detailed accounting of a farmer's activities and expenditure. By any standards he was a busy man, rarely taking holidays.

HODKIN, WILLIAM (1830–99) His diary for 1864 gives a picture of life on a small Derbyshire farm on the Chatsworth Estate, the daily routine, and the inhabitants of the village of Beeley. Little mention, however, is made of Hodkin's wife, who bore him four sons and a daughter. According to his great grandson, T.A. Burdekin, he was as much a dealer as a farmer, buying and selling a variety of goods, such as coal, wool and flour.

HOLDEN, EDITH (1871–1920) Author and illustrator, born in Birmingham. Brought up a Unitarian, her family believed they had psychic powers and participated in seances where Edith was encouraged to demonstrate her powers of automatic writing. She exhibited her paintings and taught art at a private girls' school. In 1906 she encouraged her students to paint wildflowers in their sketchbooks and select suitable verses to accompany them. Privately she compiled her own notebook, which she called 'Nature notes for 1906'. In 1977, this was published as *The Country Diary of an Edwardian Lady* and became an instant, international and exceptional bestseller, translations of which appeared in thirteen languages.

HOLLAND, WILLIAM (1746–1819) Born at Tyrdan, Denbighshire, he served as rector of the parishes of Over Stowey in Somerset and subsequently Monkton Farleigh, near Bath. Not all of the ninety-nine volumes of his diary survive, but that those that do give an incomparable, frequently amusing and unvarnished picture of rural life.

HOPKINS, GERARD MANLEY (1844–99) English poet and Jesuit priest, born at Stratford, Essex, and educated at Balliol College, Oxford. He wrote poetry from an early age but many of his early efforts were destroyed when he decided to become a Jesuit. His greatest poem, 'The Wreck of the Deutschland', was rejected as too difficult by the Jesuit journal *The Month*. Other well-anthologised poems include 'The Windhover', 'Inversnaid' and 'Spring and Fall'. His journals were published in two volumes in 1959.

ISHAM, SIR THOMAS (1657–81) His diary (1671–3), which was kept at the behest of his father, was written in Latin. It gives a lively picture of the everyday country life of a boy of gentry class in his early teens. He studied at home initially, and then at Christ Church, Oxford, where his father placed him just before his death.

JEFFERIES, (JOHN) RICHARD (1887–1962) A novelist and naturalist, he was born near Swindon, the son of a Wiltshire farmer. He started as a journalist and became known by a letter to *The Times* in 1872 about Wiltshire labourers. His first real success was *The Gamekeeper at Home* (1878), which was followed by other books on rural life. He is perhaps best known today for *Bevis: The Story of a Boy*.

JOSSELIN, REV. RALPH (1617–83) Educated at Jesus College, Cambridge, he spent some time as a schoolteacher before his ordination in 1640, the year in which he married. He became vicar of Earls Colne, Essex, in 1641 where he stayed there until his death. He was also schoolmaster there from 1650 to 1658. His diary starts with a summary of his life up to 1644; the period from 1646 to 1653 is the most detailed.

KESSON, JESSIE (1916–94) Born illegitimately into extreme poverty in the slums of Elgin in north-east Scotland, she was moved into an orphanage at the age of eight. Though clever, she was thrust into domestic service when she was sixteen. She married and worked at various menial jobs, often as a farm worker. Desperate to make ends meet, she began contributing stories, essays and poems to magazines such as the *North-East Review* and the *Scots Magazine*, for whom she kept a country diary for a year. Her novels, including *The White Bird Passes*, *Glitter of Mica* and *Another Time, Another Place*, capture elements of her rural past.

KILVERT, REV. (ROBERT) FRANCIS (1840–79) One of six children, he was educated privately, went up to Oxford, was ordained, and for a time acted as curate to his father. For seven years he served as curate to the vicar of Clyro in Radnorshire, on the border between England and Wales. It was the happiest time of his life. In August 1879 he married Elizabeth Anne Rowland but he died a month later of peritonitis. His wife inherited his diary and is said to have destroyed two large sections of it for personal reasons. What was left was contained in twenty-two notebooks, only three of which survive; the rest were destroyed by an elderly niece of Kilvert's who had inherited them from her brother. The diaries were first published in a three-volume edition, 1938–40, edited by William Plomer.

LASCELLES, SIR ALAN FREDERICK (1887–1981) English courtier. In the First World War he was awarded the Military Cross. Subsequently he became assistant private secretary to the Prince of Wales (later Edward VIII), with whom he became disillusioned, believing him to be in a state of arrested development, and of whom he was a caustic critic. As a royal adviser he was cautious of change. Outwith royal circles he was, among other things, chairman of the Historic Buildings Council for England. His letters and journals, published in the 1980s, are reflective of his character.

LEES-MILNE, JAMES (1908–98) English author and rescuer of decaying country houses, born in Worcestershire and educated at Eton and Oxford. Invalided out of the army in 1941, he spent the war years, at the behest of the National Trust, trundling up and down the country in his car interviewing the owners of remote and dilapidated country houses, many of which he saved from oblivion. His autobiography, *Another Self*, published in 1970, is a model of self-deprecation. His voluminous diaries are full of well-turned anecdotes.

LE RUEZ, ANNIE MARGARET ('NAN') (1915– ) Born on a farm on Jersey in the Channel Islands, she was the second of ten children. She left school at sixteen to work on the family farm. She kept a diary 'on and off' throughout her schooldays and continued to do so during the German Occupation. At the end of the war she placed the volumes in a Red Cross box, where they remained unopened for fifty years.

LISTER, ANNE (1791–1840) An outwardly conventional upper-class woman who lived at Shibden Hall, Halifax, West Yorkshire, Lister had passionate affairs with various women which she chronicled with extraordinary frankness in her diaries. When she inherited Shibden Hall, she spent her time managing the estate, studying languages, mathematics and literature and occasionally travelling. Her diaries cover the years 1817 to 1824.

MACLEAN, ALASDAIR (1926– ) Scottish poet, born in Glasgow. He left school at fourteen, later attending Edinburgh University as a mature student. He worked in the Clydeside shipyards, as a laboratory technician, and did National Service. His poetry has been collected in various volumes, including *From the Wilderness* and *Waking the Dead*. His diary, which he published alongside his father's in *Night Falls in Ardnamurchan: The Twilight of a Crofting Family*, is a moving evocation of the passing of a way of life.

MAY, DERWENT (1930–) Formerly the literary editor of the *Listener*, the *Sunday Telegraph* and the *European*, he is the author of a number of books, including a novel, *Dear Parson*, *Critical Times: The History of the Times Literary Supplement*, and studies of Proust, Robert Graves and Hannah Arendt. Currently, he writes daily for *The Times* on the natural world.

MILLAIS, SIR JOHN EVERETT (1829–96) English artist, a member of the Pre-Raphaelite Brotherhood, which included like-minded colleagues such as William Holman Hunt and Dante Gabriel Rossetti. He was determined to paint things as he found them. In the summer of 1851 he began his masterpiece of outdoor painting, *Ophelia*, which shows the Shakespearian heroine sinking to 'a muddy death' in a brook. Only someone immersed in nature could have captured the painstakingly observed plants and flowers in the background.

MITCHISON, NAOMI (1897–1999) Prolific Scottish writer, born in Edinburgh and educated at Oxford. Her brother was the scientist J.B.S. Haldane. She married G.R. Mitchison, a barrister and later Labour MP and life peer. Her early historical novels, including *The Conquered*, *The Bull Calves* and *The Corn King and the Spring Queen*, are among her best. She also wrote science fiction, biography and memoirs. From the late 1930s onward she spent much of her time on her farm at Carradale, Kintyre. Her friends included E.M. Forster, W.H. Auden and Aldous Huxley. She was an official tribal mother to the Bakgatla of Botswana and a member of the Highlands and Islands Advisory Board.

NEWTON, REV. BENJAMIN (1761–1830) Educated at Jesus College, Cambridge, he served in various parishes on the Welsh borders, in Wiltshire, Somerset and Yorkshire. He was also a magistrate and wrote on civil liberty and morals.

NICOLSON, SIR HAROLD (1886–1968) Born in Teheran, the son of a diplomat. He, too, was a diplomat, a politician and, unhappily, a journalist. He was a friend and, for a while, follower of Oswald Mosley. He married Vita Sackville-West, who did not attempt to hide from him her affairs with Violet Trefusis and Virginia Woolf. He was a prolific author, particularly of biographies, his subjects including Verlaine, Swinburne and King George V. His monument, however, is his diaries and letters, 1930–62, published in three volumes, which run to some three million words, many of them highly entertaining.

POTTER, BEATRIX (1866–1943) English author and illustrator, famed for *The Tale of Peter Rabbit* and its successors. Between the ages of fifteen and thirty, she kept a secret journal written in code. It was not until more than twenty years after her death that the code was cracked by the patient work of Leslie Linder. When it was published in 1966, under the title *The Journal of Beatrix Potter 1881-1897*, it revealed a remarkable picture of upper-middle-class life in late Victorian Britain. `

REDFERN, ROGER (nds) A regular contributor to the *Guardian's* 'Country Diary' column, he is a teacher and the author of a number of books, including *Peak District Diary*, *Snowdonia Country Diary* and *Walking in the Hebrides*.

SACKVILLE-WEST, VITA (1892–1962) English poet and novelist, born at Knole House, Kent. With her husband, Harold Nicolson, she created a garden at Sissinghurst, Kent, which remains a place of pilgrimage for horticulturists. Its colours and relative wildness are reflective of her character. She had passionate affairs with many women, including Virginia Woolf. In 1947, she wrote a weekly column for the *Observer* called 'In Your Garden'.

SAMUELS, LANCE P (nds) An accountant, he contributes to the *Guardian's* 'Country Diary' column.

SASSOON, SIEGFRIED (1886–1967) Brought up in Kent and Sussex. His mother earmarked him at an early age as a poet. He enjoyed country sports, particularly hunting. He was awarded the Military Cross but discarded it. Sent, 'shell-shocked', to a hospital in Edinburgh, he met Wilfred Owen, whose poems he helped polish. Revered as a war poet, he also won acclaim for his autobiographical trilogy, *Memoirs of a Fox-Hunting Man* (1928), *Memoirs of an Infantry Officer* (1930) and *Sherston's Progress* (1936). His diaries cover the years 1915–25.

SCOTT, SIR WALTER (1770–1832) Born in Edinburgh, he was the first international best-selling author. He virtually invented the historical novel, influencing countless authors, and is credited with popularising a romantic vision of Scotland which is still potent today. In 1826, at the height of his fame, his printer and his publisher, Ballantyne & Constable, suffered a financial crash, dragging Scott down with them. Determined to pay off his debts – which he managed just before his death – he threw himself even more strenuously into writing. These difficult times are recorded in his diary, his 'Gurnal'. 'I have all my life regretted that I did not keep a regular [journal],' he wrote in his first entry, on 20 November 1825. 'I have myself lost recollection of much that was interesting and I have deprived my family and the public of some curious information by not carrying this resolution into effect.'

SHARP, ROBERT (1773–1843) From the Yorkshire village of South Cave near Hull, he juggled the roles of schoolmaster, policeman, shopkeeper and tax inspector. He was born the son of a shepherd in the East Yorkshire village of Barmston. From 1786 to 1804 he lived in Bridlington where he made his living as a shoemaker. He was a compulsive letter writer and diarist and portrayed a rich and intimate picture of a rural community in the period between the Napoleonic wars and the Victorian era.

SKINNER, JOHN (1772–1839) A keen antiquarian, he bequeathed to the British Museum ninety-eight manuscript volumes of travels and researches with watercolour drawings. Educated at Trinity College, Oxford, he was ordained as a priest in 1799. His wife and other members of his family died of consumption. He committed suicide.

SMITH, EMILY (1817–77) Born in Paris, she lived in Bath until her marriage to the Rector of West Stafford near Dorchester. Cultured and gifted, she was admired as a singer and painter of water colours. Her diaries for 1836, 1841 and 1851 cover her marriage and births of eight of her twelve children. West Stafford in the heart of Thomas Hardy country. Smith knew him well and he counted her son Bosworth in particular among his friends. Her diary was published under the title *From Victorian Wessex: The Diaries of Emily Smith*.

SOUTAR, WILLIAM (1898–1943) Scottish poet, born in Perth. His parents came of farming stock and his father was a master joiner. During the First World War Soutar contracted a spinal disease which left him bedridden from 1930 onwards. From then until his death he kept a day-to-day record of his experience and observations. As a poet he specialised in 'bairnrhymes', delightful Scots children's poems of great vigour. His diaries were first published in 1954 under the title *Diaries of a Dying Man*. Reviewing it in the *Observer*, fellow diarist Sir Harold Nicolson greeted it as a 'brave and animating book'.

STOVIN, CORNELIUS (1831–96) A tenant farmer who had a large farm high on the Lincolnshire wolds. He was also a Methodist preacher. His journal, which covers the years 1871–5, details his concerns as rents and wages rise and prices are depressed. But he was also a lover of the English countryside, despairing of the loss of hedgerows and lamenting the chopping down of trees, 'sacrificed', as he wrote, 'to sanatory laws'.

STURT, GEORGE (1863–1927) Coming from a long line of wheelwrights, Sturt himself became one, entering the firm at Farnham, Surrey, in which his forebears had worked since 1706. Using the pseudonym George Bourne, he wrote a number of books, including *Memoirs of a Surrey Labourer* (1909), *Change in the Village* (1912) and *A Farmer's Life* (1922). He was a teacher until 1894, when his father died, after which he took over and ran the family wheelwright shop, where he continued to live for the rest of his life.

TAYLER, WILLIAM (1807–92) Born in Grafton, Oxfordshire, England. He entered domestic service, became a footman and began to keep a journal.

THOMPSON, J.M. (nds) A contributor to the *Guardian*'s 'Country Diary' column.

TEONGUE, HENRY (1621–90) Until financial circumstances forced him to boost his income, he was a respectable parish priest in Alcester, Warwickshire. While his son saw to the needs of his parishioners, he served for four years as a naval chaplain. His diary, covering the years 1675–9, was first published in 1825.

TURNER, THOMAS (1729–93) Born in Groombridge in Kent, he started out as a schoolmaster, but became a shopkeeper in East Hoathly in Sussex. He was twice married. He kept a diary – a record of drunkenness, debauchery and retribution – for twelve years between 1754 and 1765, a period overshadowed by the Seven Years War.

VAUGHAN, KEITH (1912–77) English painter, educated at Christ's Hospital, London. His father died when he was a child and he was brought up by his mother. He worked for an advertising agency until 1939. Initially a conscientious objector, he later served in the Pioneer Corps and as an interpreter for German POWs. His diary, which he kept from 1939 until he took his own life, is, in the words of its editor, Alan Ross, 'a self-portrait of astonishing honesty: devoid of disguise, in any shape or form, or hypocrisy'.

VICTORIA, QUEEN (1819–1901) In 1840, Queen Victoria married Prince Albert. Though she had inherited three royal residences with the crown, each had its disadvantages. The need for the couple to have a home of their own was pressing. In 1848, after several visits to Scotland, they purchased Balmoral, which provided privacy and a taste of freedom unavailable elsewhere. There they embraced Highland culture enthusiastically. Albert, for example, studied Gaelic, wore the kilt and stalked stags. When even Balmoral became too much, they retreated to humbler dwellings used by the ghillies. All of which activity is related in her *Journal*.

WAUGH, AUBERON (1939–2001) Novelist and journalist, and the son of Evelyn Waugh. At Downside School he held the record for the most beatings in one term. He did his National Service in Cyprus where, trying to unblock a jammed machine-gun, he shot himself six times in the chest. He wrote five novels before abandoning fiction and embracing journalism. A wilful and indefatigable mischief-maker, he wrote prolifically, principally for the *Daily Telegraph* and the *Spectator*. He also edited the *Literary Review*. He was *Private Eye*'s diarist for sixteen years.

WAUGH, EVELYN (1903–66) Widely regarded as one of the foremost English novelists of his generation, he was born in London and educated at Lancing and Hertford College, Oxford. After an early sortie into schoolteaching, he produced his first novel, *Decline and Fall*, in 1928. Other notable books include *Scoop*, a newspaper farce, the 'Sword of Honour' trilogy, and *Brideshead Revisited*. He was a dyspeptic wit whose unvarnished self is revealed in his letters and diary, which he kept almost continuously from the age of seven until a year before his death.

WELCH, DENTON (1915–48) Born in Shanghai, he spent part of his childhood in China. He trained as an artist, intending to be a painter, but in 1935 he was involved in a bicycle accident from which he never fully recovered. Thereafter he embarked on a literary career. He published *Maiden Voyage*, a volume of autobiography, in 1943, and *In Youth is Pleasure*, a novel, the following year. His journals, comprising more than 200,000 words, were kept between 1942 and 1948, and were often written during periods of intense pain.

WESLEY, JOHN (1703–91) English evangelist who founded Methodism, opening the first Methodist chapel in 1739. He preached all around the country, and it is estimated that he travelled 250,000 miles and gave 40,000 sermons. Nevertheless, he wrote reams: grammars, abridgements of the classics, collections of psalms, hymns and tunes, his own sermons and journals. In 1751 he married a widow who deserted him twenty-five years later. His *Journal* describes his journeys and spiritual odyssey.

WHITE, GILBERT (1720–93) Born at Selborne, Hampshire, he became a fellow of Oriel College, Oxford, but spent most of his life as a curate in his home town. In 1751, he began to keep a 'Garden Kalendar' and later a 'Naturalist's Journal'. He kept a correspondence with two distinguished naturalists, Thomas Pennant and Daines Barrington, which formed the basis of *Natural History and Antiquities of Selborne* (1788), which is redolent of his love for nature, wildlife and landscape. It subsequently went through many editions and remains a landmark in the literature of natural history.

WHITE, HENRY (1733–88) Younger brother of Gilbert White, who died shortly after receiving a copy of *Natural History*, which he declared in his diary was 'a very elegant 4to with splendid engravings'.

WILLIAMS, HOWARD (1854–1933) Born in Greenwich, he grew up in London, the son of middle-class parents. In the summer of 1875, accompanied by his two brothers and two friends, he went on a tour through the centre of England, starting in Oxford and ending in London. During the holiday he kept a diary similar in tone to Jerome K Jerome's novel *Three Men in a Boat*.

WILSON, ENID J (nds)  For more than three decades she contributed to the *Guardian*'s 'Country Diary' column, as its Lakeland correspondent. She was the daughter of George Abraham, the renowned photographer and climber. Her *Country Diary* was published in 1988.

WITTS, REV. FRANCIS EDWARD (1783–1854) He was rector of Upper Slaughter in Gloucestershire from 1808 to 1854 and vicar of Stanway from 1814 to 1854.

WOODFORDE, REV. JAMES (1740–1803) Born in Somerset, the sixth of seven children; his father was a vicar. He went to Winchester College before being admitted to New College, Oxford, where he began to write his diary. After graduation, he worked in Somerset, most of the time as assistant to his father. He never married, though he proposed to a cousin who, he told his diary, 'proved herself to me a mere Jilt'. In 1774 he found a good living in Norfolk worth £400. He was a man of modest aspirations and even more modest talent. His diary, published in five volumes, is his monument, full of mundane but fascinating details and evidence of its author's gluttonous habits.

WOOLF, VIRGINIA (1882–1941) Novelist and essayist, born in London, daughter of Sir Leslie Stephen, first editor of the *Dictionary of National Biography*, and wife of Leonard Woolf, a publisher. Her social circle encompassed many of the leading intellectuals of her day, including the Bloomsbury Group. Her novels include *Mrs Dalloway*, *The Waves* and *To the Lighthouse*. Her essay *A Room of One's Own* is a landmark of feminist literature. With James Joyce, of whom she was not a fan, she is regarded as one of the innovators of the modern novel in English. *A Writer's Diary*, edited by her husband, was published in 1958. A five-volume edition of her diaries, edited by Quentin Bell, appeared from 1977 to 1984.

WORDSWORTH, DOROTHY (1771–1855) Sister of William Wordsworth, born in Cockermouth, Cumberland. Throughout the poet's life she was his constant companion, and she was described by Coleridge as Wordsworth's 'exquisite sister'. Her celebrated journals were kept at Alfoxen in the Lake District in 1798, when her brother and Coleridge were composing *Lyrical Ballads*, and at Grasmere from 1800 to 1803, when she and William were living at Dove Cottage.

# Bibliography

Ackerley, J.R., *My Sister and Myself: The Diaries of J.R. Ackerley*, edited by F. King, London, 1982.

Allingham, William, *William Allingham's Diary*, introduction by G. Grigson, Centaur Press, Fontwell, Sussex, 1967.

Barbellion, W.N.P., *The Journal of a Disappointed Man*, Penguin, London, 1948.

Bennett, Alan, *Untold Stories*, Faber & Faber and Profile Books, London, 2005.

Bennett, Arnold, *The Journals of Arnold Bennett*, selected and edited by F. Swinnerton, Penguin, London, 1954.

Birchall, Dearman, *The Diary of a Victorian Squire: Extracts from the Diaries and Letters of Dearman and Emily Birchall*, selected and introduced by D. Verey, Alan Sutton, Gloucester, 1983.

Blodgett, Harriet (ed.), *The Englishwoman's Diary*, Fourth Estate, London, 1992.

Blythe, Ronald, *Each Returning Day: The Pleasure of Diaries*, Viking, London, 1989.

Boyd, Arnold, *The Country Diary of a Cheshire Man*, Collins, London, 1946.

Brett, Simon (ed.), *The Faber Book of Diaries*, Faber & Faber, 1987.

Brown, George Mackay, *Under Brinkie's Brae*, Gordon Wright Publishing, Edinburgh, 1979.

Case, Janet E., *Country Diaries*, River Press, Salisbury, 1939.

Clark, Alan, *Diaries: Into Politics*, edited by I. Trewin, Weidenfeld & Nicolson, London, 2000.

Clark, Alan, *The Last Diaries: In and Out of the Wilderness*, edited by I. Trewin, Weidenfeld & Nicolson, London, 2002.

Clifford, Sue, and King, Angela, *England in Particular: A Celebration of the Commonplace, The Local, The Vernacular and The Distinctive*, Hodder & Stoughton, London, 2006.

Cocker, Mark, *A Tiger in the Sand: Selected Writings on Nature*, Vintage, London, 2006.

Condry, William, *A Welsh Country Diary*, Gomer, Dyfed, 1993.

Deakin, Roger, *Notes from Walnut Tree Farm*, edited by Alison Hastie and

Terence Blacker, Hamish Hamilton, London, 2008.

Dudeney, Mrs Henry, *A Lewes Diary: 1916–1944*, edited by Diana Cook, Tartarus Press, 1998.

Evans, G.E., *Ask the Fellows Who Cut the Hay*, Faber & Faber, London, 1956.

Evelyn, John, *The Diary of John Evelyn*, selected and edited by J. Bowle, Oxford University Press, Oxford, 1983.

Fea, Patrick, *The Diary of Patrick Fea of Stove, Orkney, 1766–1796*, edited by W.S. Hewison, Tuckwell Press, Edinburgh.

Fowles, John, *The Journals, Volume 2*, edited by C. Drazin, Jonathan Cape, London, 2006.

Fox, Barclay, *Barclay Fox's Journal*, edited by R.L. Brett, Bell & Hyman, London, 1979.

Gibson, Rosemary, *The Scottish Countryside: Its Changing Face, 1700–2000*, John Donald, Edinburgh, 2007.

Gower, J. (ed.), *A Year in a Small County*, Gomer, Dyfed, 1999.

Guinness, Alec, *My Name Escapes Me: The Diary of a Retiring Actor*, Hamish Hamilton, London, 1996.

Harland, Elizabeth Margaret, *No Halt at Sunset: The Diary of a Country Housewife*, Boydell, London, 1951.

Hill, Henry, *The Diaries of Henry Hill of Slackfield Farm*, edited by J. Heath,

Centre for Local History, University of Nottingham, 1982.

Hodgson, John Crawford (ed.), *Six North Country Diaries*, Surtees Society, Durham, 1910.

Holland, *William, Paupers and Pig Killers: The Diary of William Holland, A Somerset Parson, 1799–1818*, edited by J. Ayres, Penguin, Harmondsworth, 1986.

Hopkins, Gerard Manley, *The Journals and Papers of Gerard Manley Hopkins*, edited by H. House, completed by G. Storey, Oxford University Press, London, 1959.

Ingrams, Richard (comp.), *England: An Anthology*, Collins, London, 1989.

Jefferies, Richard, *The Nature Diaries and Notebooks of Richard Jefferies*, edited by S.L. Locker, Grey Walls Press, London, 1948.

Johnson, Alexandra, *The Hidden Writer: Diaries and the Creative Life*, Doubleday, New York, 1997.

Johnson, Alexandra, *Leaving a Trace: On Keeping a Journal & The Art of Transforming a Life into Stories*, Little, Brown, New York, 2001.

Kilvert, Rev. Francis, *Kilvert's Diary 1870–79*, selected and edited by W. Plomer, Penguin, London, 1977.

Lascelles Sir Alan 'Tommy', *End of an Era: Letters and Journals of Sir Alan Lascelles*, Hamish Hamilton, London, 1986.

Le Ruez, Nan, *Jersey Occupation Diary:*

*Nan Le Ruez, Her Story of the German Occupation 1940–45*, Seaflower Books, St Helier, Jersey, 1994.

Lees-Milne, James, *Diaries, 1971-1983*, abridged and introduced by Michael Bloch, John Murray, London, 2007.

Lees-Milne, James, *Diaries, 1984–1997*, abridged and introduced by Michael Bloch, John Murray, London, 2008.

Lister, Anne, *I Know My Own Heart: The Diaries of Anne Lister, 1791–1840*, edited by H. Whitbread, Virago, London, 1988.

Macfarlane, Robert, *The Wild Places*, Granta Books, London, 2007.

Maclean, Alasdair, *Night Falls on Ardnamurchan: The Twilight of a Crofting Family*, Victor Gollancz, London, 1984.

Mallon, Thomas, *A Book of One's Own: People and Their Diaries*, Pan Books, London, 1985.

Mansfield, Katherine, *Journal of Katherine Mansfield*, edited by J. Middleton Murry, Constable, London, 1954.

May, Derwent, *A Year in Nature Notes*, HarperCollins, London, 2004.

Mitchison, Naomi, *Among You Taking Notes: The Wartime Diary of Naomi Mitchison 1939–45*, edited by D. Sheridan, Victor Gollancz, London, 1985.

Muir, John, *Nature Writings*, The Library of America, New York, 1997.

Harold Nicolson, *The Harold Nicolson Diaries: 1907-1963*, edited by Nigel Nicolson, Weidenfeld & Nicolson, London, 2004.

O'Hagan, Andrew, *The End of British Farming*, Profile Books and the London Review of Books, London, 2001.

Page, Jeanette (ed.), *A Country Diary: Selected from the Guardian by Jeanette Page*, Fourth Estate, London, 1994.

*The Past Times Book of Diaries*, Past Times, Oxford, 1998.

Potter, Beatrix, *The Journal of Beatrix Potter*, transcribed from her code writings by Leslie Linder. Abridged with an introduction by G. Cavaliero, F. Warne, London, 1986.

Sassoon, Siegfried, *Diaries 1915–1918*, edited by R. Hart-Davis, Faber & Faber, London, 1983.

Sassoon, Siegfried, *Diaries 1920–1922*, edited by R. Hart-Davis, Faber & Faber, London, 1985.

Sassoon, Siegfried, *Diaries 1923–1925*, edited by R. Hart-Davis, Faber & Faber, London, 1981.

*The Scots Magazine*, John Lang and Co. Ltd and D.C. Thomson and Co., Dundee, 1946

Scott, Sir Walter, *The Journal of Sir Walter Scott*, edited by W.E.K. Anderson, Canongate, Edinburgh, 1998.

Scott-Moncrieff, George, *The Lowlands of Scotland*, B.T. Batsford, London, 1939.

Smith, Emily, *From Victorian Wessex: The*

*Diaries of Emily Smith*, Solen Press, Norwich, 2003.

Soutar, William, *Diaries of a Dying Man*, edited by A. Scott, Chambers, Edinburgh, 1988.

Stovin, Cornelius, *Journals of a Methodist Farmer, 1871–1875*, Croom Helm, London, 1982.

Taylor, Irene and Alan (eds.), *The Assassin's Cloak: An Anthology of the World's Greatest Diarists*, Canongate, Edinburgh, 2000.

Taylor, Irene and Alan (eds.), *The Secret Annexe: An Anthology of War Diarists*, Canongate, Edinburgh, 2004.

Turner, Thomas, *The Diary of a Village Shopkeeper*, edited by David Vaisey, Folio Society, London, 1998.

Vaughan, Keith, *Journals 1939–1977*, John Murray, London, 1989.

Victoria, Queen, *Queen Victoria in her Letters and Journals*, selected by C. Hibbert, Penguin, London, 1985.

Wainwright, Martin (ed.), *A Gleaming Landscape: A Hundred Years of the Guardian's Country Diary*, Arum Press, 2006.

Waugh, Auberon, *A Turbulent Decade: The Diaries of Auberon Waugh 1976–1985*, edited by A. Galli-Pahlavi, Private Eye/Deutsch, London, 1985.

Waugh, Auberon, *Way of the World: The Forgotten Years: 1995–6*, Century Books, London, 1997.

Waugh, Evelyn, *The Diaries of Evelyn Waugh*, edited by M. Davie, Weidenfeld & Nicolson, London, 1976.

Welch, Denton, *The Journals of Denton Welch*, edited by M. De-la-Noy, Penguin, Hardmondsworth, 1987.

Wesley, John, *The Journal of John Wesley: A Selection*, edited with an introduction by E. Jay, Oxford University Press, Oxford, 1987.

White, Gilbert, *The Natural History of Selborne*, edited by R. Mabey, Everyman, London, 1993.

White, Gilbert, *The Journals of Gilbert White*, edited by F. Greenoak, Century, London, 1986–9.

Wilson, Enid J., *Enid Wilson's Country Diary*, Hodder & Stoughton, London, 1988.

Woodforde, James, *The Diary of a Country Parson*, selected by D. Hughes, Folio Society, London, 1992.

Woolf, Virginia, *A Writer's Diary*, edited by L. Woolf, Hogarth Press, London, 1975.

Woodward, Antony, and Penn, Robert, *The Wrong Kind of Snow: The Complete Daily Companion to the British Weather*, Hodder & Stoughton, London, 2007.

Wordsworth, Dorothy, *Journals of Dorothy Wordsworth*, edited by M. Moorman, Oxford University Press, Oxford, 1971.

# Permissions Acknowledgements

Various publishers and Estates have generously given permission to use extracts from the following copyright works.

Bennett, Alan, *Untold Stories*, Faber and Faber and Profile Books, London, 2005.

Boyd, A W, *The Country Diary of a Cheshire Man*, reproduced with the permission of Selina Charlton, great-niece of A W Boyd

Brown, George Mackay, *Under Brinkie's Brae*, Gordon Wright Publishing, Edinburgh, 1979
—*Rockpools and Daffodils*, 1992. All George Mackay Brown quotations are reproduced with the permission of Steve Savage Publishers Ltd.

Clark, Alan, *Diaries: Into Politics*, edited by I Trewin, Weidenfeld and Nicolson, London, 2000.
—*The Last Diaries: In and Out of the Wilderness*, edited I Trewin, Weidenfeld and Nicolson, London, 2002.

Cocker, Mark, *A Tiger in the Sand: Selected Writings on Nature*, published by Jonathan Cape. Reproduced with the permission of The Random House Group Ltd.

Condry, William, *A Welsh Country Diary*, Gomer, Dyfed, 1993.

Deakin, Roger, *Notes From Walnut Tree Farm*, edited by Alison Hastie and Terence Blacker, Hamish Hamilton, London, 2008. Copyright © Roger Deakin, 2008.

Dudeney, Alice, *A Lewes Diary: 1916–1944*, edited by Diana Crook, Tartarus Press, 1998. Reproduced by permission of The Sussex Archaeological Society.

Evans, Christine. From Gower, J (ed)., *A Year in a Small Country*, Gomer, Dyfed, 1999.

Fowles, John, *The Journals, Volume 2*, edited by C Drazin, Jonathan Cape, London, 2006. Copyright © 2006, J R Fowles Ltd. Reproduced with the permission of the John Fowles Estate.

Guinness, Alec, *My Name Escapes Me: The Diary of a Retiring Actor*, Hamish Hamilton, London, 1996. Reproduced with the permission of the Alec Guinness Estate.

Harland, Elizabeth Margaret, *No Halt at Sunset: The Diary of a Country Housewife*, London, 1951. Reproduced with the permission of Boydell Press.

Kesson, Jessie, extracts from *The Scots Magazine*, copyright © Jessie Kesson, 1946. Reproduced with the permission of Johnson & Alcock Ltd.

The Estate of Sir Alan Lascelles.

Le Ruez, Nan, *Jersey Occupation Diary: Nan Le Ruez, Her Story of the German Occupation 1940-45*, Seaflower Books, St Helier, Jersey, 1994.

Lees-Milne, James, *Diaries, 1971–1983*, abridged and introduced by Michael Bloch, John Murray, London, 2007.

Maclean, Alasdair, *Night Falls on Ardnamurchan: The Twilight of a Crofting Family*, Victor Gollancz, London, 1984. Reproduced with the permission of Birlinn Ltd.

May, Derwent, *A Year in Nature Notes*, © Derwent May, 2004. Reprinted with the permission of HarperCollins Publishers Ltd.

Mitchison, Naomi, *Among You Taking Notes: The Wartime Diary of Naomi Mitchison 1939–45*, edited by D Sheridan, Victor Gollancz, London, 1985.

Nicolson, Harold, *The Harold Nicolson Diaries 1907–1963*, edited by Nigel Nicolson, London, 2004. Reproduced with the permission of the Estate of Harold Nicolson.

Sassoon, Siegfried, *Diaries 1915–1918*, edited by R. Hart-Davis, Faber & Faber, London, 1983.
—*Diaries 1920–1922*, edited by R Hart-Davis, Faber & Faber, London, 1985.
—*Diaries 1923–1925*, edited by R Hart-Davis, Faber & Faber, London, 1981.

Soutar, William, *Diaries of a Dying Man*, edited by A Scott, Chambers, Edinburgh, 1988. Reproduced with the permission of the National Library of Scotland.

Vaughan, Keith, *Journals 1939–1977*, John Murray, London, 1989.

Waugh, Auberon, *A Turbulent Decade: the diaries of Auberon Waugh 1976–1985*, edited by A. Galli-Pahlavi, Private Eye/Deutsch, 1985.
—*The Way of the World: the Forgotten Years 1995–6*. Published by Century. Reproduced with the permission of The Random House Group Ltd.

Waugh Evelyn, *The Diaries of Evelyn Waugh*, edited by M Davie, Weidenfeld & Nicolson, London, 1976.

Welch, Denton, *The Journals of Denton Welch*, edited by M De-la-Noy, Penguin, 1987. Reproduced with the permission of the Denton Welch Estate.

Wilson, Enid, *Enid Wilson's Country Diary*, Hodder and Stoughton, 1988.

Woolf, Virginia, *A Writer's Diary*, edited by L Woolf, Hogarth Press, London, 1975. Reproduced with the permission of The Society of Authors as the literary representative of the Estate of Virginia Woolf

# *Index of Diarists*

1771, 7 November 1773, 1 December 1773, 15 November 1774,
5 March 1776, 14 April 1776, 4 June 1776, 29 March 1777, 15 April
1778, 16 April 1778, 30 September 1778, 1 January 1779, 8 March
1780, 11 August 1780, 20 November 1782, 25 December 1782,
6 March 1783, 6 May 1783, 26 January 1784, 16 March 1785, 1 June
1785, 31 December 1785, 11 February 1788, 29 July 1788, 5 February
1790, 16 September 1791, 11 April 1794, 2 November 1794, 15 January
1795

Woolf, Virginia, 5 January 1918, 23 January 1927

Wordsworth, Dorothy, 20 January 1798, 22 January 1798, 4 February
1798, 17 February 1798, 14 May 1800, 19 May 1800, 30 May 1800,
9 June 1800, 20 June 1800, 3 August 1800, 3 September 1800,
2 October 1800, 20 October 1800, 24 November 1801, 9 December
1801, 22 December 1801, 28 December 1801, 5 February 1802,
9 February 1802, 14 March 1802, 15 March 1802, 18 March 1802,
27 March 1802, 15 April 1802, 1 May 1802, 28 May 1802, 2 June
1802, 3 June 1802, 10 June 1802, 25 June 1802, 4 November 1802

# THE ASSASSIN'S CLOAK
## AN ANTHOLOGY OF
## THE WORLD'S GREATEST DIARISTS

### EDITED BY IRENE AND ALAN TAYLOR

'A diary is an assassin's cloak which we wear when we stab a comrade in the back with a pen.' So wrote William Soutar in 1934. But a diary is also a place for recording everyday thoughts and special occasions, private fears and hopeful dreams. As a result, this wonderful collection of entries from the world's greatest diarists is as inspiring as it is enlightening.

'The content is sensational – for all the right reasons. It is stimulating and charming in equal measure, often amusing, and an endless source of pleasure.' *Literary Review*

'Utterly compulsive.' *The Times*

'A superb collection . . . Gossipy, funny, perceptive and vicious. Every dip-in is a sheer delight.' *Observer*

£12.99

ISBN 978 1 84195 459 2

www.meetatthegate.com

# THOSE WHO MARCHED AWAY

## AN ANTHOLOGY OF THE GREATEST WAR DIARIES

### EDITED BY ALAN TAYLOR

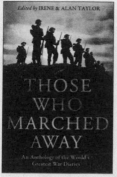

Arranged as a diary around a calendar year, *Those Who Marched Away* tells many individual stories from many wars down the ages, with several compelling entries for each day of the year. The diarists come from every walk of life; from faceless foot soldiers to those charged with orchestrating battle, from the Home Front to the Holocaust, from famous writers, political leaders and fighting men and women to ordinary working people enveloped by events over which they have no influence. Together, they contribute an intimate insight into what has been described both as 'the most exciting and dramatic thing in life' and the 'universal perversion'.

'Wonderful . . . The awesome and tragic are balanced by the humdrum and quirky.' *Herald*

'The writers are mere flotsam on the tides of war. Their words are subjective, partial, personal, sometimes prejudiced and occasionally mundane. But taken together and spanning centuries of warfare, they are the very stuff and substance of human experience.' *The Times*

'Hugely enjoyable.' *Scotsman*

£12.99

ISBN 978 1 84767 415 9

www.meetatthegate.com